swimming with maya

Praise for *Swimming with Maya*

"Powerful prose with a meaningful and memorable message."

—Lee Gutkind, Editor: *At the End of Life: Essays on How We Die*,
Founder: *Creative Nonfiction* Magazine

"How do we go on? This is the fundamental question when we are confronted with losses that seem too great to bear. Eleanor Vincent's beautifully written memoir, *Swimming with Maya*, is one woman's answer. Heartbreaking and heart healing, this compelling story of surviving the death of a child will stay with you long after you've closed the book."

—Ellen Bass, author of *The Courage to Heal* and *The Human Line*

"An important addition to the literature of loss and restoration, *Swimming with Maya* is a harrowing tale of mother love, grief, and the gradual reclamation of a daughter's life through acceptance of her death."

—Maxine Kumin, Pulitzer Prize-winning poet and author of
Inside the Halo and Beyond: The Anatomy of a Recovery

"I was riveted by Eleanor Vincent's moving tale of death and redemption. Every mother of a strong, independent child will find this memoir illuminating. And every reader who has had to deal with traumatic loss will find wisdom and healing in these brave pages."

—Chana Bloch, author of *Mrs. Dumpty* and *Blood Honey*

"In this riveting, poignant, and utterly honest memoir, Eleanor Vincent demonstrates the remarkable process of healing after the traumatic death of her daughter, Maya. This wonderfully written book can inspire anyone facing life's painful events and challenges. It shows that one *can* recover from the loss of a child."

—Judy Tatelbaum, author of *The Courage to Grieve* and *You Don't Have to Suffer*

"*Swimming with Maya* blows the reader away with its clarity, its unstinting honesty, and the searing accuracy of its vision of the medical and emotional complexity surrounding the tragic death of a young woman. It will be valuable not only to those considering organ donation, but to any psychologically aware parent struggling with the illusion of control it so movingly describes. Highly recommended."

—John Ruark, MD, FACP, author of *Dying Dignified*

"Thoughtful, honest, and beautifully written, *Swimming with Maya* chronicles a remarkable friendship between a grieving mother and the man who is alive because her daughter's heart beats in his chest. This book grabs the reader, not only because of this extraordinary aspect, but also because of the parts that are common to all parents. It is, above all, a fabulous story about what it means to be a mother."

—Wendy Lichtman, author of *Blew and the Death of the Mag* and
Secrets, Lies and Algebra

"In this powerful book, past and present weave together in strong, uplifting prose. Eleanor Vincent brings us inside her daughter's 'life after death' as we see Maya's heart beating in the body of a man who is alive because of her sudden death. Life trumps death in this beautiful memoir."

—Linda Joy Myers, author of *Don't Call Me Mother—A Daughter's Journey from Abandonment to Forgiveness,* and *Power of Memoir*

swimming with maya

A Mother's Story

Eleanor Vincent

Dream of Things
Downers Grove Illinois USA

First Dream of Things Edition, February 2013
Published by Dream of Things, Downers Grove, Illinois USA
Originally published by Capital Books, Inc., in 2004

Dream of Things provides discounts to educators, book clubs, writers
groups, and others. For more information, write to customerservice@
dreamofthings.com, or call 847-321-1390.

ISBN for this edition: 9780988439047
Library of Congress Control Number for this edition: 2012956272

The Library of Congress has cataloged the hardcover edition as follows:

Vincent, Eleanor, 1948– Swimming with Maya : a mother's story / Eleanor
Vincent.
p. cm. — ISBN 1-931868-34-4
1. Vincent, Eleanor, 1948– 2. Vincent, Eleanor, 1948—Family.
3. Lee, Maya Catherine, 1972–1992. 4. Vincent family. 5. Women journal-
ists—California—Biography. 6. Single parents—California—Biography.
7. Mothers and daughters—California—Biography. I. Title. II. Series.

CT275.V567A3 2004
979.4'37—dc22   2003018443

Excerpts from *Top Girls* reprinted by permission of Methuen Drama, an
imprint of Bloomsbury Publishing Plc. on behalf of the Author. Copyright
© 1982, 1984 by Caryl Churchill.

Excerpt from *Laughing Wild* reprinted by permission of Grove/Atlantic Inc.
on behalf of the Author. Copyright ©1988 (revised) by Christopher Durang.
Any third party use of this material, outside of this publication, is prohibited.

Book design: Susan Veach
Cover design: Jennifer Noel Huppert
Front cover photograph of Maya as a child: Kay Vincent
Back cover photograph of Maya as a young adult: Tracy Van Wormer

For my daughters
who brought me into being,
and for Sarah,
midwife to this book

Contents

Author's Note

Out of respect for their privacy, I have changed the names of some people who appear in these pages.

Acknowledgments

I am profoundly grateful to two people who arrived first at the hospital to offer support, yet make only a brief appearance in these pages, Dave and Sue. There are no truer friends. Thanks to everyone in our extended families who loved and supported my daughters and me.

To the staff of the John Muir Medical Center, I will never forget your heroic efforts to save my daughter's life. Shelley Nicholson Hunter, thank you for bearing with me and becoming my friend.

All those in the transplantation community who work so tirelessly to save lives, you are my heroes. The Compassionate Friends around the world are my inspiration and an ongoing source of support.

Chana Bloch, Diana O'Hehir, Josephine Carson, Marilyn Mcentyre, Emaz Abinader, Tom Strychacz—thank you for your support and guidance in two important areas, grieving and writing. The dedication of the Mills College women who wrestled with the early drafts of this book still spurs me on.

Norma Cowan, Granville Smith, and Virginia DeMora, my

high school English teachers who never settled for less than my best.

To my colleagues at Pacific Bell and Kaiser Permanente, I couldn't have asked for better people to share a workday with. Particular thanks to Rosalyn Kulick whose kindness is always with me. Linda Peterson has been my professional fairy god-mother, sharing her counsel and her Rolodex for more years than either of us wants to count. Linda Bine and Marjorie Little, many thanks for your fine suggestions.

Andy Black made my learning curve less steep and my "to do" list more rational, lifting my spirits along the way.

Wendy Lichtman and the Wednesday evening writing group, God love you! This book would not have taken shape without the heartfelt critiques of Kate Levinson, Susan Nunes, Kathy Bricetti, Wendy Coblentz, Laurie Kahn, Meg Jackson Reinhardt, Ronnie Gilbert, Susan Gill, Nancy Kelly, and Joanne Brown.

Paola Gianturco kept me going when I wanted to quit, and recognized the title of the book when it first surfaced in an earlier draft. Ellen Bass held my hand in person and electronically during the most challenging times. Amanita Rosenbush edited the sample chapters that ultimately brought this book into being.

Camilla Hardmeyer, Helen Crothers, Launa Craig, JoAnn Siebe, Constance Beutel, Kris Michaelis, Kenny Goldstein, and Carolyn Shaffer cheered me on, fed me, and excused me from countless social functions. John Hoey kept me standing through the early years and taught me so much about love.

Rev. Margaret Stortz and Lou Ann Kary Steiner helped me to rethink, relive, reframe, and have patience with myself.

My beloved Jay gave me the ultimate gift—time to work—and encircled every worry with humor and love. His sister

Helen recognized the core truths in the writing long before I did, and wisely said little about them.

My mother gave me words and reason to use them. My father challenged me to work harder, fly higher, and laugh longer. Undying love for them both.

To my sister, a tenderhearted and supportive friend, and to my brother who made some of the best editing catches ever and always inspires me with his practical wisdom. Thanks will never be enough.

I want to acknowledge my editor at Capital Books, Noemi Taylor, and the entire production and sales teams. Special gratitude to my agent Laurie Harper, who believed in me, in the story that had to be told, and in the future of this book.

For Meghan, the heart and soul of everything, there are no words. And for Sarah Scott Davis who gave her all to me and to the unflinching telling of this tale—honey, you rock! Here it is.

January, 2013

Publishing a book is like giving birth to a child. Keeping a book in print is more akin to the patient day-to-day nurturing required to raise that child to maturity. My thanks to Mike O'Mary for being a dedicated and creative foster parent to *Swimming with Maya* and to Madeline Sharples for connecting us. Much appreciation goes to my current writing group for practical help and skillful suggestions. To fellow writer Bob Frost and to the editors (especially Stephen Knezovich) at *Creative Nonfiction*, thanks for making my prose sing. And to readers everywhere, thank you for taking this journey with me.

Prologue

When I think of a stranger touching my daughter's clothes it feels like a violation, so donating them to Goodwill is out of the question. But then several months after the funeral, one of her cousins asks if she can have Maya's prettiest formal dress. I examine the dress, opulent as a peony, its hot pink bodice and spaghetti straps, the skirt with its cascade of pink flounces. Maya carried a little beaded purse on prom night. I find that too, then wrap the dress in tissue paper, tuck the purse in beside it in a gift box, and present it to my niece.

The shoes are more difficult. Maya's college roommates had shipped them home to me along with her other clothes. I unpack them and set them in a row in her closet with the high heels at one end, the flats at the other. Each time I pick one up and turn it in my hand I can feel my daughter's missing foot. At last, I decide to call her girlfriends to see if anyone wants the shoes. Jo Anne agrees to take them. I stack the high heels in shoeboxes on the dining room table, and Jo Anne and I stand side by side surveying the pile of shoes. "Do you want to try on a pair, just to be sure?" I ask.

She steps into a pair of black patent leather pumps and walks a few steps, pivots, and comes back. Now taller than I am because she is standing in Maya's shoes, Jo Anne opens her arms to me. As I hold her, I feel a tremor in her shoulders. Then she drives away with the shoes, and my daughter's footfalls echo in my mind.

Grief seizes me by the scruff of the neck and will not let me go. Piece by piece I reconstruct the puzzle of our life together, opening myself to the slow truth of what it meant to be Maya's mother.

PART I

Swept Under

Chapter 1

I'm dressed in my corporate clothes, a sharp crease in my brown linen pants, a raincoat thrown over my arm. The smell of rubbing alcohol pricks my nostrils. A burly man in a white coat shakes my hand. He introduces himself as Dr. Garry, the head of the Trauma Care unit.

"Your daughter is in very grave condition," he says, clicking his ballpoint pen in and out. "The fall caused considerable damage and brain swelling."

The hallway folds in on itself as if my eyes are looking down the wrong end of a telescope. Buzzing fluorescent lights make the air glow. I lean against the counter of the nurse's station in the emergency room, lightheaded with fear.

I remember her voice, equal parts taunting and tender, "Mom, *you* phone the mechanic." Maya flips her hair back from her fine-boned face. "Do it yourself," I argue. "They know you," she counters. Did that really happen this morning?

From an exam room in the ER, a voice yells, "Bring me an ampule of Epinephrine, NOW!"

I hear the frenetic voice, then the sound of pounding footsteps. I hold the image of my daughter close, pushing against the weight of the doctor's words.

Dr. Garry paints a vivid picture of her first hour in the hospital: the limp unconscious body strapped to a stretcher, paramedics rushing her in from the helicopter pad outside, nurses frantically cutting the clothes from her body. He describes leaning over her with an ophthalmoscope to examine her pupils. He says they were fixed and dilated. She showed no response to pain when he prodded and pinched her; her muscles were completely flaccid.

I picture my daughter's lean thighs and narrow shoulders. She is thin as a bird, but she works out every other day, and her body is wiry and muscular.

Dr. Garry says he ordered a CT scan and a consultation with a neurosurgeon.

His words bombard me, clinical and scary. "After the CT scan, we rushed your daughter into emergency brain surgery. They're operating now."

Like a mechanical doll, I nod. My head bobs up and down.

One of the emergency room nurses guides me down a long hallway and into an elevator. My hands and feet feel quick-frozen. As if my brain were a seismograph, I record the tremors in my body. We travel up several floors. Three of Maya's friends, including a boy she had dated in high school, are huddled in a corner of the narrow waiting room. When Alex sees me, his body gives an involuntary jerk. He stands and moves toward me. His eyes are vacant and glassy, and when I study his face it seems gaunt, much older than his nineteen years. Stiff and alert, he waits for me to say something. I motion to a row of chairs.

An orderly clanks by us with an empty metal gurney, and before I can speak a stranger's voice crackles over the intercom, breaking my concentration. We sit down beneath a bank of windows. My eyes fix on Alex's hunched shoulders.

"What happened?" I demand. "And tell me the truth."

The outing to the Morgan Territory Regional Park was Maya's idea. She wanted to celebrate the biggest triumph of her life—winning a full scholarship to the Theater Arts Program at UCLA. It was almost impossible to get into this program as a transfer student, even without the scholarship, and Maya could barely believe her good fortune.

Home from community college for spring break, Maya phoned Alex to let him know the good news. They made plans to hang out the following day with Alex's cousin George and his girlfriend Julie.

Located twenty miles from Walnut Creek, the park is a nature preserve that might as well be its own country—it is that different from the urban sprawl of the Bay Area. Rolling pastures checkerboard the hills and thick clusters of trees overhang a narrow road. A compact car is almost too wide to squeeze across the one-lane wooden bridges that lead to the field where Maya and her friends went to celebrate that afternoon. Under a canopy of trees, a green metal gate suddenly appears.

On the forty-minute ride that April afternoon, each of them had suggested at least once that they change their plans. It's too hot; there probably aren't any horses today anyway, only cows; the beer's getting warm, better to go back and get ice-cold beer from the refrigerator. Is this going to be fun or just bogus?

But each time someone suggested turning back, someone else managed to convince the others to keep going.

It was so hot that even after they reached the green gate they almost decided to stay inside the air-conditioned car to finish the beer. But one of the four, nobody remembered who, galvanized the rest of them to pile out, climb over the gate, and hike up to the field above. They had each had a beer or two by now.

When they reached the top of an oak-studded hill, they saw him. A sleek horse with a glossy coat stood by a watering tub, grazing quietly, unfenced and unsecured.

"Go on," Alex said to Maya, knowing she was always good for a dare. "See if you can ride him across the field."

If Maya felt reluctant or scared, she didn't show it. Today she was on fire with joy, a nineteen-year-old streak of a girl whose dream of being an actress had suddenly switched to the fast track. The excitement of a sparkling new future flowed through her. But she wasn't so giddy that she wanted to do it alone. She talked Julie into mounting the horse with her.

The boys gave Julie a leg up, and she sat in front grasping the horse's mane. Then Maya mounted and circled her arms around Julie's waist. They waited, but nothing happened. The horse ambled ahead for a couple of feet and then stopped.

"It's going too slow," Julie complained. The girls leaned forward to urge the horse onward.

"Giddy-up," Maya said like a child to a rocking horse. A sleeve of blond hair fell across her face.

"Kick it," the two boys urged, taking another swig of beer.

The girls hesitated, so one of the boys gave the horse a smart slap on the flank. It whinnied in protest. Then, without warning, it reared up on its hind legs. Julie started to tilt off to the side as the horse's mane slipped through her fingers. Maya, helplessly sliding backward toward the horse's rump, tried to dismount, but her leg tangled with Julie's. Like a Tilt-a-Whirl ride, she was flung backward.

As Julie slid off sideways and fell on her butt, Maya cascaded off the back of the horse, her arms outstretched in a vain attempt to grab something to stop the fall.

She could have hit the ground in a dozen ways, on her rump like Julie had, or toppling over to break the fall with her hands.

Instead, her head hit the ground with full force at the precise spot on her skull that housed the mid-brain, the section that controls the body's ability to breathe.

It was a classic cantilever fall, the kind that even football players and rodeo riders don't recover from. Maya's friends, however, had no clue. She lay on the ground face up without moving. Julie got up and rubbed her sore butt. She and the two boys approached Maya's limp body, not greatly concerned. Julie, after all, was virtually unharmed, and it wasn't unlike Maya to play a joke on her friends. They were sure she was faking.

As they stood over her inert body, it dawned on them that this was no act. They waited for a few more seconds. Maybe she would open her eyes, or moan. Alex called loudly, "Hey, Maya!"

Julie leaned down and shook her shoulder. "Maya, come on. Cut it out. Wake up!" Nothing.

Alex panicked. "You guys go down to that house we passed and call the sheriff. Get someone up here, fast!"

Unsure what else they could do and very scared, Julie and George ran down the hill to the car to find help.

Alex fell to his knees over Maya's body and lowered his face to hers, giving her mouth-to-mouth resuscitation. In between forcing his breath into her slack mouth, he called her name again and again. Once, when he shouted "Maya!" sharply into her ear, her leg twitched. She was taking in just a few breaths a minute.

A ravine full of scrub oak and laurel trees tumbled down to a dry creek bed. Alex was trapped in a bowl of grass under an open sky with a lifeless girl and a grazing horse. Silence reverberated around him.

"Maya!" he called again, hunching over her. Looking north, he could see the jagged face of Mt. Diablo through a gap in the hills that ringed the field. He glanced at his watch. Julie and

George had already been gone almost half an hour. He bent over the lifeless form again.

At last, he heard the whir of the chopper blades approaching. He looked up as the helicopter buzzed down twenty-five yards away, flattening the grass and sending the horse across the field at a gallop. George and Julie topped the hill pale and out of breath from running. Two paramedics rushed up with oxygen and a stretcher, and Alex stepped back so they could attempt to resuscitate Maya.

She had lain unconscious in the field for a long time—almost forty-five minutes. But once help arrived, everything moved at lightning speed. In one swift motion, the Cal-Star paramedics lifted her body onto a stretcher and strapped her down. They retracted her tongue and shoved a breathing tube down her throat and into her lungs. Then one of them began rhythmically squeezing the breathing apparatus, "bagging" her to jumpstart her breathing.

By air, it was a quick ten-minute ride to John Muir Hospital, where she was rushed to the trauma care section of the emergency room. Eight people immediately assembled to work on her, prodding, sticking, and probing. The respiratory therapist continued bagging her by hand to further assist her breathing, but Maya was profoundly unresponsive.

After Dr. Garry and the ER physician on duty evaluated her injuries, she was sent to the CT scanner and then rushed to the operating room for a craniotomy. Her head was shaved, and Dr. Carr, the hospital's chief neurosurgeon began to operate.

What he found was a large subdural hematoma, a blood clot. Blood was leaking throughout her brain, trapped beneath the dura, or outer covering. Massive brain swelling caused the ventricles and cisternal spaces to close in, increasing the pressure even more. Maya's brain was so swollen that Dr. Carr could not replace the bone flap he had removed from the back of her skull to facilitate the three-hour operation. Instead, her head was wrapped in a sterile turban and she was returned to the Neuroscience ICU in a deep coma. A ventilator supplied oxygen, multiple IV lines administered medications, and two computers monitored her every bodily function.

As I tried to absorb Alex's story, and piece together what had happened to my daughter, I flashed back to how this day had begun.

At six o'clock that morning, I cracked open the kids' bedroom door and looked in on them. This was the way days used to begin when Maya still lived at home. I could hardly believe she was already a sophomore in college. She was sprawled across the bottom bunk, a limp strand of hair covering her cheek, mascara smudges under her eyes. Her sister Meghan's foot peeked out from under the covers on the bunk bed above. Their even breathing soothed me like a mantra. Assured that everything was okay, I shut the door silently.

In the kitchen, three paper plates smeared with chocolate frosting littered the counter, a reminder of last night's party to celebrate the spectacular news about UCLA. I bustled around stuffing trash into the wastebasket and wiping away cake crumbs. I started the teakettle and put bread into the toaster. Now that the tension of waiting for UCLA's verdict was over, I imagined how we would relax that night with pizza and a video.

Already late for a business seminar, I hurried to my room to dress. The girls' voices began to rise and fall in their bedroom. Then, I heard Maya in the bathroom, and remembered that she had agreed to drive Meghan to school. The girls' activities, the best route to the hotel where the seminar was going to be held, and plans to continue our celebration all flowed through my mind. At last, ready for my journey, I went to check on the kids and tell them good-bye. Meghan was still dressing, but Maya sat in our big easy chair in her pajamas, her hair a rumpled mess.

"Mom, I need to get the oil changed in my car," she said. "Will you call the mechanic for me?"

"Maya, come on, can't you see I'm running late?"

Her face fell. I upped the ante. "You're the big-time actress with the big, fat UCLA scholarship. Don't you think it's time you handled stuff like this?"

"M-o-m," she stretched it out to three syllables, wheedling. "They know you. They don't know me—it will be much faster if you do it."

"Oh, all right," I said. I picked up the phone and dialed, knowing that she was gloating over what a pushover I was.

I called my good-bye to Meghan, and her voice echoed down the hallway. "Bye Mom! Have a good day."

As I headed for the door at last, Maya looked up at me and flashed an impish grin. Then she gave me the thumbs up sign, a family joke from the days when she had a crush on Tom Cruise in the movie "Top Gun."

I ruffled my hand through her hair. "I'm so proud of you, honey." I slammed the door, already planning to order her favorite pineapple, Canadian bacon, and tomato pizza for tonight.

The day went quickly, and the traffic gods were with me. Before I knew it, I was back, and it was only 5:30, plenty of time to make a salad to go with the pizza. As I walked from the car I begin to sing, reviewing our plans for the evening. When I opened the gate, still humming, I found the front door ajar. My younger daughter confronted me. Her face was drawn and pale.

"Mom, you have to call the hospital. Something terrible has happened to Maya."

Instantly, the hair stood up on the back of my neck.

Gears ground in my head. My first thought was *No! This is not true!* But already I was trembling. I stared at eleven-year-old Meghan.

With reddish-brown hair and a sturdy frame, she was the opposite of her willowy sister. As I looked at her, she seemed tiny, as if she had physically shrunk. Her voice sounded far away, like a NASA astronaut speaking to a distant command center. She backed away from the door as I came in and set my briefcase on a chair.

Since I had no cell phone, I now realized that this little sixth grader had been alone with this horrible news for the last hour.

When my feet stayed glued to their spot, Meghan urged me on. "A nurse phoned. You have to call the hospital right away." In slow motion I turned toward the dining room table. My arms felt heavy, as if lifting the phone from its cradle would be too great an effort.

"Mom," Meghan said with blatant impatience, "please, you have to call NOW." I knew I should move faster, yet I could not break out of my zombie pace. I removed a notebook from my briefcase and dialed the number Meghan had scribbled on a scrap of paper. I cradled the phone with my left shoulder, the habit of a former news reporter, and took notes with my other hand.

"Trauma Unit," a businesslike voice said, "Nurse Harris speaking."

As soon as I inquired about Maya her voice softened. "At about 3:45 this afternoon your daughter was in an accident. She has a subdural hematoma—a blood clot in her brain—and is undergoing brain surgery now. Please come to the emergency room as soon as you can."

I set the phone back in its cradle and stared down at my own spiky handwriting. Meghan said she had already phoned a friend, and Laura's mother Jean was on her way to our house. I waited until I heard Jean's car pull up out back, then gave Meghan a hug. "I'll call you as soon as I know anything more." I left my daughter hunched in a corner of the sofa and closed the door behind me.

Jean was getting out of her car as I ran to mine. "I'll take care of her," she yelled. I waved and kept going.

I gunned out of our parking space and onto Brook Street. "Okay, stay calm. She's going to be okay. *Oh God, let Maya be okay*," I chanted this prayer over and over as I raced through a yellow light and pulled onto the freeway.

I parked in the lot at the John Muir Medical Center, but I didn't know how I got there or how long it had taken me. Life had turned inside out and every move I made felt as if I was looking down on the scene from above. Nothing fit.

Then Dr. Garry delivered his assessment of Maya's condition, and the emergency room nurse guided me up two floors to the ICU waiting room and left me there with Maya's friends. Paralyzed with fear, I couldn't even remember how to get back to the front entrance to ask what was happening to my daughter. There was nothing I could do but wait.

As the hours pass, I grasp at any distraction. Basketball playoffs blare from the overhead TV above us. I hear buzzers squawking and tennis shoes squeaking as huge men skid and pivot.

Sweat falls in shiny drops from their foreheads as they stand at the free throw line. Pressure. I understand that.

I look at my watch. Almost 8:30 and still no word.

"What in the hell are they doing to her?" I demand.

"Operating," Maya's friend Oliver says. "It's going to be okay." He squeezes my shoulder and even though he is young enough to be my son, his presence reassures me. I stare into his dark eyes, survey his tea-colored face, and remember that one of the biggest fights Maya and I ever had was over this boy's borrowed car. He was her pal, never a boyfriend. They hung out together. In my mind, he is innocent because he wasn't in the field with her.

In the restroom I rinse my hands over the antiseptic white sink and look at myself in the mirror. My veneer of calm shatters. *Jesus! My child. What is taking so long? Make this bad dream end. Please God, make her be all right.*

Like an automaton, I return to the waiting room.

Alex approaches me, still stiff and pale. "I'll go get Maya's car and drive it to your apartment," he offers. I nod my head. I could as easily strangle this boy as talk to him. He shoves his hands deep in his pockets and walks away. I stare at Oliver, fixated on the warmth in his eyes.

My anger at Alex started long before this nightmare. Three years ago I went into Maya's room late one night to be sure she had not broken her curfew. To my astonishment, I found Maya curled up with a bare-chested boy in her bed. It was Alex. I went back to my room to think about how to handle this. The drawbacks of being a single mother flashed like a neon sign. A male authority figure would have been a godsend at that moment, but I was it. So, I rolled up my bathrobe sleeves, took a deep breath, and called on my best assertiveness skills.

"Guys," I said after I woke them, "I think this is not a good idea. Alex, I'd like you to go home now." There had been other incidents with Alex involving beer busts and broken curfews.

My mind begins to reel off more random memories.

One Saturday afternoon I had both girls with me shopping in downtown Walnut Creek. Driving through the McDonald's parking lot, I almost ran head on into a white Mercedes. "Mercy upon us," I shouted, slamming on the brakes.

"Mom, don't you mean 'Mercedes upon us?'" Maya quipped. The other driver backed away. We burst into laughter. Relieved, we ate our cheeseburgers and fries outside at the picnic table.

My mind skips to Maya's senior year in high school. She went to the prom with a kid she barely knew. He was wealthy and spoiled, and she ended up hating him and his posh parents, his silver BMW, his expensive tuxedo. "He's a pretentious asshole," she sniffed. When I came home from work one day, she had propped her five-by-seven prom photo on the mantelpiece. In her hot pink gown with the spaghetti straps she stands next to the trim body of her date. But to obliterate his face she cut a picture of the movie critic Gene Shalit out of a magazine and pasted it above her date's neck. The bushy hair and handlebar mustache looked ridiculous. I roared when I saw it.

A voice breaks into my memories. "Ms. Vincent?" A tall thin man in hospital greens leans over my chair. "I'm Chris Perez, the nursing supervisor; please follow me."

He leads me into the nurses' break room just outside the Neuroscience ICU. A row of metal lockers lines one wall. A few chairs are neatly arranged in the center of the room and a coffee maker sits on a counter next to a stainless steel sink.

"The operation is over now. Dr. Carr will be here in a moment to talk to you." Nurse Perez leaves me alone in the small room.

I pace between the chairs and the row of lockers. After a few minutes a dark-haired man with chiseled features comes in. When I reach for his outstretched hand, I feel the coolness of his palm, its smoothness and strength. He smells of soap, and he projects an aura of crispness. His white coat looks as if it has just been pressed.

"How is she?"

I want good answers, simple reassurance. When he doesn't respond directly I realize I am not going to get them.

"You can see her in a few minutes," Dr. Carr replies. He glances toward the window and lets his gaze linger there. "I operated for just over three hours. The outer covering of her brain, the dura, was extremely tense, and when I excised it, a huge amount of blood extruded. I must tell you, I've never seen a brain more red and angry. It's extremely swollen. So much so, that we could not replace the flap of skull we removed beforehand."

My stomach lurches. *You mean the back of her head is gone?*

He looks straight into my eyes for the first time.

"Do you have any other children?"

"Yes, another daughter." I picture Meghan, her ashen face when she told me the hospital had called, the way she sat huddled on the couch as if trying to disappear into it. "What are you saying to me?" My body bends forward involuntarily, as if standing upright is now impossible, as if his words will break my back.

"I'm saying that your daughter's odds are very slim."

Blood surges through my arms. I want to punch him hard in the center of his calm, chiseled face.

"Look, I've been sitting out there for hours thinking she has a blood clot in her brain, they're operating, they're going to take care of it. Now, you're telling me that's not the case?"

"I would say she has a two or three percent chance of survival." I feel the hammer blow of his words, but I don't believe them.

"This is not just a blood clot." He touches the fingers of one hand gently to the fingers of the other, making a tent.

"Her entire brain is extremely swollen, as I said. We've put her into a barbiturate coma, over and above the coma she's naturally in from the force of the fall. We want no brainwave activity at all. It's the only hope for bringing down the swelling."

I turn away from him toward the lockers.

"Do *anything*," I plead, turning slowly to face him again. "This child is my life."

My entire body goes numb, and I shake uncontrollably.

Dr. Carr nods his head very gently. He offers to tell Maya's friends about her condition; then he goes to a cupboard, removes a flannel blanket, and wraps it around my shoulders. Nurse Perez returns. "We don't want to take away your hope, but if you have a minister you might want to have that person here."

I stumble to the wall phone to place the call. Suddenly, there in that little room, all I have ever done and been as a mother rises up in my heart.

Up to my waist in aqua water, I propped my ten-month-old baby on my hip, holding her tight to my body. She wiggled and bounced against me as she pointed at the other little ones in water wings filling the shallow end of the pool.

I waded out deeper, away from the hordes of bobbing, jumping toddlers. Her father dived in at the deep end and swam to us under water, then surfaced inches from Maya and me. He rubbed noses with our baby girl and teasingly whispered "Peek-a-boo!" then disappeared under the water again like a glittering fish.

Maya laughed, shaking against me with heartfelt ecstasy.

"Where did Daddy go?" I whispered into her ear.

Jeff resurfaced and took her tiny body into both hands, then turned her face to mine. Their wet heads bobbed in unison. I backed away and stretched out my arms.

"Swim to Mommy."

"One... two... three... GO!" Jeff said, plunging her under water.

Maya propelled herself toward me, a look of competitive intensity on her little face. Bubbles formed as she kicked through the water. Her eyes were wide open, with a startled, mammalian glossiness.

"That's a girl. Come on, Maya!"

She lengthened her torso in one final effort. When I plucked her from the water, she snuggled into my chest, rubbing her fists against her eyes. By some deep law of the universe, this enchanted being actually belonged to me. I prepared to plunge her back under water and count, knowing her survival instinct would kick in and she would hold her breath. But I hesitated. What if the instinct didn't work? What if she forgot to hold her breath or struggle to the surface?

"What a good, brave girl you are," I crooned into her ear and plunged her under the water.

Now, all alone in a suburban hospital, I see that young mother as if she were standing next to me. She was intoxicated with her child's will to test every limit, drunk with that little girl's beauty and trust.

I pushed my daughter to take risks and applauded her when she did, believing I was encouraging her strength and independence. Until her life hung in the balance, I never considered the darker side of her behavior, or the motivation for mine.

Chapter 2

When I reach down to touch my daughter, the flaccid muscle of her upper arm is lifeless as a dead kitten. Riveted on her, I dimly register the fact that my ex-husband Dan, Maya's stepfather, has arrived and now stands across the bed from me.

The sight before us is like something out of a horror movie. A fiber optic cable runs from a computer monitor into Maya's brain, where it is attached by a large plastic screw that pokes up through the gauze turban wrapping her skull. It reminds me of a bolt on a Frankenstein monster. Her skin is so shiny it looks as if someone has waxed it. Her eyes are sealed shut, eyelids puffy. A maze of other gadgets sprouts from her body.

There's a T-shaped arterial catheter protruding from her neck; her plum-colored blood flows inside the plastic tubing. How can blood be so dark? I wonder this hazily as my eyes continue to scan my daughter's body. Another plastic tube snakes into her left nostril, and it appears to be connected to one of the bags of clear liquid hanging above the bed. An accordion-pleated breathing tube distends her mouth, hooking her to a ventilator. *That's odd, I think, she looks like a scuba diver.* Multiple IV lines administer drugs and nourishment; another set of tubes removes waste from her body. *So this is a coma.* The words form, cartoon speech above my head.

I want to gather her in my arms as if she were two years old and croon snatches of songs we used to sing—"Mockingbird" with its billy goat that won't pull and its horse and cart falling down, papa buying you everything and mama making it all better. The mechanical whoosh of the ventilator and the ticking of the computers that monitor Maya's every vital sign only underline her silence, and my helplessness.

Only twenty minutes have passed since my conversation with the neurosurgeon.

Dan looks down at his stepdaughter, fighting back tears. Together, we hover over the body on the bed.

When the hospital phoned him, he got in his car and drove like hell from remote Humboldt County, covering a distance of one hundred and eighty miles in two-and-a-half hours. Somehow I sense that Dan grasps the scene before us more clearly than I can.

I lift Maya's left hand, the pink nail polish on her fingernails gleaming under the harsh fluorescent lights. It cuts my heart to see a trace of glamour on her limp fingers. I squeeze her hand gently, hoping for an answering pressure. Nothing. I put my lips close to her ear and whisper, "Maya, it's Mom. I love you sweetheart. Dan and I are here. We're pulling for you darling. We know you're going to get well."

Dan shoots me a questioning look.

We had separated in 1984. He married again in 1987 and had recently moved to Garberville, a small town near the Eel River among the coastal Redwood trees. Every other weekend I would drive Meghan to Cloverdale, a town midway between us, and spend an hour at a local café exchanging news and parenting updates with Dan. Then he would load her suitcase in the trunk of his car, and they would drive away. Typically, Maya and I would join Dan, his wife Linda, Meghan, and assorted friends for Thanksgiving, and then reverse the visitation at Christmas.

In his mid-forties, balding yet still handsome, Dan and I lock eyes over Maya's comatose body. I telegraph gratitude for his presence and his support; his body language speaks of overt fear. What I will realize later is that he understands the gravity of the situation far more quickly than I do—perhaps because the nurse tells him when she phones his office that the accident may be fatal.

We walk slowly to the foot of the bed, and Dan motions to one of the nurses to join us there. "Can you explain what the numbers on the computer screens mean?"

Early in his career Dan had been a stockbroker. He had a degree in quantitative methods from UCLA, and numbers were his forté. When we were married, his cold logic used to drive me nuts, especially when he turned it on me in the middle of an argument.

The nurse nods. "This one shows her intracranial pressure, or ICP, and it's key to measuring whether the brain swelling is coming down or not."

Her own father was absent and unreliable, so Dan is the only father Maya has known since she was five years old. Now he looks across his stepdaughter's body at the flickering numbers on the computer. "So it measures the pressure inside her brain?"

"Right," the nurse says.

"Is it coming down at all?"

"No, it's actually gone up, but that is normal after surgery."

Her words pelt me like smooth, hard pebbles. My body feels as if it were buried under a heap of cold mud while my brain races at fever pitch.

I clear my throat. "With this much life support equipment, could you even tell if she were dying?"

The nurse glances at the chart in her hand. I clear my throat again. "I mean, I would want to know... if she were dying... I just... I don't want her to die in here alone."

Maya's hair under my fingers that morning, how soft it felt. The memory of it makes me tremble. Now it seems like half a lifetime ago when I tousled her hair, still warm and tangled from her pillow. Hurrying, late, on my way out of our front door. "UCLA here we come," I said. She grinned and gave me her "Top Gun" thumbs up, cocky self-confidence shining from every pore.

I watch the nurse intently, holding back tears. I do not want to break down in this sterile place.

"I understand," she says. "We'll call you immediately if there is any change."

I stand there rooted to the spot, longing to turn back time to seven o'clock that morning. I'd replay the hurried argument we had about getting Maya's car serviced, the argument she won, and let her win it again. Again the hair, the prideful statement, the thumbs up. But then magically the scene would change. I'd stay with her, although she wouldn't want me to.

Throughout the day I'd hover near her, watching her movements as closely as I had when she was a toddler taking her first wavering steps. I would be her guardian angel whispering warnings. Like a reel of film rewinding, the day would roll backwards in time. The bad fate erased. Then, instead of talking to this nurse dressed in crisp white, we would be back on track with what was supposed to happen.

The wall clock in the nurse's break room says 10:35. I twist the phone cord, trying to postpone delivering my news. Retreating behind a curtain of numbness to protect John and myself, I dial his number at last. He picks up immediately.

"John, it's Ellie."

Instantly, he senses something is wrong.

"What is it, sweetheart?" he asks. I hesitate. With a trace of the brogue left over from his Irish youth, he repeats more urgently, "What is it?"

"I have something really difficult to tell you," I say. "It's about Maya. She fell from a horse and hit her head." I catch my breath and forge on. "She's critically injured, John. She's in a coma."

"*What?*" John, who had lost his own son in a drowning accident eight years before, would be the last person to believe this news.

"I'm at John Muir Hospital in Walnut Creek. She survived three hours of emergency brain surgery," I tell him. "The neurosurgeon says it doesn't look good."

"I don't believe it!" John is almost shouting.

He says he will get in the car and come to the hospital now.

"No, you're too upset."

We agree that it will be best for him to stay in Salinas that night and make the two-and-a-half hour drive to the Bay Area the next morning. I lean my forehead against the cool cement block wall and set the phone gently in its cradle.

I am grateful for John's support, but cautious too because we are hanging on by a thread as a couple. We've broken up and reunited several times in the four years we've been together, and our last breakup was only four months ago. During the last few months we reached a balance point, seeing each other only every other weekend. Now, in a bizarre twist of fate, I may need him more than ever.

❀   ❀   ❀

As an Irishman, John took liberties with the truth to create a good story.

"So what do you do?" were his first words as he pulled me closer. I was in Monterey for a corporate seminar in the fall of 1988. My work buddies had dared me to ask the very distinguished looking guy at the front table to dance. Oldies played on the jukebox in the hotel bar.

"I edit a corporate magazine," I said. "I started out as a journalist and then moved into business communications," I added, pulling away from his insistent grip.

"Really?" He didn't wait for me to expand on this theme. "I worked for some big newspapers myself in London."

He quickly turned the conversation back to me, and I never found out what he had actually done. He asked if he could see me again before I left for the Bay Area, and I agreed. The next day, after my seminar ended, we went to the Monterey Bay Aquarium and then out to dinner.

It emerged that in the 1950s and 60s John had installed and repaired printing presses in London where he lived with his family before they came to California. Later, when he moved to the States, he owned an auto detailing business in Salinas.

I had a brief flicker of doubt that we could possibly have much in common, but I brushed it aside. John began telling me about his family. When he recounted the harrowing details of his sixteen-year-old son's drowning in the ocean near Santa Cruz five years before, tears welled up in his eyes.

John Jr. had been out with friends to celebrate the end of their school year. Two of his friends were swept out on a boogie board by a rip current. A football player and strong swimmer, John dove into the waves after them. He succeeded in grabbing the rope attached to the fiberglass board, and pulled the two young women to safety, but before he could swim back to shore he was swept out into the open sea.

"The sheriff called me at work and told me they were dragging the ocean for my son. I went numb," John recalled. "I drove down to the beach. I paced for three hours while they searched, but they never found him." His voice faded to a whisper.

"A week later someone found the body wedged in a crevice of a tide pool."

"Oh God," I said. Completely drawn in, I tried to imagine what it would be like to lose one of my children. "I don't think I could survive that kind of loss," I said.

He ran his fingers over the tablecloth. "I didn't think I *would*. You can't even imagine the agony..."

He told me that whiskey had become his primary tool for numbing the grief. His twenty-six-year marriage collapsed and he lost his business. He took a job selling cars at a local Ford dealership in Salinas. My feeling that any man who had survived a loss of that magnitude was bound to be a compassionate, open person blotted out whatever hard questions these revelations might have raised in me.

As we left the restaurant that November night in 1988, John put his arm low around my waist. He planted his hand firmly around my right hip, just grazing the top of my butt, and pulled me close to his side.

"Your hips are just right," he said. My cheeks burned in the cold night air because I knew he was measuring how our bodies would fit together when we made love.

As was my usual pattern in relationships, I was so starved for touch and male attention that I slept with John long before I really knew much about him. He was warm, sweet, very sexy, and he adored me. What more did I need to know?

For some reason, no one is sitting down. Little knots of people buzz in the middle of the ICU waiting room. Meghan's aunt and uncle on Dan's side are there; they had rushed to the hospital to be with me as soon as I called to break the news. Dan tells me that Jean, the mother of Meghan's best friend, brought our daughter to the hospital. They met up in the waiting room, and now Jean has gone to her job as a night nurse. Numb and distracted, I lean down to embrace my younger daughter and then stand next to her rubbing her shoulders. My minister stands in the center of the room, talking to Maya's friends. Like a vivacious little bird, Reverend Margaret's head bobs as she talks. She is a foot shorter than the tall young men surrounding her, and her red hair gleams under the fluorescent lights.

At Margaret's side is her husband Victor, also a minister. Victor opens his arms to me, and I fall into a bear hug. Margaret, the more reserved of the two, gives my arm a squeeze as if to say, "It will be all right. I'm here now."

I'm confident that Margaret will know how to help me. Over the years she has been my counselor, prayer partner, and role model as I struggled to earn a living and be a good parent to my two children. She has also counseled Maya, and now without any hesitation she asks to see my daughter.

As they approach the lifeless form on the bed entangled with life support machinery, the two ministers remain impassive. Margaret walks decisively to Maya's side and immediately launches into a spiritual mind treatment, a form of affirmative prayer that she has schooled me in.

"Maya, it's Reverend Margaret," she says directly into my daughter's ear, as if the comatose body were perfectly conscious. "You are young, and strong, and beautiful. You have everything to live for—wonderful goals and plans. I know that you will recover and go on with them."

Margaret had prayed for Maya as she was auditioning at UCLA, and took great pride in my daughter's accomplishments as a young actress.

"You are one with the life and the infinite intelligence that animates all things," Margaret continues. "The God-self within you knows exactly what to do."

My soul leaps up in agreement with Margaret's words. In this moment when a miracle is what I need most to sustain me, Margaret's faith delivers it. Maya lies as motionless as Sleeping Beauty on her hospital bed. We walk away and leave her there. For the first time since the neurosurgeon spoke to me, I feel a sliver of hope.

Chapter 3

Dan paces the waiting room, his flannel shirt hanging out of his jeans. Head bent, hands stuffed in his pockets, he looks strung out. Every so often he pauses and stands next to Meghan, absently stroking her hair.

When I look at him I feel love as well as resentment. I left our marriage with my sexual self-esteem in tatters, another reason that John's attentions overrode my better judgment. When I look at Dan, gratitude mixes with frustration and regret.

Meghan leans against her father like a small boat tethered to a dock in a storm. She still has little dimples on the backs of her fingers, and her hands and elbows are round and pudgy. She's just forming, only eleven years old. Her eyes are red and her cheeks are streaked and blotchy; she's just come back from her sister's bedside.

Dan says he wants to spend the night in the waiting room.

"Are you sure?" I'm worried about him.

"Yes," he says firmly. "I want to be here in case there's any change." We both know that he means in case Maya dies—or miraculously regains consciousness.

We agree that it would be best for me to take Meghan home

and try to get some sleep. I leave the hospital at midnight, holding my daughter by the hand.

She sits in the car, seat-belted, silent, staring out the passenger side window. I don't know what to say. What the hell kind of a mother am I, I wonder, that I cannot protect my children? I drive extra cautiously as if that could somehow make up for the dreadful sight of her comatose sister. We wind along Ygnacio Valley Road and then turn on North Broadway, driving past the pedestrian mall where I often shopped with my daughters. It jolts me to see the Nordstrom store where I maxed out my credit card shopping for Maya's prom gowns, shoes, and glittering evening bags. The night is pitch black, and there are no other cars on the city streets.

I maneuver the car onto the freeway. Pinpoints of light twinkle from big ranch houses set on the tree-studded hills overlooking Highway 24. *All the rich people secure up there on their hillsides.* The thought is a bitter one. Already I feel as if Maya's accident has put us in a separate segment of society—those that bad things happen to—and that we stand apart. Meghan's pinched, white face only confirms the doctor's frightening prognosis, underlining the nightmarish quality of the last six hours. My instincts tell me to clench up, to fall back on my obsessive need to be organized in the midst of chaos.

At home in Lafayette, I park the car precisely between the lines in the parking garage under our two-bedroom apartment. When we go in, I head directly down the hall to the kids' room where I lay out Meghan's pajamas while she brushes her teeth.

A pair of Maya's jeans lies heaped together with Meghan's school clothes, and the unmade beds hold piles of aging stuffed animals. Disorder makes me feel claustrophobic in the small room, so I begin folding the clothes. Then I make the beds. I try to avoid looking too closely at Maya's open suitcase overflowing with dirty laundry, cosmetics, and a dog-eared Steven King novel. I nudge the suitcase into a corner with my foot as gingerly as if it contained a bomb.

Meghan puts on her pajamas as I fuss around moving things here, then there. Finally, I tuck her in bed, and smooth her hair.

"The nurses will take good care of Maya tonight," I say, trying to reassure her. "We can see her again tomorrow."

"I don't want to," Meghan whimpers. "It's too sad." She clutches her stuffed furry rabbit. When I kiss her forehead, she wraps her arm around my neck.

"It's okay," I whisper. "You don't have to see her if you don't want to. It's going to be okay." This is the beginning of many lies I will tell myself in the coming days. I slip out and leave the door ajar with the hall light on.

When I get in bed I prop myself up on pillows and stare at a blank page in my journal. I carefully date the page, "Thursday, April 2, 1992." I move my pen as if it were a magic piece of kryptonite and write, "Please God let my daughter live and be whole and vibrant again. I love you, Maya. Live, honey, live!"

Still groggy from the sleeping pill I had taken, I swim up out of sleep and find Meghan curled into a ball next to me. Her deep, relaxed breathing immediately reminds me of the forced rise and fall of my other daughter's chest, the tubes snaking into her, the swollen, puffy eyelids.

Stumbling out of bed, I put on my bathrobe and head to the kitchen to make tea. As I pass the bookshelf in our living room, I stare at the paper banner I had taped to the top shelf for Maya. "UCLA SAYS YES!" is scrawled in red magic marker.

God can't let this happen to us. It's too unfair. Not when Maya's dreams are coming true. I drop to my knees before the bookcase, as if the banner were a graven image that could save us. The achievement it represents is the god I had worshipped, the god I taught Maya to worship. Not God, the capital-G, the force I trust against all reason to bring us safely through this. But one of many little gods—brains, wit, speed, beauty, skill, commitment—I lean on day to day. Now I beg all those little smashed gods, "Please bring her back to life!"

Maya's senior portrait stands next to the banner. I stand up and study my daughter's animated smile and gleaming blond hair, suddenly overcome with an urge to break things. I want revenge for this sudden shattering of our lives. I spin wildly around to face the apartment's sliding glass windows, which suddenly seem too solid and confining. I scan the shelf for a book heavy enough to hurl at them. But an inner voice tells me to get a hold on my emotions. Trembling, I walk into my kitchen and lean against the counter to steady myself. As I had from the moment Meghan broke the awful news to me, I root myself in the awareness of my eleven-year-old child's need for routine and a semblance of sanity in the midst of this chaos.

There are other responsibilities to face as well. Maya's boyfriend of one year, Dale, has to be told about her accident. Dale is every mother's dream of a potential son-in-law: good looking, articulate, and responsible. If he had been in town and available to celebrate Maya's triumph, instead of Alex, it is probable that none of this would have happened. Alex and Maya had dated only briefly in high school, but they were still friends and they had shared the drive home together from Santa Barbara for spring break. Somehow, I have to find a way to recount yesterday's events to Dale.

"Dale, it's Ellie," I say when he answers his phone. "I'm sorry to call you so early this morning, but I have some bad news. Maya's been in an accident."

"An accident?" Sheets rustle as he sits up in bed, and I imagine his grip on the receiver tightening. "A car? How bad is it?"

"No, not a car. She fell from a horse she was riding bareback..."

He pauses. "Is she dead?"

"No, but they aren't holding out much hope. She's in a coma. I think there's a chance she could pull through." I speak mechanically into the phone, "She's completely unresponsive and..."

"I'm coming," he says. "I'm leaving right now. I'll call work..."

"No, Dale," I underline each word for emphasis. I picture him speeding north on the twisty section of Highway 101 from Santa Barbara. "You could have an accident. Please call your folks first, and figure out the best way to get here safely."

His parents, Allen and Jean Ann, live in a small town in Nevada, refugees from the Los Angeles suburbs where they raised their two kids. Dale had taken Maya home to meet them at Christmas, and Maya told me that Jean Ann was hoping that Dale would propose to her soon. "I'm sorry, Dale," I say. I hang up the phone, images of the first time I met him filling my mind.

I had rented a cabin on the Russian River in August of 1991. We were there for the entire week to celebrate Meghan's eleventh birthday. She was allowed to invite three friends for her party. As a concession to Maya for putting up with the pre-teen mayhem, I said she could bring Dale. I had never met her new, more serious boyfriend.

"Mom, this is Dale," Maya said, releasing her hold on his hand and giving him a little shove forward to shake hands with me.

I grasped his warm outstretched palm and saw my daughter's face light up with pride. His sincere manner, his low-key intelligence, and his obvious feelings for Maya impressed me.

I wince remembering how tender Dale had been with Maya on our vacation—and how heated they both were in competitive pursuits—everything from video poker to a hard-fought game of Scrabble provoked fierce lovers' quarrels.

Grateful for any distraction, I lean against my kitchen sink mechanically sponging yesterday's dishes. I don't know whether hours or minutes pass until the sound of our warped wooden gate scraping against the cement patio signals John's arrival. His purposeful stride, more choppy and rapid than usual, echoes from the patio. Then his key turns in the lock. *I should go to him*, I think, but my body stays frozen in place at the sink.

When he takes me in his arms I release a pent-up shudder and gulp for air, feeling his need to comfort me coursing through him like an electric current. "Oh baby," he says, "this can't be. She's so beautiful, so alive."

An image of Maya ripping open a gift box at Christmas flashes before me. She lifts the perfectly tailored wool jersey and matching black pants up to examine them and grins up at John. Later, when she tries on the outfit, twirling before us in the living room, he lets out a soft whistle.

I shake the image out of my head and lean back to look at him. "I don't believe this is really happening either. It's just a bad dream."

As a child I used to put my hands over my eyes and tell my mother, "You can't see me," really believing that she couldn't. With the same childlike logic I want to believe that John is right, all that has happened in the last sixteen hours simply can't be real.

In an earlier era, John would have been called a dandy. He kept his silver hair neatly trimmed, and he was meticulous about his clothes, carefully brushing his black wool coat with a clothes brush every time he took it from the hall closet. He was just an inch taller than I was, and when we hugged I could easily slip my arms around his neck. His skin was tan and leathery, his eyes the cloudy blue of agates. I loved his slightly musky scent and the unfailing ardor of his embrace. In his early fifties, he was an incorrigible flirt who traded on his innate Irish charm.

He had won my jaded teenager over quickly. The first Christmas we were together, in 1988, he bought Maya a gorgeous sweater. Since she never received Christmas presents from her own father in Minnesota, my new boyfriend's attentions were especially welcome. John and Maya became allies, raising their eyebrows in unison and making whispered comments whenever I was in a bad mood as if, together, they could bring me in line.

John pressed for a commitment early in our relationship, and we decided to look for a larger house to rent together. At forty, I was emotionally needy and on the edge financially, despite a new corporate job. I nurtured a fantasy that somehow having a man around would provide more stability for my kids. When I told Maya that John might move in with us, she seemed genuinely happy. I think she sensed that I needed a mate to take some of the pressure off—and she may have felt it would make her less vulnerable to my emotional needs, and freer to start exploring boys, an undertaking she had begun a year earlier when she was fifteen.

I was drawn to John's heart, his Irish charm, and his romantic nature. It never occurred to me to ask him if whiskey was still one of his coping mechanisms. I figured the worst that could happen was that I would get stuck with a three-bedroom, two-bath house and have to find a roommate to cover John's portion of the rent. I began scanning the want ads, and soon found a vacant home in our neighborhood.

As moving day approached, I was filled with relief at the prospect of leaving our tiny duplex. My daughters and I had been cooped up together in 850 square feet, and I was sick of the cracked plaster on the walls and the cheap beige carpet. Just the prospect of no longer sharing a bathroom with my teenage daughter made me so jubilant that concerns about the future seemed unimportant.

We moved in January of 1989, and John found a job selling cars at a nearby Ford dealership. He got along well with both my daughters, but he and Maya grew especially close. He had raised four kids himself, and was a sympathetic listener. He appreciated Maya's energy and her humor.

"She's a charmer, that one," he said to me once, an extra Irish lilt in his voice. "You'll have to beat the boys off her with a baseball bat."

My first inkling that something was amiss with John dawned one Saturday afternoon in March. We had just come back from a trip to the grocery store, and I noticed him storing cans of food in the refrigerator. It made no sense.

"Honey, this stuff goes in the cupboard," I said waving a can of soup at him in exasperation. "Why did you put it in here?"

"Oh," he said. "Okay, if that's what you want." But he made no move to relocate the cans or explain his behavior. When I pushed the point, he angrily rejoined, "Could you just drop it? I won't do it again."

I also noticed that he was an extraordinarily forgetful driver. I would have to restate simple directions many times. He seemed dense and out of it, and I grew weary of having to repeat myself and impatient with him. But then he rubbed my shoulders or told me how pretty I was, and I would be won over and think my complaints were minor.

Whenever we discussed his son's tragic death, John blamed himself for his son's drowning because it had been his decision to immigrate with his wife and children to the United States. He reasoned that if they had not moved to California, John Jr. would not have drowned. When he talked to me about his feelings of loss and remorse, I saw that although the death had occurred six years ago, he still had not resolved his guilt or his grief. I wondered if he ever would.

Soon after we moved in together, my professional life intensified. That spring I was named editor of the corporate magazine I helped to produce. The new job was a promotion, and along with an increase in pay and responsibility came a renewed sense of pressure to succeed in such a visible position. I was working long hours. Meghan was now spending her school week with her father and stepmother in Lafayette. I saw her on Wednesday evenings, and she spent every weekend with me in Walnut Creek.

Maya was about to hit her peak as an acting-out teen—something I didn't connect to my own history of troubled relationships until many years later. If anything, I put Maya's problems down to her status as a latchkey kid, and I blamed her absent father in Minnesota for not paying child support and putting me in the difficult position of being both breadwinner and primary parent. But it was becoming increasingly difficult for me to minimize the signs that my daughter was in trouble—especially after the police had to be called twice in one night by irate neighbors to break up a party she had hosted that spun out of control. She had lied to me, and I felt betrayed. Yes, I had been out of town for the weekend, but we had agreed she would stay at a girlfriend's while I was gone. She was strictly forbidden to have friends over when I was away.

One night I arrived home after a long day and a rugged commute. I noticed there were no lights on in the house, and that seemed odd. John should be home by now, and where was Maya? Pinned to the front door I found a note from my daughter saying she was spending the night at a girlfriend's house. That answered one of my questions. When I pushed open the front door I sensed more than saw that something fundamental had changed. I flipped on a light in the living room and called John's name. My voice echoed in the empty house.

Exasperated, I dropped my coat over the couch arm and walked down the hall and into the bedroom. The bedside table light was on and beneath it stood an empty bottle of Jim Beam. Next to that was a crumpled sheet of white notebook paper. Scribbled on it was a largely incoherent message from John that ended with a stark conclusion, "I have a problem..."

Stunned, but somehow not surprised by either the bottle or the admission, I went to check the closet. All of his clothes were gone. I remember feeling a wave of relief. "What the hell, if this is what he's into, good riddance," I thought. The forgetfulness, the vague look in his eyes, his sudden temper flares all slid into place like pieces of a puzzle. When he called a few days later to say that he had checked into a recovery clinic, I congratulated him. "Thank God," I thought, "he's doing something about his drinking."

"Do you want me to stay out of your life?" he asked. "Yes," I said. I had seen enough of addiction's impact on my two former husbands.

"I can't go through this with you—and I don't want to put my kids through it either," I told John. At that point if you had asked me to bet on the odds of our ever getting back together, I would have said it was a hundred to one against.

When John, Meghan, and I walk into the waiting room of the neuroscience ICU later that morning, we learn a brand new routine spelled out for us by Maya's doctors and enforced by the hospital's protocols. Fifty minutes out of each hour the nurses and doctors are at Maya's bedside tending to life support equipment, adjusting fluids, calibrating her medications.

Each hour, hospital policy allows me ten minutes with my comatose child. I may take one person with me. In various combinations, we begin our hourly vigils at mid-morning on Friday, April 3.

In the midst of a crisis there are two opposite but equally powerful forces at work. A new kind of silence descends and the mundane drops off the radar screen entirely. Work, grocery shopping, bills, meetings—all these shrink until they seem tiny and unimportant. At the same time, life and death decisions bear down quickly, and people and their emotions swirl constantly. That day, I move to the eye of the storm.

Sometimes John is at my side gripping my hand, while I hold Maya's and whisper words of encouragement. At others, Dan stands across the bed from me as we try desperately to pull her back to consciousness.

To bring a touch of humanity to the grim scene on the bed, I tape two of Maya's senior pictures to the gleaming metal IV pole. In one, she wears a deep blue sweater, smiling her dazzling smile. In the other, the photographer poses her in a black drape, blond hair swirling over her left shoulder. During one of our ten-minute visits, a male nurse dressed in hospital greens motions me to the foot of the bed.

"So," he asks as if the inert figure on the bed has nothing to do with the pictures he is staring at, "that's your daughter?" I nod. "She had beautiful hair," he glances from the photo to the turban-wrapped head on the pillow. Why is he talking about her in the past tense, I wonder. "And those eyes. She looks like a real hell-raiser." Then he takes the clipboard with her vitals from the foot of her bed, winks at me, and heads back to the nursing station.

Raising hell? Oh yes, she did do that. But for years I dismissed her over-the-line behavior. She was high strung, imaginative, difficult, but so was I. And in the two years she had been away at college, all that teenage acting out had been transformed into a single-minded ambition to succeed as an actress. My daughter had become a straight-A student who was on the Dean's List every quarter she attended college in Santa Barbara. Until her accident, I had enjoyed a sense of fulfillment as a parent that I had not dreamed would ever be possible—I was the proud mother of a budding young actress.

In between visits to my daughter's bedside, I call relatives. On my list today are Maya's paternal aunt and uncle in Minnesota. I don't know how to reach her father, whom Maya and I have not seen in more than ten years.

Jeff and I divorced in 1976, at first amicably and later with rancor and arguments over child support and visitation. The year Maya turned five, she and I moved to California, and despite a court order, Jeff stopped paying child support. I suspected that drinking and smoking pot were pushing him over the edge when I began receiving letters full of gibberish. When I phone from the ICU waiting room, his brother's wife tells me that Jeff, once a talented and popular jazz drummer in Minneapolis, is too mentally unstable to be told of our daughter's condition. I agree that whatever his family decides is for the best.

Later that day Dale and his mother Jean Ann arrive. They join the hourly pilgrimage to Maya's bedside. We huddle in the envelope of pale pastel curtains that surround her bed. The corners of Dale's mouth tremble as he plays with Maya's limp unresponsive fingers.

As the hours pass and she remains lifeless, I begin to focus on the parts of Maya that are whole. Like a mother cat that knows every inch of the blind, bald kitten she nudges to life with her raspy tongue, I know my daughter's body. The brisk arches in her two strong feet. The little knobs of her ankle bones. The way her sculpted calves curve beneath her knees. The lean muscled thighs, then the bump of pelvis and smooth flat abdomen. Her firm little breasts. The valley on the upper side of her collar bone, and the white flute of neck lifting out of shoulders that are narrow but square and powerful. I remember the feel of her pudgy infant body against mine, the warm dimpled arms against my chest as we waded deeper into that hotel pool all those years ago. Clinging to my memories of her, I hold on to my belief that she will ultimately recover.

Back in the ICU waiting room, flowers in Mason jars accumulate on the end tables. Someone props a silver balloon on a stick in the corner. That Friday afternoon, the day after the accident, Alex and his cousin George come in. Looking back, I marvel that I wasn't angrier with them. The boys amble toward me, hulks in jeans and bulky running shoes. A brunette who looks about Maya's age trails behind them.

"This is Julie," Alex says.

The other girl on the horse, the girl Maya got tangled up with before she fell. "I'm sorry," she whispers. "I'm really sorry." She wears a yellow sweater with an angel pin at the neck. I stare at the silver pin, a protective talisman intended to celebrate the fact that she was unscathed by the accident.

"Thank you for coming," I say. We sit and leaf through magazines, staring out the window at the rolling hills and sprawling homes surrounding the hospital, waiting for the next visit with Maya. Her closest girlfriends tell the nurses they are her cousins so that they will be allowed to see her. When they come back from the ICU, their faces are pale and strained. One of them makes a collage out of photocopied pictures of school dances, birthday parties, sleepovers, and ski trips. She signs the photo collage, *Maya I (heart) U, love always...* We prop it up on one of the end tables in the waiting room to remind us of who she must become again.

Suspended by a thread of forced air, like a spider hooked to her web of gadgets and medicinal fluids, Maya drifts in her coma. Alex and the other young people leave after an hour. The family holds vigil. I call my brother in Ohio from a pay phone in the waiting room. His voice is steady and eerily calm.

"We're praying for all of you," Tim says.

"Pray hard," I tell him.

When I replace the pay phone in its cradle, I see my blurred reflection in a stainless steel panel below it and realize that I had put on earrings and makeup that morning. The phrase *pulled together* runs through my mind.

For three straight days I hover over my daughter in the white sterility of the ICU. Each night I dutifully take a sleeping pill to drown out the forlorn beeps and hisses of the computers that punctuate her silence. Dan sleeps in the waiting room, folded across the faux leather chairs, on the chance that something about Maya's condition might suddenly shift.

I make elaborate plans for how I will teach my daughter to

walk again, how I will coach her first words, and work with the hospital staff to help her regain all of her functions. Each time I go to her, I lean in close to her face, obsessively looking for a flutter of eyelid or a raised eyebrow—the tiniest sign perceivable that Maya will beat the odds and come back to life.

By Sunday afternoon, four days after the accident, I am angry and snappish. When John reaches for my hand, I squeeze his and then pull away accusingly, as if it is his fault my daughter is in a coma.

"Let me go," I say, rising abruptly.

I look out of the waiting room windows. Below me, stick figures move around their lawns, people who know nothing of this waiting. I stare at the tableau that passes for normal life. Then I look at my watch. It's time to see her again. I steel myself, turn to face John, and together we go to the ICU doors for what feels like the hundredth time. I lift the house phone to request permission to enter.

"This is Maya's mom. Can we see her now?"

"Yes," a nurse answers. "I'll buzz you in."

People who voyage through Arctic waters in summer say there is no way to describe the sound of tons of ice breaking up, the creaking and groaning before the roar of separation.

I walk toward my daughter's bed, past the curtains surrounding families bent over other silent bodies. After almost four days of nursing my hope, of making myself believe she will recover, the thought of the impossible dawns—*Maya might not make it.* When I reach her bedside, I am vibrating with this new possibility. I take her hand in mine. "Sweetheart, it's Mom. I've been telling you that you will get well. But maybe that's not right; maybe what I want isn't what matters."

A roar fills my brain as I speak to her, saying out loud what I still cannot accept. John stares down at her. He seems oblivious to my words. I pause, watching her face for a sign. "You decide, honey," I say. "It's between you and God. If you need to go, I won't hold you back."

Maya's face is smooth and inanimate as ice, bride-like with her pink skin and white bedclothes. The gadgets are only gadgets. They have no power, and I can see that now. I lean into her cheek and whisper the biggest lie of my life, "I'll be all right sweetheart, if you need to go."

Our life together rushes in to fill every space in my mind. As if it had happened yesterday, I see my three-year-old child jumping from the edge of the bathtub into my arms to enact our nightly ritual. Maya lands in the white terry cloth towel I hold out. I set her down on the bath mat and dry beads of water from her skin. Then, I lead her into our game, draping a towel over my own shoulders. Together we call "Wonder Woman!" "Wonder Woman!" The towels, which in our shared imagining have become two white capes, billow behind us, as we run through our apartment in Minneapolis. We extend our arms like airplane wings, grasping the edges of our capes, two beings as one in flight. The fantasy of being all-powerful ends at the side of her bed where I help her into her nightgown and tuck her in, a little girl again.

As I stand looking down at her now, I know that I have no magic bracelet, no supernatural powers, and neither does she. As the hard core of determination dissolves, all I want to do is throw myself across her chest and give in to hours of suppressed weeping. But the moment of acceptance quickly gives way to a new thought: *If I break down, it will be too hard for her to die. My task now is to let her go.*

I remember the night Maya graduated from high school and I came home alone before the others to prepare for the party.

One look at her senior picture sitting on the mantel and I broke down. I had to stop bustling around the living room. I sat in our beat up old rocking chair and sobbed. On that night when I acknowledged that my daughter was moving away from me, I never dreamed that anything more difficult could happen, that any greater surrender might be asked of me. *Forever* yawns like an abyss.

Maya's chest rises and falls. The ventilator hisses, the computers beep, fiber optic cable snakes into her skull to measure the pressure inside her brain. I never knew love could be large enough to allow even this. I have a premonition of lifelong grief rolling toward me, but I know that, once again, I am being asked to step aside and give my daughter her freedom.

God must be mad! I must be mad to say, "Yes, go."

A few hours later, her temperature soars. When John and I return to Maya's bedside, two nurses are hovering over her.

The doctor paces at the foot of her bed, thumbing her chart.

"Okay, what's next?" I ask, afraid to hear his answer.

"Just some routine blood tests to see what kind of bug might be causing this fever. Meanwhile, I'm having her packed in ice. We have to bring the fever down or she could go into convulsions."

"Should I spend the night?"

"No, you go home and try to rest. I'll call you if there's any change."

One of the nurses hands me a plastic bag embossed with the hospital's name. She says it contains some of Maya's things. As we prepare to leave the hospital parking lot, I set it carefully in the back seat of John's car, reminding myself to take it into our apartment and look at it in the morning.

At eleven o'clock John and I are sleepless, lying in bed with our fingers laced together, peering into the darkness. Car headlights flash across the blinds. Maya's black and white cat Bizbomb purrs at the foot of the bed.

"I'm afraid," I whisper. "Oh, John, I'm so afraid."

I feel the answering pressure of his hand and know that his unspoken wish is the same as mine—*Please God let this be a bad dream that will vanish when we wake up.*

Chapter 4

I settle into the same easy chair where Maya sat four days earlier when I said good-bye to her. The cat jumps into my lap. The living room is quiet and peaceful, filled with books and family photographs, and for the moment, the sterility of the hospital recedes. Bizbomb cocks her head at me, purring loudly. I scratch her ears and rub under her chin, cuddling her against me. Eight-year-old Maya used to wrap Bizbomb in a flannel blanket and drag the rocking chair out to the porch so she could hold and rock her kitten. Later, she and the grown cat used to butt their heads together as a sign of affection, the blond head snuggled in against the black.

I set Bizbomb down on the carpet and prepare to open the bag of Maya's belongings the nurse gave me the night before. I reach in and my fingers touch something smooth. When I open the mouth of the bag wider and look in, I see a pair of grass-stained cutoffs with ragged edges. They fall open when I lift them, cut in two by nurses when Maya first arrived at the hospital. Digging deeper, I find a bra with its elastic band snipped in half, and a pink T-shirt that has been cut down the middle. *They stripped her naked in under a minute.*

Buried beneath her clothing is a smaller bag.

As I reach into that bag, I feel something soft. Curious, I open the bag wider. Thick strands of Maya's hair lie coiled in my fingers. My mouth falls open, and I hear the sound of someone screaming. I snatch my hand out of the bag.

"Oh, God," I gasp. "Her shaved hair! My daughter's hair!" I jump up from the chair. The cat races under the dining room table, cowering there.

John rushes into the living room, sees me, rigid, staring into the bag, and takes it from my hands. The finality of that nest of hair is like a slap across the face. John holds me while I sob.

His fury at the nursing staff escapes in elaborate curses as he bustles to the kitchen to make tea. "Bloody hell," he mutters, "what were they thinking?"

I stuff the bag of hair back in with the shredded clothing and put the entire sorry mess on the floor by the chair.

"Look love, you're shattered," John says, guiding me to the dining alcove and setting me down in a chair. "Have some hot tea." Strong black tea with milk and plenty of sugar is his answer to any crisis. After drinking several cups I feel more composed.

As we wind along the curving streets of Walnut Creek, I brace myself. We pull into the parking lot on yet another warm spring morning. If it weren't for the medical center, we could be in a park. The acacia trees and oleanders are in full bloom, their pink blossoms spilling down onto the pavement with each gust of wind.

The hospital's new wing faces Ygnacio Valley Road, towering six stories above the smaller office buildings and homes surrounding it. I can look up and see the second floor where my daughter's body lies in a sea of white, where the stiff plastic chairs outside of the Intensive Care Unit will hold us for another day as we wait. John maneuvers the car into a parking space near the emergency room entrance, and for a moment I sit there unmoving, staring at the dashboard. I am not sure that I can face Maya's limp, unresponsive body for a fifth day.

Many specialists have offered opinions about Maya's condition. They all concur that she has developed multiple complications of diffuse brain swelling, including a mild form of diabetes, anemia, and low blood pressure. They think that she may have ruptured her spleen or kidney, but this is never confirmed. Meanwhile, the pressure inside her brain remains elevated, and blood flow to critical brain tissue is inadequate.

One of her doctors, a cardiologist named Tim Carlton, tries desperately to support her blood pressure with drugs in order to improve the perfusion pressure in her brain. But despite vigilantly reformulating the many medicines she is receiving, no one is able to reduce the intracranial pressure or completely offset the after-effects of the craniotomy during which she lost three units of blood.

Shortly after our first ten-minute visit with Maya that morning, her neurosurgeon hustles us into a nearby conference room.

"We need to run some additional tests," Dr. Carr tells me. I am instantly on guard. "We have to find out if any blood is still flowing into her brain."

The procedure involves shooting radioactive dye into her bloodstream, then evaluating how much of the dye reaches the brain. They will have to move her three floors down to the Radiology area. In my mind this evokes images of a cold dark basement with technicians swarming over her body, a prospect I find completely unacceptable given the trauma she has already suffered.

I shake my head violently. *Leave her in peace,* I think. And don't take her out of my sight. Later, I will see that I am trying to postpone the finality of a terminal diagnosis, which I fear above all else.

I begin to argue. "I can't understand why you need to do this. The nurse told us earlier that her fever has come down and the intracranial pressure has improved from last night. Why can't the procedure be done here in the ICU?"

He smiles indulgently. "That's impossible. This has to be done in Radiology."

"I want to talk to Dr. Garry," I shoot back.

Dr. Carr drums his manicured fingers on the conference table, then finally agrees. "All right. I'll have the nurse call him."

"No," I snap at him. "I want to speak to him *here*, in person."

John gives me a look that telegraphs "Calm down!" Raging with grief and pumped full of caffeine, I feel reckless and determined. I don't give a damn what either of them thinks. I'm her mother. No one is taking Maya away unless it is truly necessary.

Ten minutes later I stand outside the conference room door with John and Dr. Garry. "If Maya's getting better, why does she have to be moved?"

Dr. Garry looks at me hard, but kindly, then flips through the pages of Maya's chart with a puzzled crease between his eyebrows. He glances up from the file in his hand and assures me that Dr. Carr knows what he's doing and that she will not be jostled or disturbed on the way to the Radiology area. I give in.

He disappears through the metal sliding doors into the ICU. Suddenly, the air closes in around me. The smell of antiseptic makes me want to vomit. I turn wildly to John. "I have to get out of here. I can't take this another minute!"

We make our way across the hospital parking lot, walk down the sidewalk for a few blocks, and then climb a steep path that is part of the regional trail system. The dirt crumbles under my feet. Gulping down air, I let the rhythm of my legs take over as we pass dozens of flowering trees. It was only a week ago when Maya arrived home for spring break. That Monday night, we watched the Academy Awards ceremony on TV. When a cool, self-possessed Jody Foster claimed her prize for "Silence of the Lambs," I watched my daughter studying the actress and knew she was dreaming of what she would say if she won the Oscar someday. When we heard the news of her acceptance at UCLA two days later, we felt like we had won the lottery. Luck rained down on us. The future was expansive, limitless, rich. Now it was crumbling like the dirt at my feet.

My legs churn up the path. At the crest of the hill, I turn east to gaze at Mt. Diablo. Its sawtooth outline cuts through a ribbon of clouds, a big grandfather of a mountain hulking over the lush green foothills. I imagine the horse that threw Maya standing on one of those hillsides above Morgan Territory Road calmly flicking his tail, pushing his muzzle deeper in the grass to search for tender clumps. His owner had heard about the accident and sent her minister to the hospital to comfort us. An earnest middle-aged woman with glasses and a somewhat too sympathetic smile, she had patted my shoulder and assured me that her congregation was praying for Maya's recovery. My thoughts veer to the limp form, the gauze turban, the tubes running from her body to machines. I turn away from the mountain to face my lover. I see my fear and sorrow reflected in his eyes.

"If she dies," I say, "at least it will be a good death. She's going out on a high."

"Oh, honey, just pray that she won't," he says.

I look at my watch. It is just after 1:30 in the afternoon on April 6, 1992.

Almost a hundred hours have passed since the accident.

When we arrive back in the ICU waiting room, Dan says that Dr. Carr wants to speak with us about the results of the cerebral blood flow study. One of the nurses asks if family members will please come to the same windowless conference room where we met with Dr. Carr earlier. When we enter, I recoil.

A hospital social worker sits at the opposite end of the table looking grave and sympathetic. There are boxes of tissue sitting on the end tables. Dr. Carr comes in, his white coat flapping, and sits down.

"Did you feel it?" He asks as if he were addressing all of us, giving no time for an answer. His voice is choppy, like a pitchman selling something on late-night TV. "Did you feel it coming?" He leans forward in his chair and with characteristic bluntness says, "Bad news. Bad news."

Why does he say everything twice? My hands are ice-cold. I clench them in my lap and search his handsome, dispassionate face with another surge of amazed fury at his pure detachment.

"The test we did shows the blood flow to the brain." He speaks to the wall now. "There is none, absolutely none, zero blood flow. I've declared her brain dead."

I don't move. I don't even blink. A collective gasp echoes through the cramped room as if a sudden gust of wind had swept through. Dale groans. Dan covers his face with his hands.

"I've called in a second surgeon to confirm the diagnosis," Dr. Carr says with infuriating calm, as if oblivious to the emotions swirling around him.

Others file in and pandemonium breaks out. Dale's mother Jean Ann screams, "No, no, no! Oh, no! Oh God, Dale, *no*." Meghan leans against her father and weeps.

I stare at the doctor with a hatred so absolute I don't know if I can stop myself from killing him. How can he tell such a lie? How can he sit there, so smug, so above it all, so white and clean and antiseptic? Hot tears of disbelief trickle down my cheeks. John squeezes my hand so hard his rings cut into my flesh. Of all the people in the room, I am the only one who does not move, or cry out. I feel granite-hard, yet sensitive as a tuning fork, paralyzed with grief. The social worker passes out tissue like party favors.

"We did all we could," the doctor says lamely.

I nod. This is the one thing I do believe.

Out of nowhere Dr. Carr turns to me and asks, "Would you consider organ donation?" He looks straight at me for the first time since he entered the room. His eyes are as prominent as icy blue marbles.

His question hangs in the air for a long moment. In that instant I see my baby the day she was born, pink and bald, her eyes squinting up at me as if the light might blind her. My diabetic mother plucking at the sheets on her deathbed as her kidneys fail. Then the image of the pink donor sticker pasted on the front of my driver's license. I see Maya stride on stage for a final exuberant bow. I think of families in other windowless hospital conference rooms sobbing when a doctor confirms their worst fears.

"Yes," I hear myself tell him.

Dr. Carr nods. "At least it won't be a total waste."

He gestures at the hospital walls, and beyond at the high-tech gadgetry keeping Maya's heart beating, her lungs pumping, her blood circulating. He means that all the effort and resources spent over a hopeless case will not be in vain. What I mean is that the love and energy I poured into my daughter, her very life, must continue. I can no more accept that Maya is truly dead than

I can fly to the moon or allow any vital part of her that could save another human being to go to her grave.

Dr. Carr says he will contact the California Transplant Donor Network. There is not a moment to waste because as long as the ventilator is supporting Maya there is an increased chance of damage to her organs, especially her lungs. People are waiting with desperate patience for what Maya has to offer: heart, liver, kidneys, corneas. These parts of her like ripe fruit in her perfect, otherwise unmarred body.

I made the decision. I said yes. Now, I sit at the table and tremble uncontrollably trying to encompass the impossible consequences.

The social worker immediately begins taking relatives to Maya's bedside to say their final good-byes. If she is to be a donor, everyone now has to move quickly, Dr. Carr reiterates. Meghan files out with Dan and one of her aunts.

John stands behind me in the airless room, squeezing my shoulders.

"Can I get you something?" he asks. Yes I tell him, please, water.

One of the ICU volunteers who spoke with us several times during the last four days comes into the room. He has gray hair and a welcoming smile, and every morning as we arrive, he greets us warmly. His own son died here in the hospital. I did not want to become a member of his club.

I stare at him blankly. He kneels down on the carpet next to my chair. "Eleanor," he says, grasping my hand. I turn to face him, focusing on his eyes. I can see that he knows everything I feel—the shock, the disbelief, the hot anger, the searing grief. He leans his forehead against mine and clasps me by the shoulders.

"Do this with dignity for your daughter's sake," he whispers.

"Eleanor, can you hear me?" I nod. I understand him perfectly. "Hold your head up, be proud of what you are doing, be proud of Maya," he says ever so softly.

I am about to give my daughter away in pieces. *If I had fought harder, could I have held her here?* I gave Maya ultimate freedom, and she took me up on it.

I clasp his hands. "Yes," I tell him. "I understand."

The social worker leans in the doorway and announces that my ministers Rev. Margaret and Rev. Victor are on their way to the hospital. The hospital volunteer turns and speaks to John as if they are co-conspirators in the world of grief, old hands in a secret society I am just joining. "If there is anything you need, anything I can do..."

As I wait for Margaret and Victor to come, I drift into a trance, suspended in a state of numbness that alternates with stabbing pain so intense it feels as if it could propel me out of my own body.

If something so outlandish can happen to Maya, I must say yes to another thing that is extreme enough to equal my grief. In that moment, I will do anything to protect others from the kind of suffering that is tearing me apart. Donating Maya's organs seems like the only way to salvage her lost life. My yes is an act of hope, of defiance—a way of keeping my child alive.

Across the San Francisco Bay, a figure shrouded in white lies on a hospital bed near death. Semi-conscious and oxygen starved, the man's heart failure is so profound that his fingernails have turned blue, and his doctors are on the verge of giving up hope. This critically ill Chilean businessman is a blip on the computer screen of the national donor registry, where he waits with four thousand others on the heart waiting list for someone else to die so that he can live.

By his side at the University of California Medical Center in San Francisco on the afternoon of April 6, his wife stands looking down at the semi-conscious body of her husband; she knows that even the ventilator can't force air into his lungs much longer. She watches the rise and fall of her husband's chest. The backs of her hands are wet with tears she rubs away without noticing.

Dozens of times in the last ten years she has stood over his crumpled body after the defibrillator implanted in his abdomen knocks him to his knees with a shock powerful enough to restart his failing heart. Her two children are reading magazines in the waiting room, fidgeting with their candy wrappers. Their lives are a constant limbo. She turns her back on her husband's bed and prays for a miracle, not knowing that her prayer has just been answered in another hospital only thirty miles away.

With John sitting by my side in the hospital conference room, I prepare to sign away the contents of my daughter's body. A young nurse who is our donor coordinator sits across from me with a checklist on a clipboard. She begins to read me a list of Maya's vital organs as if they were car parts, asking permission to salvage each one.

"Do you give consent for her corneas?" I say yes, then initial a blank line next to the organ with the pen she handed me earlier.

The nurse's cheery smile doesn't mask her discomfort. "Do you give consent for her lungs?" When she begins listing the right and left ventricles of Maya's heart, I am ready to reach across the table and slap her. *Do you have any idea what you are asking?*

I know she is only doing her job, but surely she must realize that to a mother this is torture. I can't sit in a windowless conference room while this businesslike woman ticks off an inventory of the contents of my first-born's body.

"Look, I can save us both a lot of agony." I lean toward her across the table. "Just take it—take it all."

She shakes her head apprehensively. "The law requires that I must go through each one... I know this must be hard for you..."

"It is unbearable," I snap at her. "Do you have any children?" She shakes her head no.

I smile sardonically. "I am going to initial each of these blanks and sign this form here at the bottom," I say slowly. "Then we are both going to agree that we did this legally, and John can witness that I gave my consent. But I am not going to sit here while you read me a list of my daughter's organs."

John gives me the same look he had earlier when I insisted on seeing Dr. Garry, as if I am mildly insane. I squeeze his hand under the table to let him know that my mind is made up.

I press through the triplicate form with the ballpoint pen she gave me.

"You understand that you are giving consent for them to take bone, skin tissue for grafts, and inner ear bones as well," she says, a quiver in her voice.

"Yes," I reply. "You have my permission to take anything that will save lives or reduce pain. Just don't make me stay here another minute."

She asks if I want to see Maya one last time. I am so grateful to hear my daughter's name spoken out loud, to bring some humanity back into this surreal drama.

"Yes," I say, turning to John. "Can I see Margaret and Victor now?"

Rev. Margaret and Rev. Victor are in the waiting room talking to other family members and comforting Maya's grief-stricken friends.

John holds the door open for the transplant network nurse, who must be as relieved as I am that our interview is over. I push back my chair and begin pacing back and forth behind the table.

When Rev. Margaret enters the room, my agitation calms. Her down-to-earth wisdom had guided me through the challenges of parenting without a partner or immediate family nearby. Margaret had once looked me straight in the eye during one of our counseling sessions when I was fretting about dividing myself between writing in my scant spare time and the pressures of my corporate job.

"Get with the program," she had said. "You have two daughters to raise. You have the rest of your life to write—you're not a ballerina with a limited time horizon. Writers can work until they're old."

Margaret holds me close. For the first time in four days in this hospital, I let sobs rack my entire body. "That's good," Margaret says, patting my back. "Just let it out."

Glazed with weeping, I lead the way to my daughter's bedside in the ICU for the moment of final good-bye. Margaret and I stand across from each other at the head of Maya's bed; John, Victor, and Betty, a grief counselor from our church, gather near the foot of the bed. A nurse draws the curtains, and the five of us form a protective circle around Maya's prone body.

The ventilator still distends her mouth, but the fiber optic cable that had run from the computer to her bandaged skull has been disconnected. She looks more tranquil than I have seen her in the last four days. Her cheeks are rosy and some of the puffiness has left her face. She is so like the little baby I held in my arms almost twenty years ago; she has that same swaddled look, the same clean smell.

I lift her warm, limp hand. The October morning Maya was born they wrapped her in a blanket and gave her to me on the delivery table. It was her fingers I noticed first. Long, thin, strong, with perfect miniature fingernails, as delicate as a tiny china figurine. I extended my index finger to her and she latched on tight with her little fist.

"Look, she has piano player fingers. Those hands could straddle an octave," I said to her father Jeff, delirious with fatigue and happiness.

Now, it's as if no time has passed. As I lift Maya's still warm and pliable fingers in mine, the instinctive mother's recognition of her child's body takes over. I slide my right hand under her shoulder and gaze down at her serene young face.

Rev. Margaret leans over her. "Maya, this is your graduation from life on earth. You are going on to a school far greater than UCLA. We release you with all our love and blessings." She looks at me from across the white mound of sheets covering Maya's body. "Can you let her go, Mom?"

The question takes my breath away, and my chest tightens as if something monstrous is squeezing the air from my lungs. I look down at the rosy cheeks, the distended mouth, and smooth neck. My lovely, lovely girl. She seems to be merely sleeping deeply. So still and peaceful.

"I love you, Maya," I whisper. "You are as beautiful to me as the day you were born. I will be your mother forever. But I'm letting you go now with all my heart, with all my love."

I stroke her cheek again and again.

"Do you want a few moments alone with her?"

Margaret's voice startles me.

"No." I move my head mechanically from side to side, tears sliding down my cheeks. I am afraid to be left alone with my daughter's body for fear I will go mad.

I put my head on Maya's chest, resting my cheek against the soft cotton of her gown. The rise and fall of her mechanically powered breath is like a whoosh of ocean tide—in and out, in and out. The steady drumming of her heart fills my senses. At last, I raise my head. There will be no last breath to signal the end. I simply have to walk away and leave her, something I don't have the strength to do on my own.

I look at the other faces in a ring around the bed. Without speaking and as if we had planned it beforehand, we each bow our heads toward Maya's body. Then we walk away from her silently, past the row of beds in the ICU, and back to the waiting room for the last time.

Chapter 5

Arriving in my arms three weeks early, Maya Catherine Lee was born in a Minneapolis hospital on October 4, 1972. She weighed little more than five pounds, but she was strong and healthy. When we brought her home two days later, the sky was azure and the air crackled with the crisp scent of a perfect autumn day.

Jeff sold his 1964 Corvette to pay the hospital bill. My husband and I were young and distinctly not rich. I was a graduate student in the School of Journalism at the University of Minnesota and Jeff was a drummer in a jazz trio, so we had no health insurance. We lived in a two-story townhouse on Queen Avenue in North Minneapolis overlooking a park.

One afternoon after we brought Maya home from the hospital, I stepped out on our deck. Being confined to the house with a newborn's bundle of needs and my own seesawing hormones was driving me crazy. The air smelled ashy, suffused with moldering leaves, and I could see their inexact piles sliding with every gust.

My mother had taken a Greyhound bus from Cleveland to Minneapolis to help me look after her first grandchild. She was a young grandmother, only fifty-one, but her dark brown bob had turned an iron gray, and she already had a stoop in her shoulders.

"Ellie, I can watch the baby," Mom offered. "You go for a walk."

My fingers fumbled impatiently with the buttons on my sweater, and I stepped out of our front door as if I had just been freed from prison. Shuffling through the brown and gold leaves in the park, I let my mind fall with the sun's rays through the arms of majestic elms. "I've just done the most amazing thing," I said aloud to my twenty-four-year-old self. "If I can give birth, I can do *anything*."

Old feelings of anxiety and powerlessness dropped away like useless scales, as if I could shed the past and shine forth in this new skin called motherhood. I had a purpose. I had a role. The circumstances of my daughter's conception only three weeks after I first met Jeff receded to a far corner of my mind.

Goose flesh raised on my arms, and my spine felt electric. I could hear my own thoughts; they were that lucid and compelling. As my feet brushed the leaves, and the autumn light poured down, I thought, *Now I understand. God is in these leaves, in the light, in my baby, and in me.* I suddenly knew, without a doubt, that it was all one thing and in that moment I was experiencing it directly. God was not a judgmental bearded old man, the far off omniscient being I had read about in my Baltimore Catechism as a child. Buoyed by all I had experienced in the last week, I knew instinctively that divine energy was right here, in me, right now. Giving birth was a miracle.

I returned to our townhouse feeling renewed. In the blur of changing diapers, breast feeding, endless laundry, and sleepless nights, my life finally seemed to come into focus. After my mother returned to Ohio, I lasered my attention on my infant daughter.

She was an energetic and fussy baby, and in the evening her colicky wails echoed through the townhouse. Wisps of blond hair appeared on her smooth pink skull, and her eyes changed from gray blue to deep brown. Dressed in the red and green Calico dress my sister had made, Maya looked like a pixie with an impish grin. The first time she smiled I yelped with happiness. Slowly I began to knit my life to hers.

Four-and-a-half years old. Maya sitting at our yellow Formica kitchen table in Worthington, Minnesota, where she and I moved the year after I left her father. I was a staff reporter for a local newspaper and meal times were one of the few hours in the day that Maya and I spent together. I had made our usual fast food—a broccoli omelet and fried potatoes.

Maya picked at her potatoes, then looked at me and asked, "Mommy, what happens when we die? What do we eat?" I hesitated. She cocked her head to one side, waiting for a real answer to her logical question.

"Well, we don't eat anymore, because our bodies are dead."

"But our souls won't be dead, Mom, right? I remember you told me that." The depth in her eyes was mesmerizing.

"That's right. Our spirits won't die, just our bodies," I said, marveling at her memory and her ability to ponder.

"What would happen to me if you die, Mommy?"

I tried not to flinch. "Lots of people love you, honey, and they would take care of you. Your daddy would take care of you," I lied. "Besides, Maya, nothing is going to happen to me. I promise."

But she was not convinced. "I don't want you to die, Mommy," she wailed. She got up from her chair and ran to me.

She put her head against my chest and sobbed. I stroked her back over and over.

Then I asked her, "What do you think I would do if *you* died first?" Without hesitating, she said, "You would cry for a long time. Do you think you would cry for forty days, Mom?"

"I don't know, Maya, but I would be very, very sad for a long time."

Leaving the hospital the day of my daughter's death, I realize that "sad" and "long" aren't even in the same emotional universe with what I feel now.

On the morning of Tuesday, April 7, following the surgery to remove her organs, bone from her legs, and tissues for donation, Maya's body is transported from the hospital morgue to the County Coroner's office for an autopsy. This is a required procedure following the accidental death of anyone under the age of twenty-one. Meanwhile, relatives from Minnesota, Ohio, and New York are making travel preparations to attend the funeral, converging like pieces in a kaleidoscope.

If only I were a dog! Then I could howl over the sudden absence of my own flesh and blood; run in circles seeking her scent, her warmth, her voice. But I'm a human being with social obligations to fulfill—there are mourning rituals to arrange, guests to welcome, a memorial service and burial to plan and to somehow endure.

So that afternoon, I make the strangest shopping trip of my life, searching for something to wear to my daughter's funeral.

I leave my car in the Nordstrom parking lot, feeling sick to my stomach and as lost as the skinny seven-year-old who worked so hard to fit in. The humiliation of the day when our teacher took a pair of big-handled scissors and cut out brown paper sack tunics for all the children whose parents could not afford, or had not bothered, to buy costumes for the Halloween parade drills into my memory. In my brown sack and construction paper headdress, I stood red-faced and stiff. I was supposed to be an Indian. The rough paper armholes chaffed my arms. As my girlfriends lined up in fringed Dale Evans cowgirl skirts and vests, toy guns gleaming at their sides, my heart congealed with shame and envy. That sack represented everything that set me apart as a child.

My mother was oblivious to how desperate I was to blend with the other kids, and blind to how much her aversion to convention weighed on me. A devotee of *The Catholic Worker* socialism espoused by Dorothy Day, Mom wore baggy pants and sensible shoes. She looked and acted the complete opposite of the June Cleaver mothers of the 1950s.

Since my earliest days, I was obsessed with appearance as the ticket to social acceptance. I did not follow my mother's example with my daughters, no matter how tight my budget was. I racked up credit card debt to buy them good clothes, and always found the means to dress stylishly myself. Even as a child, I loved clothes and makeup. "You're too vain," my mother scolded. I made my credo the opposite of hers.

Mom hated department stores and avoided them at all costs. She never wore makeup unless she was acting in a play. She would have preferred to dress her three children like the Amish in dark handmade clothes with no buttons. Everything I knew about appearance and how to get along in social situations, I learned from my mother's mother. My grandmother Eleanor, the woman whose name my parents pulled from a hat when I turned out not to be the boy they had anticipated, became my role model.

My mother and grandmother were poles apart on many issues, but it is my grandmother's ways that I lean on now.

Despite the tragedies in her own life—my grandfather's manic depression and erratic drinking bouts, his ultimate death in a state mental hospital—I never saw Grandma cry. She was a woman who invested heavily in looking elegant, whatever the conditions of her life. Shiny Charles of the Ritz makeup bottles, silver and crystal perfume decanters, pots of rouge, and a round container of loose powder decorated her dresser. We visited her every Christmas, and lived with her each summer in her five-bedroom house on the shores of Lake Erie outside of Cleveland. I would thumb through her *Vogue* magazines, admiring the expensively dressed models, drinking in the elegance. I embraced my grandmother's commitment to grace under pressure, her notion that projecting beauty and sophistication in public was paramount. Later, I saw that her obsession with appearance was her defense against the pain and shame of my grandfather's alcoholism and mental illness.

But in that moment of loss, all I knew was the bedrock comfort of her values. These were the values I taught my daughters, and Maya absorbed them readily. In fact, she taught me how to enjoy shopping. When she was in high school, the mirrored dressing rooms of Macy's and Nordstrom reflected the body of a lithe young blond in a prom dress and an admiring mother adjusting straps or straightening flounces.

Now there is only one big event left for Maya, not the graduation or wedding I had fantasized about. I am determined to make her funeral beautiful. I will be beautiful for *her*. The idea of burying my daughter makes me ache; I know that something is terribly off kilter, but I can't fathom that any of this is actually real.

Inside the Nordstrom store, smooth Cole Porter riffs from

the piano only intensify my bewilderment. I gaze down from the escalator at the people wandering among potted palms and stacks of expensive merchandise. When I reach the second floor, I head straight for a rack of black suits. A saleslady approaches, asks my size, and what I am looking for. I say I need something dressy, no more. Let's try a size eight, or maybe a ten. Then I go to the dressing room and fumble in and out of black skirts and tailored jackets. The shock and grief of the last week has already carved away pounds, and these expensive designer suits hang loosely on me.

"How are we doing in there?" the saleslady chirps.

"Fine," I say, re-hanging a jacket whose outsized shoulder pads make me look like a scarecrow on steroids. I emerge from the booth and make a quick escape to the ladies' room. There I pull out my make-up bag and push the mascara wand against my eyelashes, careful not to leave any clumps. I still believe that looking together is some kind of magic glue that will mend the broken pieces.

Fragmented images of my parents dance in my psyche. "The show must go on!" My father's oft-repeated slogan has become the subconscious mantra of my life. He was a charismatic actor and director who would not let anything—whether illness, fatigue, or family emergencies—interfere with a performance. Like him, my credo is to keep moving, keep the mask on.

But my mother's asceticism made its mark also. A vivid picture of the day she sprained her ankle springs to mind. Ever the stoic, she refused even the minor remedies of ice or rest. Bruised flesh ballooned over the side of her shoe as she hobbled from the stove to the kitchen sink, acting as if walking on a sprained ankle were normal. *Her* heroes were not drawn from the pages of *Vogue*. A lapsed Catholic who returned to the church with the fervor of a convert after I was born, she read the lives of the

Christian martyrs and attended morning Mass each day, riding to church on her bicycle.

And then there was my stoic grandmother, her white permanent-waved hair and perfectly manicured nails, her square closet with its row of silk dresses from Lane Bryant and Higbee's. I can still see her hatboxes, and her suede gloves sitting neatly in the drawer; each implement, each perfume bottle resting in its place on her cherrywood dresser. She never lost control in public, never complained, never cried.

I flick my hair in place with my fingertips and lift my purse from the counter, picking up the habits of half a lifetime. Like Grandma, I save the sorrow for later.

At the Ann Taylor store, I find a white silk skirt and matching black and white jacket with pearl buttons. The combination of the two colors appeals to me as less stuffy and formal than an entirely black ensemble.

"I'll take it," I hear myself say. I watch the saleslady swath my funeral clothes in plastic, and then I walk along Broadway Plaza in Walnut Creek carrying my new costume. I am a mother in mourning, a role for which I am now outfitted, but for which I have no script. Grandmother would approve.

The coroner classifies Maya's death as an accident. In his neatly typed summary of the external examination of her body, he notes: "The body is that of a well-developed, well-nourished white female, who appears the stated age of nineteen years. The body measures five foot seven inches in height and weighs approximately one hundred and twenty pounds. Rigor mortis is fully and uniformly developed in the lower extremities. Rigor has been broken in the upper extremities."

Today, I have to choose a casket. John stays at home to unpack Maya's suitcase and launder her dirty clothes, a chore I can't face.

Dan phones, and we agree to meet at the cemetery. We meet at Oakmont Memorial Park, high on a hill overlooking the entire Diablo Valley, and the parents of Meghan's best friend join us there to help with making the arrangements. I could bury Maya at the Lafayette City cemetery, but it's tiny and crowded, and it overlooks Highway 24. The noise would drive me insane, and I already know I will be spending many hours by her grave. Dan's father offers to pay for the plot at this more expensive place with its manicured hillsides and identical flat headstones.

Our friends John and Jean Cox get out of their car at the mortuary office. John is a former priest with a gift for gab, and Jean is a nurse, a woman so rock-solid I trust her with Meghan's well-being. These two are weekend parents to my younger daughter, and I have tried to be the same for their daughter Laura, coaxing her to eat a few bites of broccoli when all she wants is a hot dog. The girls spend their after-school hours together, and they are fiercely loyal, having met in the second grade. Now, Laura and her family surround us like a human shield.

John Cox happens to sell caskets for a living, and he doesn't let the salesmen at the cemetery or the funeral home get away with a thing. "No, that's not what she wants," he tells them. "Keep it simple—she wants a birch casket. Show me what else you have."

Jean and I lock eyes, sharing the misery.

Back in my car on the way home, I turn on the radio just as the announcer reads the traffic report. "Highway 24 is backed up to the 680 interchange. Brake lights again from South Main to Livorna Road." He intones this meaningless information as if it were the most important news of the day. I slam the off button.

"Who the hell cares?" My voice echoes in the empty car as I snarl at a person I don't even know and then burst into tears. I yearn to be with my daughter, not in the mundane grocery-store world of dense, slow-moving bodies, of traffic and weather reports where nothing makes sense to me anymore.

Later, I walk to the florist's a few blocks from our apartment in Lafayette. I order flowers to drape over the casket: white tulips, curly willow, pink Gerber daisies, sprays of forsythia. I specifically instruct the sales person, "Absolutely no carnations." I want a display to match Maya's beauty and sophistication.

Leaning into the counter, I bend towards the sales assistant to calculate the cost. At that moment, a chill runs up my spine. I can feel Maya's presence as surely as if she had put her arms around me; there is a warmth that lights up the entire left side of my body. I understand then that Maya is there to help me choose the best flowers. I have to stop myself from turning to speak to her in the store.

But as I walk home, I talk to her through my tears.

"I can't believe I have to do this. I thought I would be choosing flowers for your wedding, not your funeral.... *Where are you?*"

In the blur of making arrangements, the most difficult task becomes choosing the clothes in which Maya will be buried. For some reason, I am terribly worried that she will be cold. Warmth and style become my selection criteria. Determined to choose some bits and pieces of mine that will keep us close, I riffle through my own dresser drawers searching for intimate apparel.

"What can I do to help?" John stands on alert, watching me closely.

"Make this *not* be happening," I answer, slamming a drawer shut.

John sighs and leans against the doorframe. If it were in his power, I know he would fulfill my wish. His patience comforts me, but it doesn't stop me from taking my emotions out on him. Buried under my shock and sadness is fury at the ultimate injustice of my daughter's death. Feeling cheated and abandoned pervades my every thought.

At last, I choose a cotton camisole trimmed with lace. I fold it neatly and set it on the center of my bed. Then I go into the girls' bedroom to sort through the clothes John has washed and ironed. I have never seen a young person's body in a casket before, and the older bodies I have seen were always formally dressed.

"Doesn't it seem bizarre to put Maya in a dress?" I call to John who hovers outside the bedroom door. "That isn't her style."

"Pick something she would have chosen for herself," he advises.

So with angry tenderness, I choose a pair of brand new navy blue painter's pants, with loops below the hip pockets. She had purchased them on sale at Sun Valley Mall a few days before the accident and bragged to me about what a great bargain they were. There's a blue and white polka dot shell with a wide neck, which can be pulled over her bashed skull. For extra warmth, I pick the voluminous white V-neck sweater her boyfriend gave her for her nineteenth birthday the previous October. I lift a pair of clean white athletic socks from her drawer, and then wonder about which shoes I should select for her. Suddenly, an idea hits me. I hoot bitterly. I go to the closet and pick up a pair of white imitation leather cowboy boots that she loved, but that I hate.

"Let's get these hideous things six feet under." I hold the boots out in front of me like a noxious dead skunk. Scooping her purse from the side of the bed, I carry her things back to my room.

When I click open her purse, I find keys for her car, her bicycle lock, and the house she's been renting with college classmates in Santa Barbara linked together on a brass Mickey Mouse key ring. A miniature red corduroy coin purse in the shape of a gym bag holds a few quarters. A hot pink and green cardboard tag attached to her gym card declares, "I'm not hungry or thirsty... I'M HORNY!"

"Look, John." I hold up the tag. He laughs, and then groans.

Digging deeper, I find a plastic Bic lighter and a crumpled pack of cigarettes. The little sneak! "If she weren't dead already, I'd kill her," I tell John. Besides being angry with God, I am furious with Maya, yet I finger the lighter gently in case I might be rubbing away her fingerprints.

When I open her wallet, there is her driver's license, the hard facts of her life. "DOB: 10-4-72," I read. Beneath her picture are these words written in red letters, "Age twenty-one in 1993." I trace each letter with my finger, filled with black anger at some nameless state bureaucrat for taunting me like this.

Finally, at the bottom of the handbag, I find her brush with strands of hair still tangled in its bristles. When I hold it to my face, her scent is strong and sweet.

The fistfuls of shaved hair are still sitting in a plastic bag at the bottom of my closet. "I can't bury her bald." My words seem so puny and unreal compared to the immensity of Maya's death and yet this one detail grips me. Because her brain was so swollen, and Dr. Carr had cut away her skull bone, a hat is impossible. Still obsessed with the idea of keeping her warm, I find a blue and white cotton bandanna of mine to wrap around her forehead.

At last, John helps me put everything on a hanger. Then I tuck a pair of cotton bikini underpants that he has washed by hand, and that I have neatly ironed, into a bag. After pinning the intimate apparel inside the sweater, I pull a dry cleaner's bag over it all.

Now my daughter can be as snugly dressed as if she were still my baby, tucked in her crib in a fuzzy sleeper suit with her toy Calico cat for company. And she will also be as stylish and beautiful as she was just one week ago. Her burial clothes are ready.

Chapter 6

Wmen others try to comfort me I want to set them straight—my daughter is *not* dead—she'll be coming back. Blindly, I search for her in our apartment, wandering into her room. Instead, I find her neatly folded clothes, her makeup bag, her empty shoes.

The family assembles for her funeral. My brother Tim and my sister Tess fly in from the Midwest and meet my father's flight from New York. They crowd around my dining room table with John, Meghan, and me. Black and bitter, the coffee I brew cuts the sugary taste of meringue-topped pies and home-made cakes that seem to appear out of nowhere.

Since Mom died in 1990, I haven't seen my Dad. Maya's funeral is the first time my sister has visited us in the fourteen years we have lived in California. Now that I know what real trouble is, this old sore point fades. She's here and she's my sister and my lifeline. Tim travels on business, so we see each other often. Of the three of us, he's the calm presence, the emotional rock. With only three-and-a-half years between us, from oldest (me) to youngest (Tim), we are a small tribe.

Contact with my father has always been sporadic. Reaching out to Dad is a tentative process, one complicated by my memories of him as an overbearing, erratic, and angry parent. It's a surreal family reunion, but I'm glad to have them with me.

Photos capture Tim at the kitchen sink, a middle-aged man in a pullover sweater preparing to plunge his hands into a stack of dirty dishes as if he were cleaning up after a holiday meal. My father, too, looks unusually jolly considering we are about to bury his first grandchild. Intent on coping well, the two men keep conversation flowing.

Only my sister grieves visibly. Covered by a rose and white comforter taken from Meghan's bed, Tess looks into the camera with red-rimmed eyes rendering bewilderment, sorrow, and exhaustion. Her only daughter is ten months younger than Maya. When they were toddlers, the two girls played together during our visits home.

My sister hovers over me like a mother hen. I welcome the comfort she offers yet dread the mirror of sorrow and vulnerability she holds too close to my uncomprehending eyes. We stay up late talking in the square white box of my living room, trying to piece together the past like an old frayed quilt.

Tess wants to know why Maya's father Jeff isn't attending his daughter's funeral. I explain that his brother and sister-in-law decided not to tell him about her death, afraid that he might come to the ceremony and make a scene.

"I don't want him here," I say. "We haven't seen him for ten years."

Tess shakes her head. Her marriage is long and enduring, and I know she can't even imagine my life as a single mother.

Jeff stopped supporting Maya financially when she was five years old, in spite of a court order. He let her slide out of his life and rarely even wrote to her. I can't contemplate the horrible tragedy this is for him—I'm still too angry at his desertion of our daughter. Everything about his life is erratic, and I stopped depending on him for anything long ago. Maya was nine the last time we saw Jeff. He took her to a park and smoked marijuana in front of her and then began talking to people who were not there, mumbling gibberish. She came back terrified. He never asked to see her again, and I never offered. I can't picture him mourning a child he barely knows, one who grew up far from his dreamlike world.

On the morning of my daughter's funeral, I enter the dim chapel with Dale and walk with heavy limbs toward the casket. The only sound is the soft swishing of my skirt. I have asked for a private viewing of my daughter's body and invited her grieving boyfriend.

Hull's Funeral Chapel is humid as a greenhouse and each breath I take feels clammy. The chapel smells like Lemon Pledge and stale cigar smoke. Two stained glass panels shaped like church windows are recessed into a faux brick wall at the front. On either side of the fake windows are two identical potted palms. Maya's casket rests on a wooden dais above a carpeted riser. A lectern and a pipe organ stand nearby.

The funeral director's assistant hovers by my left elbow. He addresses me with exaggerated politeness and his movements are stilted and deliberate.

Dale and I hold hands, staring numbly at the simple wooden box. I have not seen my daughter since I walked away from her hospital bed on Monday. Seeing her now is the only evidence that will make me believe she is really dead. When the assistant asks if he should raise the lid of the casket, I nod my head.

He fumbles with the lid and raises it slowly.

With my friends' help, I had selected the simplest possible casket, but even so, I am shaken by what I see. Lying on a garish white satin lining, my daughter's body looks like a precious object someone has carefully polished and placed on display. In her deep coma, at least she was warm and pliable. The body before me now is a rigid caricature of my daughter.

In life, Maya was movement at gale force, flying over the beach boardwalk in Santa Barbara on her roller blades. Now she appears almost mummified, a heavy layer of rouge and lipstick covering the pallor of her face like a mask. Her lips are dry and cracked where the hose from the ventilator held them open, and the dark red lipstick, a brassy color she would never have worn, is clotted and bumpy. The assistant clears his throat and moves away.

I study Maya's body. She looks unutterably old, and a beatific suffering is etched on her face. A pang of guilt shoots through me along with a raw jolt of awareness—I agreed to save other lives at her expense.

Dale's hand grips mine, and when our eyes meet it's hard to comprehend that he is twenty-three years old, the age I was when I married Jeff. Last Christmas, he gave Maya a promise ring, and I had hoped that he would eventually propose marriage. With his lost eyes and brooding face, Dale brings a lover's grief to this ritual. And it all began over a bet in a sports bar in Santa Barbara. "Twenty bucks says the Raiders lose this game," Dale challenged the pretty blond next to him. "You're on," she said.

Dale lost the bet, and to pay Maya back he took her out to dinner. Romance ignited quickly. For me, the calculus was simple. Maya was happy. After a string of romantic disasters, she had finally found a guy who was wonderful. I know I can't

make it better for him, but I desperately want to. This is too
unfair.

Earlier that morning, we each wrote Maya a note. Dale's
message is on one half of the folded card. On the other side is
mine. "Maya, I love you heart and soul forever. Mom." I lean
forward and tuck the paper into the satin lining next to her
shoulder.

When I lift her right hand to attach a charm bracelet with
her cat Bizbomb's ID tag on it, I almost scream with fright. That
arm feels as cold and heavy as something just removed from a
meat locker. With trembling fingers, I put the bracelet on her
wrist.

Then I turn back to Dale. "Shall we put the ring around her
neck now?"

I had attached the opal and diamond promise ring to a gold
chain. With a face as rigid and mask-like as hers is, Dale nods
his head. I can't bear to touch her broken skull so I motion to the
assistant. "Please, can you help me?"

He takes the chain from me and gently lifts her head, fas-
tening the clasp behind her neck. The ring gleams above her
breastbone. I note with satisfaction that she is warmly dressed
in the clothes I provided, and that the white cowboy boots are
on her feet.

Next, I put her baby blanket in beside her—kittens in yellows
and pinks on an oblong of white flannel. It doesn't strike me that
sending her into the earth with a receiving blanket is deranged;
it's a comfort I want for her. Her dingy white Polar bear, the one
stuffed animal she refused to part from and even brought home
on spring break, gets tucked in next, snuggled against the blanket. Dan has given me a stone from the Eel River and a feather
to give to her.

My mother's long-time companion, Serena, sent a small bottle of specially blessed water from Mom's old church. Catholic rituals still are meaningful to me even though I left the church long ago. I rub a few drops of holy water on Maya's frozen temples, and place the bottle next to her.

Earlier that morning, I took her nest of blond hair and placed it in a woven basket. I kept a small lock for myself, but Maya's hair was her trademark, and I want it buried with her. I set the basket near her left foot, the pointy tip of the white boot visible beneath the satin cover.

We step back from the casket, and I study her face for the last time, knowing that this is not the version of her I will remember. The assistant closes the casket lid. When he latches it shut, I set a framed photograph of my daughter on top. As I wait for the ceremony to begin, I keep my eyes focused on my daughter's platinum hair, her radiant smile. This is the girl I know.

Maya's funeral is simple—no bible passages or organ music— just the calm presence of Rev. Margaret reflecting on a young person's death. She holds up a many-chambered Nautilus seashell to illustrate the phases and changes of a life. When my sister stands in front of the sixty of us in the chapel to speak, she breaks down describing Maya as a toddler. I want to run to her and hold her in my arms, tell her that it will be okay, that the little Maya she remembers is still alive.

Dan moves to the front of the room. I have no idea what he will say, but since he is the only father Maya knew for the final fifteen years of her life, it will be his memories that are most vivid for me today. He is the closest to Maya, besides Meghan and me. He recounts the difficult years when Maya was a rebellious teen—the time she threw a keg party when I was out of town, the dozens of times I grounded her, the awful week when she refused to speak one word to me. This other-daughter bond was not an easy love, "It was love in the trenches," Dan says. Few here know how true his words are.

Tim stands and reads a letter he wrote to me that morning, looking up at me each time he pauses to take a breath. "You gave so much to Maya, and she gave so much to you in return. I can see each of you in each other—such a zest for the challenges of life, open and free-spirited. It seems to me Maya died as she lived." The words blur and my mind can no longer absorb any more.

When the ceremony is over, her three uncles and her male cousins lift the casket from its platform and carry Maya's body outside to a long black hearse. They struggle to slide the coffin in, and I realize she is heavy now, a corpse.

An oppressive silence falls in our limousine, its funeral flag waving in the breeze. The cortege drives past sprawling ranch houses with rose gardens and clipped lawns. Tucked away in the hills, Reliez Valley Road epitomizes the genteel wealth of Lafayette, a place where we were always on the margins. As the car winds up to Oakmont Memorial Park, I stare out the window at the trees lining the road, dreading what is still to come.

Maya will be buried in "The Garden of Remembrance" under an oak tree.

The pallbearers lift the casket from the back of the hearse and carry it down a steep rise to her grave. "It's so beautiful here," my sister whispers to me as we walk to the graveside. Tess is holding Meghan by the hand. I lean on John's arm trying not to think about how dark and cold the hole in the earth will be.

The grave sits near a large oak tree with branches that spread a canopy above us. The hole has been covered by a piece of Astroturf. We gather around it in a circle. I force myself to focus on Rev. Margaret's voice.

Standing at the foot of the grave, she speaks. "Man's earthly body is a sacred temple in which he dwells, and when he leaves it for a new experience in higher life, it is fitting that the former temple be honored. So we do now commit with love the body unto the elements from which it came, knowing the Spirit is no longer here."

The acres of grass in this place are green and manicured, with a regimental line of brass vases attached to each headstone. Farther off, Mt. Diablo looms. Soon they will lower the casket. Rev. Margaret signals the two men who are waiting. She guides each of us to walk forward and place a white rose on the coffin lid.

"God's natural beauty is all about," she continues, "and our thoughts will be of the living Spirit triumphant, now free, and ever unfolding wherever unfolding. And we shall meet again."

At these words, my knees buckle. John squeezes my hand. The men begin to lower the wooden casket, pulleys creaking as they inch it down. My disjointed mind remembers that Abraham Lincoln had the body of his young son exhumed three times so that he could look at the child's face. As Maya's body is lowered into the grave, I suppress a wave of madness that tells me to follow her down.

The grave faces the implacable mountain where she spent her final conscious moments. Hillsides, a stupid, beautiful green, hold trees and a flagpole. Looking down again, I see the litter of white petals on the casket as it disappears into the hole. Then, one of the younger cousins dances around the edge of the grave and almost falls in. "Stop it!" his mother hisses at him, pulling him back by the shoulder.

I stare at the dancing boy's downcast face, the clipped grass under his feet, the tree limbs above his head. The world I now inhabit has become a form of hell.

The gravediggers shovel brown blotches of earth over the ivory rose petals, and soon they are covered. The sharp thud of each falling clod builds to a crescendo that sounds like a hail of earth.

We will stay here until she is fully buried. Most funeral parties walk away at this point, but I told them ahead of time. "I have to see it all." I stood beside my mother's grave like this too, as everyone else wandered off, vowing that no one I love will ever be buried by strangers without me as a witness to the entire process. Maya must be safely tucked in, the last shovel of earth tamped down. When that final ritual is done, I blank out. The next thing I remember is being in my former brother-in-law's backyard standing in front of his wife's prize rose garden.

People are talking in low tones. Sandwiches and soft drinks are spread out on tables. John urges me to eat something, but the bread tastes like sawdust in my mouth. Meghan stands with me. She puts her arm around my waist, and I stroke her silky hair, drinking in her comfort. But it doesn't erase the stab of knowing that I have just buried my firstborn and that I will never see Maya again.

Wrapped in the cotton wool of frozen emotion that clings to me now, I sit in the front pew of the First Church of Religious Science in Oakland. When the church is almost full, the organist begins to play. The massive stained-glass window radiates hues of blue and purple light over the sanctuary, bathing our faces in its glow. We buried Maya yesterday. Today, at her memorial service, I am told that the aim is to celebrate her life. To me, it feels like a grand game of make believe.

Dale takes my hand, and I see a lover's yearning in his eyes, and wonder if it is anything at all like a mother's. "She was so unique," he whispers to me. *Was?* Why is he saying this? Even for him, she is already moving into the past. I squeeze his hand to let him know I hear him, and I sympathize, yet the ways we know Maya are so different. Surrounded by people I love, I feel completely alone.

A mass of flowers puts forth a perfume that overpowers any other scent. Only the physical solidity of John's shoulder next to mine reminds me that any of this is real.

Dressed in formal ministerial robes, Rev. Margaret opens the service.

"I think of Maya as sensitive and bold, a risk-taker, and her passing fits her boldness," she says. "We must make her life as meaningful and as filled with impact as if she had been with us for eighty years. We have to love her enough to let her go." I know I said I could do this in the hospital, but now suddenly I *can't* let her go. It's impossible.

Margaret invites some of Maya's friends forward to share their thoughts. Oliver, who waited by my side the night of Maya's accident, reads a poem he wrote for her.

"The burning you feel inside is not illness or pain. It is part of the love from Maya's overwhelming soul touching each one of our souls."

As I listen to his voice, I notice that Alex is sitting with his family in a pew across the aisle from us. A flush of anger rises in my chest. If only Dale had been with her that day, none of this would have happened.

One of her best friends talks about dissecting cow's eyeballs in Biology class with Maya when they were in the tenth grade. Somehow, Maya convinced Jenni to close her eyes and hold out her hand. She felt something slimy drop into her palm. When she looked down, there was the cow's eye staring up at her. "It was as big as a golf ball." Everyone laughs. I hear my own hiccups of laughter and then an echo in my brain—the practical joker in Maya is partly what killed her. Is this supposed to be funny?

My seventy-two-year-old father rises in the pew behind mine. I notice it's harder for him to climb the steps to the podium than it seems like it should be. His baritone voice booms out, "Your children are not your children," from Kahlil Gibran.

When he reaches the part about the parent as a bow and the child as an arrow, I realize that now I am stuck here behind, the bowstring still quivering, no longer able to see the arrow I shot from my own body. "For even as He loves the arrow that flies, so He loves also the bow that is stable." Except that my father either misreads or intentionally changes that last word to "subtle" instead of "stable." An interesting choice of words.

Dad reads the entire poem and then returns to his pew without ever uttering one personal word about Maya. He barely knew her, I realize, so perhaps he is more comfortable in his actor's voice than his grandfather one.

I can't stand and eulogize my daughter, risking a breakdown in front of three hundred people. Instead, Rev. Margaret reads a letter that I have written to Maya. It contains words like "joy" and "remember" and "forever." Little anecdotes. The time she tried to comfort me and said, "That's the way life lives." That funny saying of a quirky little girl makes everyone laugh except me. I hate life for living this way.

Afterwards, I stand outside in the courtyard greeting people, letting words of pity wash over me. After five minutes of platitudes I think I will scream if one more person hugs me, or murmurs that she is in a better place now, or says what a beautiful girl and how tragic and mysterious life is. They don't know.

Only one person says anything I treasure. And it comes later, after the formalities are over and we are all listening to Maya's "Talking Heads" tape on a portable player in the other building. Helpers clear the remains of tea sandwiches and cake. People drift by. Out of the blue, one of Maya's college roommates approaches me. "I want to tell you something. I hope it's okay. I don't want to upset you."

Oh honey, I think, *nothing you can tell me now can upset me because I am more disturbed than you can possibly imagine.* "It's all right," I say, "tell me."

The girl says that a few days before they left for spring break, the roommates were playing a game that had little cards with questions about personal topics. Maya drew a card asking who she admired most and why.

"She picked you," the girl says. "She said, 'My Mom. Because she raised me and always kept everything together no matter what.' I thought you would want to know. She loved you more than anything."

"Thank you for telling me this," I say, feeling tears rise for the first time today. Then she drifts away too, one more person I will never see again.

Finally, only a few family members and Rev. Margaret remain. Someone turns off the music. Margaret and I page through a photo album. On the last two facing pages of the album are eight-by-ten photos of Maya and Dale side by side.

"What a handsome couple," Margaret says. "You know, someone told me once that when a child dies you never completely get over it, you just get used to it."

I can't imagine ever getting used to this, but I nod my head because there is nothing else I can do. God knows I can't let myself feel the bonfire of rage burning beneath my carefully made-up exterior in its black and white silk suit and pearl earrings.

Chapter 7

I stand at the kitchen sink, filling the teakettle, and gaze out of the window at the familiar shapes of trees in the predawn light. From there, I can see the narrow lane behind our building. Surrounded by gigantic pines and sturdy California oaks, our apartment is enfolded by greenery, surroundings that remind me of my childhood home.

My younger daughter's bedroom door squeaks open. She pads down the hall toward the bathroom. It's time to start breakfast, time to construct—again—the pretense that life is safe, that routine matters, that we can go on without Maya.

When the teakettle whistles, I lift it from the stove. The boiling water hisses as it fills the cup. I sit at the table in the dining nook turning the cup in my hands to take the chill out of my fingers. The permeating cold in my extremities began in the hospital, deepened during the week of Maya's funeral, and although life is supposed to be getting back to normal, remains as relentless as frostbite.

Meghan comes to the table and reaches down for a hug.

"Did you sleep okay?" I try to affect a casual tone. Meghan has had vivid dreams and difficulty sleeping since her sister's death. I search her face, pale and creased from her pillow. Her nightshirt is bunched and wrinkled and her hair sticks out at odd angles.

"Yeah," she says. She props her bare feet on the rungs of the wooden chair, twirling a lock of hair with her fingers. "In my dream, Maya called me on the phone."

"She called you?"

Meghan nods solemnly. "Yeah, we were talking on the phone, and she asked me if I wanted her to come visit me."

"What did you say?"

"I told her not to visit me because it would be too scary. But then I said, 'Mom really wants you to visit her.' Then she said, 'I know. But I can't—it's too painful.' "

"Are you sure?"

Meghan nods dreamily. "Then we talked some more, and I asked her if she had seen Jesus. She said, 'No, I'm not on his committee.'"

It was exactly the sort of thing Maya *would* say. Meghan reports it nonchalantly, but her words tear at me. I lean on my elbows, head in my hands. So Maya *knew*. I had been praying for a bed-thumping apparition, no matter how frightening. I would risk anything to see my daughter again. Meghan interrupts my thoughts.

"Mommy, do you think Bizbomb will ever come back?" Her gray-green eyes look puzzled and sorrowful.

In the midst of a raw outburst of tears, I had let Maya's cat out onto the patio and she didn't come home again. It was almost as if Bizbomb understood that Maya was never coming back, and she also knew that I was not her real mistress. Another part of Maya had vanished.

"I hope she will... but I don't know sweetie. She's been gone for more than a week." I miss the soft black and white fur, the white whiskers, her body rubbing against my legs in the morning.

I reach out and squeeze Meghan's shoulder; it reassures me to feel her solidity. She returned to her sixth grade classroom on Easter Monday, just two days after her sister's funeral. The routine of getting up, packing her lunch, making breakfast, and seeing her off to school gives me a reason to get out of bed. By rote, I produce cold cereal, fruit, and toast and then pack her a lunch for school.

Three weeks have passed since the funeral. It's time to get on with my life, whatever that means now. But the remnants of my daughter's existence—two bank accounts, clothes, a rental lease on a shared house in Santa Barbara, some furniture, a car and car insurance—all have to be concluded. My neatly written list for this Tuesday morning reminds me to close Maya's two bank accounts.

By ten o'clock I am sitting across from the young branch manager at Patelco Credit Union where Maya had a checking account. I fumble in my purse for my daughter's death certificate. It feels embarrassing to put my daughter's death on display so publicly. He looks so young and sweet, curly ginger hair and a sprinkling of freckles on his cheeks. *Surely he is not old enough to do this,* I think.

The manager reads the official declaration, calmly makes a photocopy, and then requests her VISA and ATM cards. He methodically cuts the cards into pieces. The snip, snip of his scissors cuts through my numbness. Shards of red and white plastic drop onto his desk blotter. Then he sweeps the pieces into his hand and drops them in the wastebasket. I stare at the top of his head as he bends over to do this dreadful act.

From his window, I can see walnut and locust trees in the

parking lot, but they look like the plastic trees that used to be part of Maya's toy farm set—small, hard, far away. At my request, he transfers the final balance of $128 from Maya's account to mine and produces a copy of the transaction for me to keep.

I mumble something polite and leave the bank, holding my breath to keep my composure. The yellow slip of paper I clutch in my hand is now the only proof that my daughter existed as a bona fide member of society with a bank account and spending power. Maya has just been officially obliterated.

I remain dry-eyed through the next errand, picking up copies of Maya's high school graduation picture in wallet size that I had ordered from a local photo shop. I plan to include them with thank you messages for the dozens of sympathy cards that I received. As I look at the photographs, studying the glint in my daughter's brown eyes, her infectious smile, her shining hair, something in me cracks. The car speeds along the freeway from Walnut Creek back to Lafayette without any conscious guidance from me. The towering bulk of Mt. Diablo recedes in my rear view mirror. I clench my jaw.

At the second bank, Wells Fargo in downtown Lafayette, I can't maintain my veneer of calm. I sit at the branch manager's desk weeping openly as she cuts up my daughter's debit card before my eyes, then spreads fifty dollars and some change before me on the desk. Maya had a gold account with the bank, an account she had opened because there was no Patelco branch in Santa Barbara. The manager says that there is a small accidental death benefit to be paid out, and pushes a form toward me to sign, followed by a box of tissues. I take one and dab at my eyes.

"I'm sorry," I say. "I thought I could get through this."

She smiles sympathetically. How often does she meet with grieving parents I wonder—two or three times a year? The tragic car accident on prom night, the inexplicable drowning, or the long struggle with cancer after which the exhausted parents send in an aunt or uncle to do the job. She must be used to it.

When I stand up to leave, the manager extends her hand, "Time will heal," she says, shaking my wooden palm and icy fingers.

I stifle my sobs over this attempt at condolence and flee to the parking lot. *Time will never heal the loss of Maya.* Cars pull into the gas station across the street and swarm through the traffic light into the post office parking lot. They look like blurry bits of red and blue metal, the sun radiating in painful waves from their floating shapes. Flooded with memories of my daughter, I race my grief home.

"Watch me, Mom. Are you watching?" Maya never took her eyes off the water below, but waited until she could feel my attention on her.

She folded her arms across her chest, bounced on the end of the diving board to test the spring, then dropped her arms to her sides, backed up three paces, and straightened her body.

"Yes, I'm watching," I called.

She took three quick steps, lifted one leg, and leapt— hard— on the end of the board. Her chest rose as her arms came up in a perfect V. Her body lifted into an arc, her arms outstretched as if to catch the air on either side and she hung, suspended, for a fraction of a second. Then her body sliced the water, parting it without a splash.

Even before she surfaced, I could see the grin on her face.

"That was perfect," I called. "You really looked like a swan!"

"What would you give me? Was that a ten?" She swam to the side of the pool and looked up at me, water dripping from her hair.

"Your position was perfect, your back was arched, your entry was clean. Yes, a definite ten," I replied.

Her cousins applauded—even the boys. She continued her methodical performance in her step-grandparents' pool while I kept score for her. Evening unfolded over the hills of Walnut Creek as her step-grandfather's video camera whirred, taping her swan dive, her back dive, her back flip. Just fourteen, her body glistened with determination while I settled deeper into the terry cloth cushions, admiring my daughter's skill and her precision.

Now I push open the apartment door, lock it, and lean my back against it, choking out hoarse cries, torn in two by feelings of longing and remorse. Was I to blame for her death? Had I been blind to the dangers of her willingness to try anything?

I had aided and abetted Maya's fabulous competence, told her she could do anything she set her mind to, applauded her daring, and overlooked its darker side—the lure of speed, the sharp edge of risk. Maya pushed the envelope with her wiry, muscular body, cutting through the water, and with tenacious vulnerability dove headfirst into her acting. I had seen her on stage tear open her innermost heart and spill it out for an audience. They applauded her daring performance. So did I, proud and self-satisfied.

I sob with such force that my eyes are bloodshot and red-rimmed. But several hours later when Meghan returns home from school, I am calm and numb again, and we sit at the dining room table working on her math problems. John makes dinner and urges me to eat something. I take a few bites and then push my chair away from the table. After I tuck Meghan in bed at nine o'clock, I go to my room and sit on the bed staring out the window, listless, without the will or strength to move.

I had intended to read one of the books on grief that sit unopened on my night table, but I am overcome with a feeling of torpor so profound it is as if the walls of my room have collapsed on me. I'm enveloped in a dark pit where I can cease to exist simply by giving in to an unspoken invitation. I want desperately to dissolve and reunite with Maya. *I have to be with her. I am her mother.*

John comes into the room, but I sense this more than see it. My vision narrows as if I were looking down a dark tunnel. I can't speak, and I can barely breathe. My heart begins to race. I feel as if I will suffocate.

"I don't know what's happening to me," I say into the stifling air. He is hanging something in the closet. He turns, studies me, and then quickly comes and sits down on the edge of the bed next to me.

"I want to die. Everything inside of me and outside of me is so dark, I just want to be with Maya..." I drift into silence, then more words come. "I want to get out of here..."

He grasps my hand. His palm feels solid and warm.

"I know," he says.

We don't speak for several minutes.

"I know," he repeats, "I know exactly where you are now."

Searching for an anchor, I look into his eyes and sense understanding emanating from them almost as strongly as a comforting touch.

"Am I crazy?" I ask. "I've never felt like this before..."

"You *are* crazy," he says calmly, "and you will be for a while. But that is normal when you lose a child." I stare at him, wild with fear over my own suicidal impulses.

"Were you like this?"

"Yes, on and off for a long time."

He must see the fear in my eyes.

"One thing I can promise you," he says, squeezing my hand, "is that this feeling will come again, but it will never be as intense as it is now. Each time you go down, you go a little less deep."

I nod and grip his hand because it is a living thing, and I am an empty shell, a dark presence caught in some level of hell. What used to pass for reality, the daily ticking off of minutes, the errands, the meals, now seems not only unreal, but also unendurable. We sit like this for a very long time until the death wish passes and the searing ache in my heart returns to tell me I am still alive.

Grief is a jagged piece of glass I carry with me. In the spring of 1992 doing something ordinary—driving the car to the supermarket, walking home from the BART station after work, even fixing dinner in my own kitchen—I may see or hear or remember something. My emotional range is swift and wide, and the triggers are everywhere.

Early in May I drive to the grocery store. As I approach the intersection at Mt. Diablo Boulevard, a family of four walks in front of the car in the crosswalk. I slam on the brakes and stop inches from the painted lines. One of the kids looks up at me, unaware that he is facing a woman about to explode, and smiles with a wide, innocent grin. He and his sister are towheads and usually that would reduce me to sobs, but at that moment my emotions swing in another direction. They all look so damn happy, so blissfully unaware that their precious family togetherness can shatter in an instant. I have a sudden impulse to gun the accelerator and run down this bright, happy family. What right do they have to be whole when I am so broken?

"C'mon kids, let's go!" the father urges his children across.

I press harder on the brake pedal and grip the steering wheel so tightly that my arms begin to shake. After the light changes, I drive through the intersection and into the Safeway parking lot. I pull into a parking space and close my eyes. Images of my daughter when she was the same age as the boy swim in front of me. Her lean little arms, the way wisps of hair worked their way free of her barrettes where her cowlick stubbornly stuck out. Her hair the day of the accident, the way the cowlick made the hair on the right side curve into an unmanageable arch and I ruffled it down on my way out the door. Then the image of the blue and white bandanna wrapped around her bald skull in the casket. I pound on the steering wheel. *Why, why, why?*

Just the day before I had told my therapist, a psychiatrist I began seeing after my mother died eighteen months earlier, about my overpowering urge to die so that I could join Maya. What would he say about *this?*

I gather my purse and my list. Meghan will be home from school in less than an hour so falling apart now is not an option. In the bread aisle, as I reach for the brand of sourdough that both my daughters prefer, I hear a harried voice shouting, "You are a bad, bad girl." An exasperated mother grabs her three-year-old daughter and shakes her. The child's head rocks back and forth. Her eyes bulge and her chin quivers.

I am seconds away from intervening. *You have no idea what you have, how lucky you are, and how very foolish,* I think. But I force myself to reach out for the loaf of bread I came for, put it in the cart, and move on to the checkout counter. Wails echo through the store.

I stow the grocery bags in the trunk of my car, and then sit behind the steering wheel unable to move. Tears roll down my cheeks. At last, I can cry in public.

Just rising from the sofa takes all my energy. Coming to grips with the reality of my daughter's death is sucking the life out of me. But, eager for structure and distraction, I return to my editing job at Pacific Bell headquarters in San Francisco six weeks after Maya's funeral.

One warm May evening, I round the corner of the main street in Lafayette on my walk home from the BART station. There I see a young fair-haired woman leaning in to talk to her mother at a café table on the sidewalk. In an instant, I see the same closeness in these two strangers that Maya and I had often shared. Their heads meet in the center of the table. My chest constricts. I cross the street, passing office buildings and then houses in a blur. On Brook Street, I break into a run.

I pull open the apartment door and lock it behind me. The thump of my purse and then my briefcase against the dining room table sound like karate chops. I pace wildly, weeping and calling Maya's name. I am walking in circles. Then I double over and hold my arms over my aching heart. I lurch toward my bedroom, leaning against the walls for support. When I reach the side of the bed, I drop to the floor. I always thought the phrase "wracked with agony" was hyperbole. Now I know exactly what it means. I struggle to my knees and clench my hands together, begging God to return my daughter.

"This is a terrible mistake," I am shouting this prayer. "Give her back! I need her here!" I rant for what seems like hours.

When thoughts of death descend again after the storm of grief, I know that I need help. More help than I could ever have imagined. John provides as much support as anyone could, and to some extent I hide the intensity of my feelings even from him, because I know that he worries about me terribly. I see it in his eyes, and feel it in the urgency in his arms when he reaches for me in the night. And there is another reason too. If I keep John a little distant, I am able to shield myself from the full reality of how crazy and unmoored I am. And the psychiatrist? Despite his empathy and skill, he is not a bereaved parent and I know, on some fundamental level, that he just doesn't get it.

I need help from others who have been torn by the same wild mixture of disbelief, rage, sorrow, and guilt; other parents who know what it feels like to want to die, to pray for death, and to live with those feelings day after day, week after week. My hands shake as I page through the phone directory searching for the number of The Compassionate Friends, a peer support group for grieving parents my sister told me about. When John returns home, I tell him about my need for more support, and he urges me to call TCF.

After dinner that night, John is working a crossword puzzle at the dining room table while Meghan watches TV. I phone the number I scribbled down earlier and leave a message with an answering service. An hour later the phone rings.

A soft voice asks for me. "Eleanor, this is Sandy from The Compassionate Friends. I understand your daughter died recently. I know this must be so painful for you, but I thought you might like to talk..."

I walk into the bedroom with the portable phone pressed to my ear, tears already streaming down my cheeks. "I think I'm losing my mind..."

She laughs very gently. "Oh, yes, I know the feeling..."

I sob quietly as I clutch the phone, drinking in every word.

Sandy says that she had twin sons who were severely disabled. One died at birth. The other, to whom she had devoted her life, died when he was nineteen. That had been almost ten years ago. "I still miss him every day," she says.

"Are you able to sleep at all?" she asks almost apologetically.

"I take sleeping pills," I confess. "Sometimes I get up and write in my journal. I try to read, but I can't concentrate. I have no sex drive... I don't know who I am anymore."

"All those things are normal in the early stages..."

Normal? How could these feelings ever be normal?

Sandy explains, as John had, that the feelings will fade in intensity—but never go away entirely—and that, in time, I will reach what she calls "a new normal." I ask what that means.

"Do you ever feel joy again?"

She hesitates. "Yes... but it's different. You learn to go on in a new way."

I shake my head. "I can't go on without Maya."

"It takes time," she says. "Everyone is different, so there are no formulas I can give you."

Sandy encourages me to come to the next support group meeting, held the last Tuesday of every month. She reassures me that there are several mothers whose children have also died suddenly in accidents and promises to introduce me to them. When I hang up the phone there is a wadded up pile of tissues next to me on the bed. But for the first time in weeks, I am able to sleep through the night.

Chapter 8

Meghan gathers with her girlfriends in a tight little clump to snap photos, their pastel dresses swaying like upside down tulips. Musical names ring out as they strike their poses—Brooke, Ia, Sarah, Laura—"Over there, move in closer." "Smile! No, that's too cheesy! Smile the *right* way."

On this sweltering June evening, my daughter will graduate from the sixth grade at Happy Valley Elementary School. The grounds are pristine and clean, and the buildings tucked back from the road in an exclusive neighborhood of Lafayette.

I sit in the bleachers, taking in the scene as if I were a cardboard facsimile of a proud mother that has been rented for the evening. Dan and Linda drive down from Humboldt County for the occasion, and they are sitting next to John and me. But there is a huge gap where Maya should be. Her absence feels like a phantom limb. I reflexively stroke the polished wood where she should be sitting and leaning toward me to whisper witty observations and delicious secrets. She would have played her role of big sister to the hilt, showering Meghan with teasing compliments.

After the ceremony, we clamber down to join Meghan and

her friends. She beams up at her two sets of parents. The next day she'll drive north for a two-month summer vacation among the giant Redwood trees at Dan and Linda's house.

As I look around the gymnasium, it's hard to picture a tragedy like ours happening to any of the stylishly dressed parents who arrived in the school parking lot that night in BMWs, Jaguars, and safe, shiny Volvo station wagons. I have checked Meghan's class list and noticed—as in every other year—that she is the only child who has two parents living at separate addresses; the only child who, when asked to draw her home, makes two peaked roofs with two square windows in the center of two identical side by side houses.

Of course our houses look nothing alike. I am living in a tiny downtown apartment in order to keep Meghan in the wealthy Lafayette schools after her father's move to the country. The blocky white rooms and beige carpet, the little front patio, and the shared laundry room in the basement seem a worthwhile arrangement for the privilege of providing what amounts to a private school education for Meghan. She sits in class with the sons and daughters of investment bankers and high-powered attorneys. The school principal personally greets her each morning.

"Ellie, let's go." John puts his arm around my shoulder.

We all walk out to the parking lot together. When we reach Dan's car, I lean in to hug my daughter. They'll be leaving for Garberville first thing in the morning.

"Call me when you get there," I remind Meghan. Then I kiss her forehead and watch as she gets in and buckles her seat belt. The tail lights flash and the car backs out and turns away. I wave, even though she's not looking. John takes me by the hand and leads me to our car.

He drives along the side streets of Lafayette, and then into the lane behind our building. On the other side of the lane is a neighborhood park with a rubber tire swing, a small slide, and a few picnic tables. I look longingly at the children playing there.

The sun has set, and they are playing in the dusky evening with the joy and focus of young kids, digging in the sand near the slide, oblivious to the grownups around them. Groups of parents stand and chat with each other as they watch the kids play. The children are safe, their parents unconcerned. Everyone is together sharing an ordinary moment. The children's voices waft toward me like music when I open the car door.

We walk up the sidewalk from the parking area to the front gate, ivy draping over the fence. When John opens the front door with his key, I look in at the empty living room, stunned by the quiet.

Meghan's just away, I tell myself. She'll come home again. Then it hits me. That's what I tell myself about Maya too. There's a place in my mind that I seal against the impact of her death. I pretend she's on a long trip. She'll be back. But staring at my empty home I see that "away" and Maya don't fit together. I wonder what new stories I can invent to keep the reality at bay.

PART II

Reflections

Chapter 9

After Meghan leaves for Garberville, there is no one to be strong for. The grief takes over. At night I pace my apartment sobbing. Each morning I catch a BART train to San Francisco, attempting to put on a brave face and do my work but often breaking into tears in my office too.

"Do you think Maya will wait for me to die so that we can reincarnate together?" I've pondered this question for the better part of a week, and now I have to know what John thinks about it.

"Ask her," John advises.

"What do you mean?"

"I talk to my son all the time. Don't you talk to her?"

"I write to her..."

Days after she died, I began writing to Maya. The previous fall I had enrolled in the creative writing program at Mills College to begin work on my MFA degree. Now my weekly fiction writing seminar is a place where I can get support for expressing my grief on the page. A classmate and I have formed a writing group and I share drafts of my stories about Maya there.

"No, I mean talk out loud," John says, as if it were the most natural thing in the world. He reaches over and gives my bare foot an affectionate squeeze.

That night in the shower, with the water to drown out the sound of my voice, I speak to my dead child. "Look," I say, "wherever you are, whatever you are doing, I want to be with you. I don't care how far away it is, or how much time has to pass, just let me know where and when. I'll be there..."

That night I dream in short, vivid bursts. The images are hyper real.

Dressed in a pink party dress, four-year-old Maya lies on a heap of garbage in the back of a truck driving slowly along a road. The dress seems too large on her wiry body, its ruffles and bows garish and out of place. Maya's limbs sprawl across a mass of crumpled papers, banana peels, and coffee grounds.

I walk by the side of the truck, holding her hand as she slides around, trying to pull her up, but she only laughs, seeming to enjoy slipping away from me. I tug at her hand, holding her tighter. On the other side of the truck is a woman dressed in slacks and a jacket carrying a reporter's notebook. She walks along observing everything and entering it in her notebook.

Suddenly Maya's legs get caught in the truck's giant rollers. They jerk her away and I lose my grip on her hand. She is slowly being sucked away from me. "Help us, please help us," I scream at the reporter. But she keeps looking straight ahead, taking notes in her notebook.

I wake from the dream panting with fear, my mind swimming with disturbing questions. For twenty years I had marched ahead being a professional—like the reporter in my dream—supporting first Maya, and then her sister. There must have been clues that something was terribly wrong. How did I miss them? As I re-examine our past, my immaturity stands up in my memory and slaps me awake. I had been consumed with building a career and acting out my own shortchanged adolescence during Maya's pre-school years.

When I left her father, I was twenty-seven, and Maya was only three. Survival—financial and emotional—became my entire focus. After I took the job as a staff reporter on a rural paper and moved us away from friends in Minneapolis, I felt forlorn. Soon, I began an affair with the editor of the paper, a man I had known at the University of Minnesota. The following year, he looked after Maya while I took a two-week trip to California in the spring of 1977. It was my first-ever grown-up vacation. It was also the first time I had ever been away from Maya for more than a day. In her letters, dictated to my boyfriend who typed and mailed them for her, Maya said they had planted potatoes in the garden. "Please hurry up and come home, Mommy," she wrote.

I wrote back describing the beauty of San Francisco, Golden Gate Park, the ocean, the wonderful scents of flowers I had never even imagined. I fell in love with San Francisco, and I made up my mind—somehow—to move to California. A friend I was visiting in the city took me to a trendy Sausalito nightclub. A strikingly handsome man with sun-baked skin asked me to dance.

"So what do you do?" he asked in between songs.

"I'm a reporter," I said. "I'm here on vacation."

"Oh, who do you work for?"

"A paper in Minnesota you never heard of," I said.

"Really? I do some writing myself," he said.

The music started again and instead of shouting over it, he asked if I would like to go outside and talk. We sat on a wooden dock, dangling our feet over the San Francisco Bay, watching the stars, and talking. He pulled a joint from his pocket, lit it, took a deep drag, and then offered it to me. I took a puff and handed it back. He said he was working on a book about metaphysics. Intrigued, I asked him to tell me more.

A few days later we drove to Carmel for a picnic on a panoramic white sand beach. I was awestruck by the beauty of the ocean and already swept up in a vacation romance with Dan Wright. He had a mischievous grin that spread across his peaked face and sharp cheekbones that faded into the most amazing blue-green eyes. All his features seemed to tilt up so that I couldn't help smiling when I looked at him. Two years my senior, he was witty, urbane, and seductively warm. My life in Worthington, Minnesota, had always been temporary, anyway, I told myself, and besides career opportunities would be better in California.

I bought Maya a T-shirt when we stopped in Monterey to visit Cannery Row. Dan looked at the pictures of her I carried in my wallet and told me what a beautiful child she was. A few days later I sadly kissed him good-bye and spent the entire flight back to the prairie fantasizing about when I would see him again.

As the plane circled Sioux Falls, the vast, barren ground rose into view. At the gate, Maya ran toward me. "Mommy, mommy. You're back!" It hadn't occurred to me that two weeks was an eternity to a four-year-old and that she must have thought I had abandoned her. If Daddy can disappear, why not Mommy too?

"I'm back," I said, holding her tight, relieved and happy to see her, and depressed by the thought of returning to our daily grind.

I had only the vaguest of plans for escaping from Worthington, but somehow I knew that I would do it and that Maya and

I would eventually live in California. Dan would be part of the picture; I pinned my hopes on that.

❀   ❀   ❀

Dan flew to Minneapolis on a business trip in December. Maya and I met him there. He fell in love with her, and within hours of being introduced to her, he was holding her on his lap and they were chatting like old friends. I was ecstatic. I redoubled my efforts to find work in California.

In February of 1978, ten months after my vacation, I flew back to California, ostensibly for a job interview, but really to spend a few days with Dan. We spent a long weekend in Nevada City, a quaint mining town dotted with restored Victorian houses where Dan had recently moved. Downtown Nevada City looked like a movie set for a town in the Old West; it was known as the Carmel of the Sierra. That seemed auspicious since that was where Dan and I had spent a picture-perfect afternoon.

He was persuasive about our moving to California to join him. The long-distance phone bills mounted after I returned home. Early in March I made up my mind. By the last week of March, I had quit my job at the newspaper, and Dan was flying out to help me pack. Maya seemed excited about the move, but she must have been totally swept up by my feelings, and besides, she really had no choice. I sold our modest three-bedroom ranch house for a few thousand dollars more than I paid for it, but I had no idea how difficult it would be to replace it at West Coast prices. I had obtained sole custody of Maya; now I applied for and got a court order permitting me to relocate with my daughter.

The day before our departure, puffy clouds scudded across

a barren sky. Patches of melting snow re-froze as evening approached. Footing was treacherous. That didn't stop Dan from taking five-year-old Maya to the park for a few last trips down the slide. He had a son by his first marriage, but we did not speak much about this nine-year-old boy who lived in the Los Angles suburbs with his mother and her new husband.

The next morning we bundled into the car and left for California like gypsies, carrying scraps of our old life with us. It didn't occur to me that I was volunteering for loss—of routine, of income, of friends, and of place. I had no idea how thoroughly Midwestern I was in values and outlook. That realization didn't sink in until months later when I woke up in the bed I shared with Dan disoriented, depressed, and wishing I could turn back the clock.

On the blustery March day we left town, I was giddy with the thought of starting over, and wildly in love. We hit the interstate with the radio blasting oldies, a supply of marijuana-laced brownies in a plastic bag, twist-tied to keep them moist. Since I had met Dan, I had smoked more pot than in all my previous years combined. I thought it was hip and a badge of acceptance in the California social scene I was about to enter. A long car trip seemed like the ideal time to indulge. For me it was a rite of passage, for Dan it was an everyday routine.

Maya alternately napped and looked out the back window as we sped along Interstate 90 through Sioux Falls toward Rapid City. Frozen fields swept by like gray-white sheets of newspaper. Dan and I discussed Carlos Castaneda's books, argued over the teachings of the psychic Edgar Cayce, then debated whether the little cabin on Banner Mountain he was renting would work as a permanent home for the three of us.

"Mommy," Maya interrupted from her perch in the back.

"What?" I responded, an irritable edge in my voice.

"How do the horses get water when the troughs freeze over?"

I looked out the window at the shaggy herd picking its way across a frostbitten field. "I think the rancher probably comes and makes a hole in the ice for them," I said, hoping that this was true.

"Oh," she said, "yeah I bet that's what he does..."

She had her doll, a blanket, and a few favorite books in the back seat. I turned and ruffled her hair, and she settled down again for a nap.

On the second day of our odyssey, Dan told me that he was thinking of starting a public relations business. He had quit or been fired (exactly which was not clear) from his job developing and marketing a line of greeting cards for a small publishing house. In the year I had known him he had collected unemployment, worked as a counselor in a boy's home, and then moved to the mountains to take the greeting card job. I felt a surge of uneasiness.

"You take good care of her," one of my older colleagues had instructed when my new lover came to pick me up at the end of my last day in the newsroom. She gave him a piercing look. I thought her concern was sweet and old-fashioned. Driving across Wyoming discussing our uncertain future, I began to wonder if she had some sort of sixth sense.

By the afternoon of the fourth day, I had cottonmouth and a strong desire to sleep in a familiar bed. Hours went by without singing or conversation. Maya braided and re-braided her doll's hair. Dan stared out the window.

We crossed the Sierra Nevada Mountains in a raging blizzard. It was the first day of April in 1978. Nearing the summit, I stared at jagged peaks that boomed into the sky. My first love was the ocean, and I had no idea what a rugged landscape separated California from the rest of the country. I also had not bothered to research average April temperatures at higher elevations. I blamed Dan, slumped in the passenger seat of my battered green Oldsmobile, as if he had personally caused the storm.

"Can you believe this?" I muttered to myself. "Snow on April Fool's day."

Maya lay sleeping in a nest of blankets in the back seat. We wound up over Donner Pass, the snow falling in wet clumps. Donner Lake dropped away in the rearview mirror, a gray blot among white peaks. I laughed bitterly because I had just sold our snow shovels in a garage sale. Luckily, I had kept our down jackets.

An hour later we reached Nevada City. We stopped to buy groceries, loaded them in the car, and then began the twenty-minute climb up Banner Mountain. As we wound higher and higher on a two-lane road that had not been plowed, the nearly bald tires of the Olds spun on the slick asphalt.

At last, I pulled into the gravel driveway of our new home. We clambered into the tiny cabin, kicking wet snow from our boots. The cabin appeared smaller and darker than I remembered. Our breath hung in white puffs above the rusting cast iron stove as we stuffed in rolled newspaper, trying to build a fire with wet manzanita and oak logs. Smoke billowed into the living room. A drafty linoleum walkway led outside to the bathroom, an afterthought to the unwinterized cabin.

"Mommy, come look," Maya called to me from the bathroom. I joined her there, and we stood together staring down into the stained bathtub at a huge bullfrog.

During those early months in Nevada City, I felt as if I were strapped into a roller coaster. One minute I'd believe Dan was the man of my dreams, and the father Maya desperately needed,

but the next I'd blame him for dragging us away from our familiar life. It was a love-hate affair, and my emotions rose and fell
in violent spikes.

"It's as if you've taken the file folders out of a filing cabinet and
dumped them all over the floor," one sympathetic friend said.
"Now you have to sort out your life and put it back in new com-
partments." I was determined to make it work. When friends
from Minnesota would inquire about how we were doing, I put
on a brave face. "Fine," I wrote back airily, "I love California.
The people are so positive here."

I began writing for the local alternative weekly newspaper,
The Western Slopes Connection, and Dan and I started the public
relations business we planned on the trip. I used the profits from
the sale of my house in Minnesota for stationery, business cards,
and the first month's rent on our new office. Maya was settled in
daycare and registered for first grade; she would be six that fall.
I was about to turn thirty.

Maya's father Jeff came to visit us that summer. His band had
broken up; he didn't have steady work, so he decided to take a trip
to San Francisco. He showed up for an afternoon barbecue at the
Wright's family home in the Bay Area suburb of Walnut Creek
where we were spending the weekend with Dan's parents. Their
sprawling two-story house stood on a little knoll surrounded by
walnut trees as if it were a country estate, although it was only
five minutes from the town center. It operated like a bed-and-
breakfast inn on weekends—three or four of their six kids, their
grandkids, assorted friends, even ex-spouses would show up to
hang out by the backyard pool and live off the largesse provided
by Dan's parents.

Vodka tonic in hand, Dan's father would crank up the San Francisco Giant's game on the radio, or play his favorite Dixieland jazz on the tape player. Steaks and chicken breasts sizzled on the grill. It was a sun-filled cacophony of music, sports, and shouted conversation among people who were all high on something. Jeff fit right in.

Jeff towered over his daughter. He looked dazed, dressed in a T-shirt and baggy pants, a floppy white hat pulled low over his eyes. He was stoned out of his mind. Maya, a beanpole in a hand-me-down red and blue bathing suit a size too large for her, pulled at her father's arm.

"Look, Dad! Watch me swim," she said, splashing into the pool to show off her crawl. He nodded and smiled. Someone passed him a beer. He pulled his hat lower and leaned back against the steps.

"That's great, honey," I said, a little too enthusiastically, trying to drum up interest in Maya. "Show Daddy how you can swim underwater."

Her body slid beneath the surface and, dolphin-like, she glided from one end of the pool to the other, skinny legs churning. Maya learned early that showing off her skills got my attention. Jeff glanced at her and looked away, tipping his beer can to his lips. He left that evening, and promised he'd call before we left for Nevada City, but he never phoned. We didn't hear from him again until the following summer when he wrote a note on a scrap of yellow paper.

"Writing to tell you of my latest adventures of Zag-Back. My mother is a soldier for shout, a local politician. They keep throwing me out of the house. They had the gall to tell me to go to work when they gave this guy $900 for this roof work—they use marijuana to promote workhouses. (SCREW)"

Scrawled up the side of the paper was this message: "I

couldn't afford the car so here's a token." Enclosed was a red and white decal of a sports car with the black outline of a driver at the wheel. Jeff had printed "me" with an arrow pointing at the driver.

I tucked the note away in a file folder. Whenever Jeff sent letters that were at least partly intelligible, I would show them to Maya, but more often they were filled with strange drawings or obscenities. I got a call from my former sister-in-law. Jeff's mother was going to commit him to a mental hospital, but changed her mind at the last minute.

Grateful to have escaped from my first marriage after only three years, I never saw any parallels between what I considered my old life and the new life I had created in California. It was as if I had been reborn in that trip over the Sierra Nevada. As I looked back on those years from the perspective of Maya's fatal accident, I suddenly felt afraid. Patterns I never noticed before claimed my full attention now. But it would take many more years before I would have the courage to confront them.

Chapter 10

Living in Nevada City mixed rich friendships with humble economics. High paying work was almost nonexistent and our little family struggled to get by. Long after she should have had a proper bicycle, Maya was still riding her plastic Big Wheel, a toy I had given her when she was three years old.

We had lived on Banner Mountain for six months, long enough for me to celebrate my thirtieth birthday, for Maya to start first grade at Nevada City Elementary School, and for conflicts over sex, money, and drugs to drive a wedge between Dan and me. One Saturday morning, Maya went outside to play, and we began a discussion that quickly escalated into an argument.

"Look, I can't reach you when you're stoned all the time," I complained. "It's as if you've got a mistress—weed—and she's more important to you than I am."

Resistance and anger mingled on Dan's face. He thought my concern over his marijuana use was a form of obsessive hysteria. Suddenly, the kitchen door banged open and Maya ran to the foot of the ladder beneath our attic bedroom.

"Mom, Dan, come look at what I can do," she shouted.

"Not now, Maya. Your mom and I are having a serious talk," Dan yelled back.

Maya begged, "I need you to come *now*. Mom, this is so neat."

I shrugged at Dan and shouted down, "We're coming."

I climbed down the ladder propped next to the rusty wood stove, our only source of heat in the cabin. Dan scrambled down after me.

Maya's blue jeans vanished around the corner into the kitchen. The screen door slammed. Gravel crunched in the driveway as she ran to the road.

Before we reached the end of the driveway, Maya was already in full flight down the hill, hair streaming. The wobbly Big Wheel jolted over the uneven pavement, its plastic tassels sticking straight out. Maya lifted her feet from the pedals. The Big Wheel whirred like an out-of-control eggbeater as she coasted downhill.

She approached the end of the cul de sac in a blur. I opened and shut my mouth and stepped forward, heart thumping, but Dan caught my arm.

"No, wait! She's going over the bank. She *wants* to."

Filled with stubs of volunteer pine and scrubby manzanita, a deep gully yawned at the end of the road. Maya careened straight toward it.

The toy jounced to the edge of the bank overlooking the gully, then lifted into the air. Maya arced over it, clinging like a female Evel Knievel hell-bent on height and speed. She flew into the forest, her knobby spine curled around the Big Wheel, her narrow back floating airborne then sinking out of sight.

We heard a dull thud.

Dan and I ran to the end of the road and peered into the gully.

Maya was brushing pine needles from her thimble of a backside.

She pulled leaves and dirt off the seat and handlebars, set the Big Wheel upright, then turned and dragged it up the gully grinning. Dan and I gaped at each other.

"What a kid!" he said as much to the air as to me.

After the shock wore off, I felt waves of admiration.

"Wow, Maya, that was incredible," Dan said.

"I can't believe you did that," I echoed.

"Do it again," we said in unison.

Dan and I applauded my daredevil daughter as she pedaled uphill. Tree shadows wavered over the asphalt. The Big Wheel crossed in and out of reflected leaf patterns. She turned and pushed off a second time.

She flew down the road, hitting the bank at breakneck speed. She soared up, hovered over the gully for an instant, then thudded down.

We ran to the edge of the gully and looked over.

She was lying on her back whimpering, the Big Wheel toppled on its side.

"Maya! Maya! Are you okay?" I slid down the bank, panic rushing up my throat.

Her toothpick limbs sprawled in the dirt. Dan ran after me. She sat up, clutching her left hand. "Honey, let me see," I said.

The skin below the fingernails on her injured hand was scraped back. She wiped her face with the back of her good hand, streaking dirt and tears across her cheeks. "I pinched my fingers," she wailed. I put my arm around her shoulders, grateful there was nothing broken. She held up her hand so that I could examine it.

Dan leaned over her. "You were terrific, Maya. We shouldn't have asked you to do it again. It's too dangerous."

I buried my nose in Maya's hair, felt the warmth of her scalp, its piney smell leaching into me. "Let me kiss your fingers better," I said.

She offered her wounded hand.

"Do you want some hot chocolate?" Maya nodded and stretched her good hand up to mine. I hauled her up the bank.

In our dilapidated little house with its clacking roof, squeaky doors, and drafty windows, we settled into the late afternoon gloom of the dingy kitchen. Drawing our chairs close, we created a circle of safety. I put marshmallows in the cocoa. The rush of flying settled like motes of dust on the kitchen table.

Chapter 11

One winter afternoon we were marooned in the cabin with no heat. Bored with an endless round of Monopoly games, Maya had grown whiny and restless. Dan devised a brilliant stratagem to distract her at the precise moment I thought I would lose my mind.

"Okay, now just feel your way deeper into your body with each breath," Dan instructed. With each inhale her narrow shoulders rose, then slowly fell. She sat cross-legged in an overstuffed chair upholstered with faded orange and white flowers. Candles flickered on a nearby end table. Dan sat on the floor, also cross-legged, guiding her through the meditation.

She looked calm as a little Buddha.

I was going stir crazy. A monster snowstorm had knocked out the electricity and the water pump four days earlier. Our breath hung in steamy puffs in the frigid indoor air; each night we brushed our teeth with bottled water borrowed from our closest neighbors. Most days, we spent several hours huddled in their kitchen because they had a wood stove that actually produced heat, unlike our aged cast iron Box King.

After five days of virtual camping, I put my foot down and insisted we look for a new place to live. In March we moved to a rented house near the neighboring town of Colfax with a furnace, a dishwasher, and a two-car garage. I enrolled Maya in a neighboring Grass Valley elementary school.

Outgoing and gregarious, Maya seemed to be adjusting to her new school and making friends. But the wrench of our abrupt move from Minnesota, my preoccupation with the ups and downs of my relationship with Dan, and my worry over finances made me a distracted and inconsistent mother. After the move to Colfax, she overheard Dan and me discussing the possibility of getting married. She began her campaign. "Mom, please, please have a baby," she begged. "I want a little sister to play with."

My rush to remarry had more to do with my biological clock and the loneliness of single parenthood than it did with compatibility or true love. I told myself I wanted to give Maya a family, even if it was far from a perfect one. But in reality, I was the one in need of kinship, and Dan's extended clan welcomed my daughter and me as if we belonged. Their all-American way of life was a huge draw for someone raised by parents whose lifestyle was eccentric, at best.

Maya was the flower girl in my August 1979 wedding. Dan's five siblings and their partners, his parents, his grandmother, and a tribe of nieces and nephews took up three rows of chairs. My mother, the lone representative of our family, had a seat in the front with the others. Dan's son Mark sat next to Maya. Four years older than his new stepsister, eleven-year-old Mark had become her playmate and confidante during his holiday and summer visits to Nevada City.

I was thirty-one and captivated by the "go with the flow" glamour of the place and the era. We wrote the ceremony ourselves. Friends with mail order ministers' licenses married us. Then we hosted a boisterous party and potluck supper at a

Nevada City landmark. The American Victorian Museum was a converted foundry that housed a collection of Victorian bric-a-brac and old mill wheels. It was a fun affair, funky and perfectly expressing the hippie ethos of the late 1970s in the Sierra Nevada foothills. We danced into the wee hours and cleaned up the cavernous main dining room ourselves after our guests had left. My mother looked after Maya while we honeymooned at a Big Sur campground overlooking the Pacific Ocean. I spent most of that week in tears. Dan would wander off to the edge of the cliff overlooking the ocean and smoke a joint, preferring to be alone with his thoughts, rather than making love with me.

After the honeymoon, our fights took on a new, more urgent character. Stumbling over one of my husband's improvised bongs (he made them out of cardboard toilet paper rolls and tin foil) made me fly into a rage. Long after I went to bed each night, he sat in our shared office tape-recording marijuana-inspired monologues.

I compensated by spending more time with women friends and submerging myself in my work as a reporter for the local alternative newspaper. I documented the culture clash between the "old guard" loggers and real estate developers and the influx of artists and back-to-the-land enthusiasts—but what really captured my imagination was profiling a host of local characters who had been shaped by the lore and history of the place. Restless and unhappy, I found that Colfax was too far from the social and cultural center of my life. I wanted to be in the thick of the action in Nevada City, and so did Dan. Besides, a move offered a wonderful distraction from our escalating marital conflict. That winter we moved again—this time, to a rented house in downtown Nevada City.

Before I had unpacked the last of the boxes, dark circles under my eyes greeted me each morning in the bathroom mirror. I kept a stash of Saltine crackers by the bed to fend off morning nausea. I consulted a local midwife for a pregnancy test, and she confirmed what I already knew. I desperately wanted this baby, but my new marriage was foundering. Absent the pregnancy, I might have bailed out, but in the end I gambled that Dan and I could hold it together. Maya was overjoyed when I announced that the baby she had begged for was due in August. After talking over the options with some women friends, and discussing it with Dan, we decided to make it a home birth.

Among the "hipoisie" of Nevada County, home birth was a political statement. Down with the glaring lights and metal stirrups of hospitals and their mind numbing drugs. I brushed aside the irony. Consciousness-expanding substances were a staple of my life because no gathering in our Nevada City social circle took place without them. And pot was a daily routine for my husband. But an epidural? No way.

With a few months of childbirth education, and a competent midwife, it was possible to orchestrate the birth at home with ample focus on family bonding. I was determined not to repeat the experience of being separated for hours from my newborn baby, as I had been from Maya. We visited the best midwife in the county at her farm on the San Juan Ridge, and she agreed to manage prenatal care and delivery of my baby. I read all the guidebooks, gathered a knowledgeable birth team, practiced my breathing, and assumed the birth would go smoothly.

Just before midnight on July 31, 1980, contractions began. Maya was asleep, but Dan and I stayed up all night. As the labor pains intensified, we called our birth team, and by six that morning everyone had assembled in our first floor bedroom. By noon on August 1, the contractions felt like long seismic jolts. Without drugs to dull the pain, I wailed like a banshee.

Between contractions, Dan fed me ice chips and attempted to keep my breathing rhythmic and slow. Whatever residual anger I felt toward him quickly melted. We were both focused on only one thing—delivering a healthy baby. When the contractions peaked, and I was in full transition, the midwife coached me to push. But after half an hour, it was clear that my efforts were fruitless. She worked intently to coax the baby out. Her hand-prints stood out like brands on the skin of my taut belly.

After an hour of pushing with no sign of my baby's head, panic swept over me. Maya's delivery had taken forty-five min-utes. I knew this was not normal. Waves of fear grew more intense with each fruitless contraction. After the second hour of grunting and straining without results I was so exhausted that I thought I would die with the next pain. As another contraction peaked and my belly gathered into a knot, I shouted, "NO, NO, NO!"

The midwife put her face inches from mine and urged me on, "Say, yes. Say yes, Eleanor!" A burning, ripping sensation brought me to the brink.

"YES!" I wailed.

The midwife broke into a grin.

"The baby's head is crowning," she crowed to everyone in the room. Turning back to me, she instructed, "Touch your baby's head."

I reached down and felt the very top of my child's wet head, which quickly receded as the contraction ended. I fell back against my birth coach. At that moment I lost all sense that I even had another child. Seven-year-old Maya witnessed the labor and birth in a corner of the room. I had actually believed it would be as calm and uplifting as the blissful films of deliveries we had watched during the birth training.

It wasn't until I looked more closely at our birth photos, many months later, that I got a glimpse of what that afternoon was like for Maya. She is sitting on a chair in the corner of the bedroom cowering behind a pillow. Her bony shoulders emerge from a frayed pink tank top, as she buries her face and weeps. One of my friends leans over to comfort her. But what I saw in that picture—a look of pure terror on her face—pierced my heart. Sucked into the vortex of birth, I was lost to her.

When the next contraction gathered force, I pushed until I thought I would explode. The midwife finessed my baby's head into daylight. I looked down at an infant with a face so blue, it appeared to have been strangled. The midwife jammed a plastic oxygen mask over the nose and mouth. My panic began to wane as color appeared on the tiny cheeks and seeped down the neck. Weeks later, our midwife admitted to me that she was moments away from calling an ambulance to take me to the hospital for a C-section.

Home births were orchestrated to give the father a central role; we had agreed beforehand that Dan would catch our baby after the midwife delivered the head. "Mr. Wright," she now instructed, "you can deliver the body." Dan shifted into position and held out his hands. I pushed with my last ounce of strength and the shoulders slid out. My husband caught our new daughter. He gazed down at her, completely dazzled. I watched him melt as he cradled her naked body. Tears rolled down his cheeks.

At a celebration for our birth team two days later, Maya positively glowed. The terror of the birth was gone, replaced by the joy of a new life. She grinned down at the baby in her lap, looking at her half-sister with as much love and pride as if she had produced her herself.

In the following months, Maya did become like a second mother to Meghan. The boundaries between my older daughter and me were so blurred that I immediately enlisted her to be my assistant. Instead of the playmate she had dreamt of, she faced the reality of a colicky infant who wailed almost non-stop. And she had to contend with two over-stressed, sleep-deprived new parents with little time and less patience.

I strapped my three-month-old into the stroller and tucked a blanket in around her.

"Now be sure to look both ways before you cross the street," I instructed my precocious assistant. "Do you have a pacifier?" Maya, who had recently turned eight, nodded solemnly. Meghan was still colicky, and we never went anywhere without a pacifier. The stroller bumped down the porch steps onto the sidewalk. I closed the front door and sank down into the knotty gray couch for a blessed twenty minutes of silence.

I had discovered the astonishing truth that two children were more than twice as much effort as caring for one. Meghan was now the center of attention in our family, an adored baby with an involved, loving father. I couldn't have anticipated how having a biological child would change Dan's way of relating to my older daughter. It was almost as if some animal switch had been thrown where Meghan was concerned—he was completely focused on her well-being. He no longer eagerly scooped Maya up when she came to him for a hug. His attachment to his own child was intense and all consuming. Maya was out in the cold.

Just blocks from our house that afternoon, my older daughter performed a primal experiment. At the top of a hill by the Nevada City Library, she released the handles of the stroller with her baby sister strapped in. The runaway stroller bumped down the sidewalk. A patch of buckled concrete fifty yards below stopped its momentum. Miraculously, Meghan was unharmed. Maya calmly took the dollar I gave her for babysitting when she came home and never mentioned this close call. It would be years before she told me.

Maybe she was tired of playing mother. Or tired of having no father while Meghan's father, formerly one of her greatest admirers, virtually ignored her. Instead of being her passionate advocate and best pal, I had morphed into a stressed-out cranky parent who routinely grasped at her for help. Maya's childhood had taken a turn that made her angry and sad. She was grieving.

Even her attic bedroom was far from the center of family life, tucked under the eaves, a narrow rectangle that stretched the length of our white clapboard house. A window at the front end of the house looked out over Pine Street, but with only a single source of outside light, the room was cave-like. As Meghan grew rounder and more adorable in our eyes, she became more of a threat to her sister. Maya guarded her territory jealously. But she was no match for an active toddler.

Meghan would scatter the butterscotch cow and the canary yellow duck in the plastic barnyard play set, and send the fence posts skittering across the linoleum. When Maya attempted to organize a game of jacks, Meghan swept the jacks everywhere. And the worst sin—two-year-old Meghan cut the shiny acrylic hair of Maya's Barbie doll into a Joan of Arc bob with a pair of pink plastic scissors.

Maya was at the mercy of this interloper. And, as is so often the case with firstborns, she took the rap over the years even when the two of them were equally to blame.

The lined school paper of one of Maya's poems is frayed at the edges, but her printing is neat and clear. It says, "I wish for a brand new bike. I wish for my mom to feel better. I wish for a pony. I wish to live the rest of my life."

Maya got one of her wishes in 1982. We bought her a used bicycle. She careened down Pine Street to Broad Street, narrowly missing the black wrought iron lampposts and wooden benches on the sidewalks. When she turned ten, she began a troubling pattern of accidental falls. From the top of the circular slide at Pioneer Park. From the upper bunk bed at a friend's house. And, finally, tumbling from her bike over the handlebars to the street. She ended up in the emergency room with a mild concussion.

"What do you think is going on with her?" I asked Dan.

"I'm not sure," he replied. "A growth spurt?"

"Maybe, but she seems so out of it at times, like she's just not here..."

"Yeah, you're right."

We wrote a note to her third grade teacher, who had also expressed concern about Maya's clumsiness at our last parent-teacher conference. After the trip to the emergency room and our expressions of worry, Maya's balance seemed to improve.

She was also experiencing a spurt of creativity, something I enthusiastically encouraged. She took ballet lessons and pirouetted across the stage dressed in a black and yellow bee costume, gold antennae waving. Her teacher chose her for the lead role in a school play. And then, with my help and coaching, she attended her first formal audition at a local community theater. She read for a part in *Cat on a Hot Tin Roof,* as one of the bratty children, the "no neck monsters," created by Tennessee Williams. Maya got the part of Trixie, a little girl who taunts the main character Maggie—a sexually frustrated wife ignored by her alcoholic husband. The play ran for three weeks at the Nevada Theater on Broad Street.

"Look, Mom, my picture is in the paper," Maya said, handing me a copy of *The Grass Valley Union.*

"Honey, that's terrific!" I looked at my ten-year-old smiling in a grainy black and white photo surrounded by her fellow child actors. Maya is leaning toward the camera with her arms propped on her knees. What my mother's eye saw was her scuffed tennis shoes.

At the opening night performance I watched my daughter scamper about taunting a frustrated Maggie the Cat with a whiny bravado that was absolutely believable. She was a fabulous brat! I tucked the photo and accompanying article into a file folder labeled "Maya–Theater." Her energy and talent gave me hope that Maya would ultimately surmount her diminished role in our blended family. In the play, she took center stage, a feat she could not bring about at home.

Chapter 12

I n the winter of 1983, more than ninety inches of rain fell
in Nevada County, a record for the area. Perhaps it was
the rain. Or pawning my grandmother's silver spoons for
money to buy groceries. Or that when our yippy wire-haired
terrier pooped in the living room for the umpteenth time, no one
even noticed it except me. Or maybe it was the night Dan got so
drunk he had to crawl up the stairs to our bedroom on all fours.
Whatever it was, I had reached a breaking point.

Dan claimed marijuana made him more creative, and when
he had a major project due for a client, he'd binge and stay up
all night working. His income was erratic. We routinely used
"creative accounting" to manage our separate accounts, writing
checks to each other to create more float time. Sometimes we
borrowed from his parents to pay rent and monthly bills.

The worst side-effect of his dependence on pot was the impact
on our sex life. At first, I thought our problems in bed were my
fault—it took time to lose the pregnancy weight, I was often
stressed about money, and I was worn out from dividing my
attention between Maya and Meghan. My own libido fluctuated
wildly. But when Dan routinely lost his erection a few minutes

into our lovemaking, I was panic stricken. He usually wanted to stay in me, limp, and be caressed. I was repulsed.

I pushed him off, rolled away, and curled into a ball. "Why does this keep happening?" I demanded.

"You have a penis fixation," he snapped.

Had I been mature enough to understand how afraid he was, I might have found another way to respond. But I was hot-wired to sexual release. I stared at the wall, fists balled up, head pounding. "What I have is a normal sex drive, and I can't take this any longer," I snarled from between clenched teeth.

We tried couples counseling, family therapy, and even sex therapy. I spent hours in Al Anon meetings and Narcotics Anonymous trying to understand marijuana addiction and how I was enabling it. Through it all, my children kept me going.

Standing over Meghan's crib during the nights when I couldn't sleep, I watched her eyes flicker as she dreamt. Her soft reddish hair clumped in sweaty strands where I touched her forehead, and her dimpled palms curled up as if to catch the errant moonlight streaming in through the window. I gazed at my two-and-a-half year old, still so cherubic, and wondered how I could leave her father. When I looked in at ten-year-old Maya, she was curled on her side with her arms cradling her cat, Bizbomb, sleeping peacefully.

One morning when I got up ahead of the others and went downstairs to make breakfast, I was so weary I could barely lift the teakettle. My life had become just like my mother's—I was trapped in a loveless marriage in a small town, broke, weighed down by housework and kids. Our need for money propelled me toward an escape hatch.

The following summer, I began a contract writing assignment at a computer software company in Walnut Creek. We moved from the Sierra foothills to a rented house not far from Dan's family home, in a leafy suburban neighborhood with curving lanes and picket fences. This corner of the Bay Area was a long way from the small town in Pennsylvania where I had grown up, but the surrounding hills and trees bore a distinct resemblance to those of my childhood.

I was sad to leave our life in Nevada County, but as the marriage fell apart I felt more and more isolated and confined there. As I adjusted to the faster pace, I felt more solid in a place where jobs were plentiful and schools for my kids were excellent. Dan accepted an unpaid position as the executive director of a nonprofit foundation in San Francisco. I was now the sole support of our family. The girls liked being near Dan's parents, but by that point their son and I were barely speaking.

I stuck it out in the marriage so that my daughters could settle into their new schools and I could formulate a plan of action. In the spring of 1984, once I had found a house to rent in nearby Oakland, I knew the marriage had to end. I was thirty-six years old, Meghan was almost four, and Maya was about to turn twelve. The next two years passed in a blur as the challenges of being a single parent absorbed all of my energy.

Our divorce was final in October of 1986, right around Maya's fourteenth birthday. That year had been tumultuous for me—I had been laid off from my job at the computer firm and my landlady decided to sell our rented house to her son, presenting me with a thirty-day eviction notice. We were very nearly homeless during the summer of 1986, and survived only because I began housesitting for vacationing friends, moving three times in the space of three months. Confronted with the option of sending my older daughter to a crumbling public high school in

Oakland, or enrolling her in an expensive private school, I again moved to Walnut Creek to a small duplex where I could just barely afford the rent.

The following year, Dan married for a third time.

Maya was showing signs of depression that I wanted to believe were the normal hormone-driven moods of a sensitive young teen. A freshman in high school, she withdrew into her room, or spent long hours on the phone with friends, listening to music or polishing her nails. She began to defy me even over simple things. She was hyper and irritable. We had fierce arguments that ended in shouting, tears, and slamming doors.

My ex-husband now lived in a better school district than I did. He and his wife rented a large home with a swimming pool in Lafayette, one of the wealthiest communities in the East Bay. By combining his public relations skills with his wife's graphic design business, Dan had engineered a steady income. I was increasingly absorbed by my problems with Maya, and Meghan had difficulty splitting her school week between two homes as our joint custody agreement stipulated. In the end, I agreed that Meghan could live with her father and stepmother during the week, attend the better elementary school, and I would become the visiting parent. Admitting to myself that I was simply unable to cope was a devastating blow. Worse yet, I now felt I was failing both of my daughters, and I missed Meghan terribly.

In addition to a demanding new corporate job in San Francisco, a two-hour daily commute, and a teenager who was acting out, I also had a mountain of grief about giving up my seven-year-old child. But I was determined not to go under emotionally or financially. I had to be there for Maya because I was all that she had. Meghan was more fortunate, and I had to acknowledge that her father could now provide more advantages for her than I could.

Our duplex was no bigger than a doublewide trailer. Painted a dull gold with white trim, it had a cement front porch and a back patio with wide dirt borders where I planted a modest garden. Each Wednesday night and on weekends Meghan stayed with us. For the most part, Maya and I were on our own. As the next year passed, I discovered that I was more tied down and stressed out as a single parent of a teen than I had been when my daughter was an active three-year-old. Back then, I could keep her safe and under control.

One night, I was clearing away dishes after supper when Maya, now in her second year of high school, came into the kitchen and said she needed to talk. I imagined it must be about a problem with her schoolwork, or a fight with one of her girl-friends. We sat down at the table. The stove light gleamed in the tiny kitchen. She took a deep breath.

"Mom, I'm pregnant."

There before me was her slim body, her smooth oval face. She was only fifteen. Scraps of her childhood flooded back— blond curls peeking out of the plastic laundry basket she loved to play in when she was two years old, the way she always begged me to push her on the swings. "Go higher, Mommy. Higher!"

Pregnant? She was still a child. She wore size three jeans and had a pile of stuffed animals on her bed. *Pregnant?* I swallowed hard. My palms were sweating.

"Have you thought about what you want to do?" It sounded so lame, so pedestrian. I didn't know what else to say. I suppose anger would have been an option, or empathy, but in that moment all I could think of was finding a solution as quickly as possible. Becoming a teenage mother couldn't happen to *my* daughter.

Maya told me she had decided to get an abortion. She had

already met with a Planned Parenthood counselor to consider the options. "I think it's the right decision, Mom," she said. "I've thought it through."

She asked if I would go with her and her friend Courtney to the clinic on the day of the procedure. I nodded, happy she had asked me, numb with fear, and stunned by her clear, deliberate words. She pulled her hair back from her face, wrapping the long strands over her left shoulder. Her brown eyes snapped with determination. The refrigerator hummed. I clenched my hands under the table, fumbling for words.

"I'm too young," my daughter said. "I can't take care of a baby. I want to finish my education." Like an icy liquid, shock buffeted my brain. I nodded. "Dave agrees," she added, almost as an afterthought.

Dave? For a moment I couldn't orient myself. Of course, a father. How elementary, there has to be a father. I felt a surge of hatred. How could he have done this to her? Then the hatred turned to anger; simple anger toward him for the hurt to Maya, and then fury at both of them for their carelessness, followed by a sharp stab of sorrow for the loss of my first grandchild.

Just as quickly as these emotions arose, they were replaced by a stomach-churning wave of guilt. How could I have known so little about this boy? I had no idea their relationship had progressed so far, so fast. I felt I had let Maya down.

To help us through this crisis, I insisted we see our minister, Margaret Stortz, for counseling. Rev. Margaret asked us to come in separately. Maya cried after her session. All she would tell me was that Margaret had helped her deal with the guilt and fear. In my session with Margaret, I told her that I felt like a failure as a parent. She reassured me that I was doing the best I could as a single mother of two children and reminded me that many of the teenage daughters and middle-aged mothers she counseled could not even discuss something this painful and difficult. Her words soothed me.

On the afternoon of the procedure I sat stiffly in the pastel waiting room thumbing a magazine, trying valiantly to hold back memories of two pregnancies I had terminated as a frightened college student. At least it's legal now, I told myself. The clinic was full of sunlight, plants, and friendly women. But my heart was heavy. The wait seemed interminable.

"You can come in now," a young woman in a pink smock said, resting a hand on my shoulder. I walked into the recovery area. Curled up on a couch, Maya was wrapped in an afghan. She looked pale, but her face lit up when I came to her side.

"How are you kiddo?"

"I'm good, Mommy," she said. "Happy it's over."

I ran my hand across her forehead, smoothing her silky hair.

That night at home Maya and Courtney watched a rented video in the living room. I paced my cramped bedroom, crying, wondering how I could have veered so far off track as a parent. I had already taken Margaret's calming words and placed them in a corner of my brain reserved for positive thinking. I muffled my frustrated sobs with handfuls of tissue so that the girls couldn't hear me, and then sat on the edge of the bed staring out my window at the lacy carrot tops and green onions sprouting in my suburban garden, wondering what the hell to do.

Meghan was seven years old that spring and having her own struggles adjusting to a new school and a new living situation in Lafayette. I was so caught up with my fifteen-year-old daughter, and our relationship was so intense and drama-filled, that Meghan's mostly placid demeanor was a relief. With three parents instead of just one, and as an adored granddaughter in a large extended family, Meghan's advantages continued to torment Maya, and she responded with canny and well-disguised cruelty.

Often, my work kept me in San Francisco until after six o'clock in the evening, and on Wednesday afternoons Maya had almost three hours alone with Meghan when she was expected to be in charge.

One afternoon, a frantic Maya temporarily hijacked Meghan. Increasingly cocky about being a latchkey teen, Maya panicked when I returned home from work unexpectedly in the middle of an impromptu party. She instructed her high school chum Oliver to grab Meghan and a six-pack of Coors Lite and hide with them in the bedroom closet, where Oliver clapped his hand over Meghan's mouth to keep her from blowing their cover, while Maya spun out an excuse.

Maya's stories were inventive and convincing. I was an easy target for her fabrications. I desperately wanted to believe that she was okay, that our life was unfolding in a positive direction, and that being the product of a one-parent family was not an insurmountable handicap to her future. And on the surface we looked good. She was bright, outgoing, and achievement oriented; my work in a big corporation was gradually building a more solid financial foundation beneath us.

For the first time in my life, at the age of forty, I could actually afford to buy nice things. Because of my editor's job at Pacific Bell, I suddenly had spending power. Early in 1989 I could afford higher rent, and with the support of my new boyfriend, John, I found a white clapboard house not far from our duplex. There was a silver-leafed olive tree in the front yard, and the house was set on a little knoll above the street. It was a one-story rancher with three bedrooms and a huge kitchen that had 1950s-style Formica counter tops. From the kitchen, I could look out to the terraced backyard with more trees. Best of all, there were two bathrooms, and I would no longer have to share one with Maya, a perpetual source of conflict.

John gave us a set of scratched, dirty-blond maple bunk beds that had belonged to his grown daughter. He helped me set them up in the girls' room, and I carefully dusted them and oiled them with Lemon Pledge. Then I took the girls downtown to buy comforters with matching sheets and pillowcases. It was peaceful. They didn't fight, and we all agreed on the comforters—light blue with peach and white flowers and pale green stems—a pattern that worked for both a sixteen-year-old and an eight-year-old. The pillow shams had ruffles, and there were matching twin sheets. Best of all, I could charge it on my Macy's account. My daughters had pretty, comfortable beds in the room they shared on weekends. Life seemed to be on the upswing.

Chapter 13

W hat happened to you?" I couldn't hide the edge in
my voice. Maya had spent the night at a girlfriend's.
When she stepped through the front door that
Saturday afternoon, a vivid bruise on her face pushed all of my
alarm buttons.

I moved toward her. She mumbled something I couldn't
make out and attempted to brush past me. "Wait! What happened?"

She gave me a cutting stare. "I fell on a brick patio and hit my
head."

"Honey, let me see," I said, moving in for a closer look.

A large purple goose egg bulged above her right eye. There
was a jagged rip in the shoulder of her favorite T-shirt.

"I'm fine." she waved me off. As she again tried to pass by me
to get to her room, I smelled liquor, not so much on her breath as
emanating from her skin.

I stood my ground. "Listen, Maya. You need to put some ice
on that. It's a nasty bruise."

"I just want to take some Advil and go to bed." She set her purse
down by the bookshelf in the entryway as if it belonged there.

"All right," I said, stymied. I wasn't sure what more to say to my obviously hungover sixteen-year-old. She looked like her grandmother, my former mother-in-law back in Minneapolis, who frequently appeared with bruises or burns after a weekend bender. I recognized the defiant hangdog expression.

"Do you want something to eat? Some protein might be..."

"Oh, God, no!" she cut me off.

"Well let me make an ice bag," I persisted. "You can take it to bed with you."

"All right, Mom, whatever..." She brushed her hand across her forehead. Her bangs pouffed up in a blond cloud.

When I came into her bedroom, she was under her blue and peach comforter, fully clothed and fast asleep. Her mouth was open, lips parted, and I could see dark bluish purple rings under her eyes. *Had she slept at all last night?* I wondered. I propped a plastic bag of ice wrapped in a clean dishtowel between her forehead and the pillow. She stirred and mumbled but never opened her eyes.

I backed out of the room slowly and closed the door.

In the kitchen I loaded the dishwasher, looking out at the back yard, suddenly aware of all that grass I should be cutting. I wanted to run away and hide. I tried to distract myself with chores—laundry, mopping the kitchen floor—but the plain fact kept drumming in my head. Maya was drunk. It was already the afternoon of the day *after* the party, which meant she must have been so drunk at the party that she fell and hit her head, hard, and didn't feel it until she began to sober up.

I raced back over the last few months in my mind. I could hear the tap, tap, tap of Maya's suede cowboy boots over the hardwood floors in those early mornings when she came home long past her midnight curfew. My daughter's tapping woke me, and I would burrow under my own flowered comforter, sometimes groggy enough to fall back to sleep, sometimes bolt awake. It was lonely, raising her by myself, worrying alone. John was busy with work and consumed with his own furtive drinking, which I sometimes suspected but never observed. The house was full of secrets—and outright lies.

It was party season in Walnut Creek. Warm weather brought out older boys and rented beer kegs, but I knew little, at that point, about binge drinking. I did know about keg parties, I wasn't that dense, but in the two-and-a-half years we had lived in Walnut Creek, I was shocked by how acceptable teen drinking seemed to be. Some parents were so glad their kids were not doing hard drugs that they actually opened their liquor cabinets to their children. I always checked to be sure there would be supervision at the parties she attended, but Maya was an artful liar. I harped on the dangers of driving while drunk, but I had made no clear agreement with her about alcohol use.

I needed to talk this over, to tell someone what I suspected. John was a car salesman, and weekends were busy for him. He wouldn't be home until late. I considered calling Dan to ask for his advice and then thought better of it. I'm probably making a mountain out of a molehill, I reasoned.

Meghan had a friend over, and I had ordered pizza and made a big salad. It had grown dark outside. At last, Maya emerged from her room. She sat with us half-heartedly picking at a slice of cold pizza. Sober at last. The two younger girls were glued to a television show. Maya seemed subdued, almost apologetic, but offered no explanation of her previous night. I got pulled into the swell of activities—dishes, tooth brushing, bedtime stories for the younger girls—and let the undiscussable elephant sit there smack dab in the center of our living room with its big hollow eyes.

It was the summer of 1989. In a few weeks Maya would begin her senior year in high school. One August evening, she was out with some friends. I had to be up extra early the next morning. Union-represented phone company employees were on strike, and as a manager I had to cross a picket line to fill in for striking directory assistance operators. We were pulling twelve-hour shifts, and my day started at five in the morning. I went to bed before my daughter's midnight curfew. At two o'clock that morning I woke with a start. I sensed that she had not come home; her absence was palpable. I got out of bed, put on my robe, and crossed the hallway to her room. Her bed was empty, the covers in a jumble, clothes spread on the floor.

I went to the kitchen to make tea. Where was she? She had promised to turn over a new leaf. My mind raced with possibilities.

When the front door scraped open a few moments later, I held my breath. I could hear her tiptoeing toward her room, unaware that I was awake. I stood at the kitchen counter turning the mug of tea in my hands. Her door closed. I set my tea down and went toward her room.

When I knocked, there was a muffled, "Come in."

"I was so worried. Where have you been?" I demanded. I was determined not to be fooled this time.

"What do you mean?" She stared at me defiantly. She was lying in bed wrapped in her comforter.

"Don't play games with me. I know you just got in. It's two hours past your curfew."

"What are you talking about?" she sneered at me.

"You know damn well what I'm talking about. I was in the kitchen when you came in. I heard you."

She lay back on her pillow and laughed. The blood rose in my cheeks.

"Okay, Mom, if you have nothing better to do than sit up and wait for me, then you might as well stay up all night. I'm going out again."

It was my turn to laugh. The sounds emerged clotted and raspy.

"Think again, Maya. You're not going anywhere."

Her eyes flashed at me. She threw the blue flowered quilt off her bed and stood up. She was fully clothed. One leg of her jeans caught above her boots. Like a flamenco dancer, she stamped on the wood floor to bring her pant legs level. Then she scooped her purse up from the floor by the bed.

I backed up and stood against her door, heart pounding, as if I could block her from leaving the room.

"I have to take Oliver's car back to him," she said. "He let me borrow it to come home."

"Too bad. Call him and tell him he'll have to walk over here and pick it up." I knew Oliver lived in an apartment not far from our house.

"He needs his car." She looked as if her eyes might burst into flame.

"He doesn't need his car at two o'clock in the morning." I leaned into the door with clenched fists, eyes flashing, matching her fire.

"Yes, he does. We're meeting some people at Denny's."

Then she shook her head. I heard her whisper something that sounded distinctly like, "You bitch."

"What did you say?"

"You heard me." She tossed her mane of blond hair.

"Not only are you staying here," I said between clenched teeth, "you are grounded for the next month."

"Fuck *you!*" She was screaming so loudly that I flattened myself against the back of the door. "You just want to ruin my life, you fucking bitch!"

"Think what you want," I said icily, "but you are *not* going out." I glared at her, furious and humiliated. I turned and left the room, pulling the door shut, determined not to let her get the better of me.

A few minutes later I heard a scraping noise coming from her room. When I tried the door, it wouldn't open. I called her name. Then I heard a car start and screech away. I put my shoulder to the door and pushed harder. When it opened I saw that she had blocked it with a chair. Her window was open. She was gone.

Finally, I got it. My guilt over her lack of a father (and a host of other things about being a single parent) kept me from confronting her bad behavior. We were both out of control. I vowed to stop the downward spiral. After her night out, I insisted that we get family counseling. I also restricted her telephone time and TV viewing, and threatened to curb her use of the car if she did not shape up.

One thing in particular motivated Maya—her desire to go away to college. She had largely given up acting and instead focused on competing in high diving with the Las Lomas High School swim team, but it was clear that she was not living up to her academic potential. I played the college card, agreeing that if she settled down and applied herself in school, I would send her to Santa Barbara City College after she graduated. It had become her top choice once she realized that she did not have the grades for the University of California.

We settled into a routine. She went to group therapy once a week and I met, alone, with the therapist each month. The sessions were painful.

"What makes you think you should be your daughter's best friend?" the therapist asked. "Your job is to be her parent, not to win a popularity contest."

I explained that my younger daughter lived with her father and that, for most of her life, Maya and I had lived alone. No one in my life was as close to me as Maya was; we had grown up together. I had always been her best friend, and she had always been mine.

"Do you think that's fair to Maya?"

"I don't know..." I fumbled, confused and sheepish.

"Isn't that a lot of pressure for a child her age? Why should she have to meet *your* emotional needs?"

I wanted to say, "Because no one else will." But the obvious answer was that she shouldn't. However, that was our unspoken and largely unconscious agreement. My relationships with men were painful and unsuccessful. By contrast, Maya and I understood each other. Our love was bedrock.

I left the therapist's office burning with remorse. When I got home I buried my face in the arm of the couch and wept. The pain of knowing I had heaped so much emotional responsibility on Maya clawed at me. Suddenly, I could look back and see that in spite of my love for her, I had not been a wise or mature parent to Maya. In some fundamental way I had cheated her.

Later that night, I asked Maya if we could talk. She agreed and came to sit at the kitchen table with me. I told her I wanted to make some changes. I would stop trying to win her approval or lean on her emotionally. I was going to try to be a better parent, to set firmer limits, and do all the things she didn't like, but desperately needed me to do. We were about to step out on a new path.

In the movie, *Indochine*, Catherine Deneuve takes her beautiful adopted daughter in her arms and they dance a perfect, fiery tango. Mother and daughter glide from one end of the room to the other. They hold each other like lovers, sure in the knowledge of each other's bodies. Their heads swivel in unison and they lock eyes smoldering with unspoken anger. They are dancing the complex emotional terrain of mothers and daughters— the intense love, the underlying sexual tension between two women, one of whom is aging while the other is blossoming, the pride a mother takes in her daughter, the envy she feels of her child's youth, the dreams she has for her daughter's happiness. And the child's passionate but ambivalent attachment, the desire to follow the mother's lead, but also to break free, to find her own rhythm and take her own steps. My dance with Maya was reaching its emotional peak as she prepared to leave home.

My own mother was battling for her life in the spring of 1990, struggling with kidney failure and other life-threatening symptoms of end-stage diabetes. I ran my credit cards up to the limit flying back to Ohio three times that year, and each time I thought it would be the last time I would see my mother alive. My nerves were raw, and my own health suffered. But family therapy seemed to be working, and Maya's weekly group therapy helped her find ways to become more independent from me without being self-destructive. The house was calmer.

After we celebrated Maya's graduation from high school, she and Meghan and I went camping at New Brighton Beach, one of our favorite campgrounds on the California coast. We jammed our camping gear into my little car and took off for the hour-and-a-half drive to Santa Cruz.

As we unloaded our tent and cook stove, I wondered how we would ever manage to get it all set up before dark. But both girls pitched in, and we did it.

"Mom, we're roughing it without men!" Maya joked as we stood back to admire the big dome tent we had just erected on our campsite. She put her arm around me, and gathered Meghan in to her side. I closed the circle and we stood among the tall redwood trees hugging each other.

That night we roasted marshmallows and sat around our campfire telling stories, reliving our history as a family. Maya confessed to some of the horrors she had inflicted on Meghan, and we were able to laugh about it. She seemed more at peace. She and Meghan got along beautifully. During the days, I took them to the beach in Capitola, and my heart burst with pride as Maya, lithe and tan in a black and royal blue bikini, played Frisbee with her younger sister, or ran into the surf holding hands with her. I basked in the July sun and thought maybe things had not turned out too badly after all.

Maya and I began our final plans for her first semester as a student at Santa Barbara City College. After we returned from our vacation we hit the stores in search of back-to-school bargains.

She decided to leave for Santa Barbara in mid-August in order to get established and to find part-time work. With an October birthday, she was only seventeen, but she seemed so self-confident and mature that I figured it would be okay. Torn with grief over my mother's impending death, I could not possibly let myself feel how much I was going to miss my daughter. She was still my best friend, no matter what the therapist said.

Dan offered to help Maya move and settle into her new

apartment. He rented a small trailer to haul some of her furniture and household supplies. Maya invited Meghan to go along, but I was staying behind. I planned to go to Santa Barbara once Maya was settled and help her decorate her apartment.

The morning of her departure, I cooked her favorite breakfast—French toast with vanilla and cinnamon, strawberries, and chicken-apple sausage. I sat at the table watching her wolf it down.

"If you get lonely," I said, not knowing I was really trying to reassure my own aching heart, "you can always come home for a few days..."

She smiled. "Okay, Mom, I'll keep that in mind," she said gently, clearly eager to be on her way. I pushed my sadness aside and began reviewing the checklist of last-minute items with her.

"Do you have detergent? Fabric softener? Quarters for the laundry room?"

"Check," she said mockingly. "I'll be fine, Mom."

I squeezed back tears and smiled, "Of course you will."

Dan arrived with Meghan. We all trooped from the house down to the street, loading boxes into the little open trailer hitched to the back of his car. I carried hangers full of Maya's clothes from her closet to hang on a clothes bar in the back of the car. Then a laundry basket full of sheets and towels, still warm from the dryer.

Finally everything was stowed away. I opened my arms to her, and she snuggled against me. I wanted to cradle her, to tell her that it had all gone by way too quickly. I was still learning how to be a parent. But I couldn't find the words. I nestled against her body, stroking her hair, knowing I had to let her go. At last, I took her by the shoulders and turned her to face the car door on the passenger side.

"Okay, go!" I said.

She got in and slammed the door. The car pulled away. I stood on the side of the road and watched the back of her head recede up the hill. I raised my arm to wave. She waved back without turning to look at me, her hand sticking out of the rolled down window. When the car disappeared from view, I turned and walked up the stairs to my little white house, kicking rotting olives across the cracked cement of the front walkway.

I entered my front door. Silence. No blasting stereo, no hair dryer humming, the washer and dryer were finally quiet, even the dishwasher was mute. I walked in a complete circle around my living room as if seeing it for the first time. The white cotton duck couch, scratched wooden floors, overflowing bookshelves. The TV's black eye stared me down. It didn't object to my tears.

Someone watching me that afternoon would have marveled at my energy—a whirling dervish of a woman alone in her living room busily mopping the floor, waxing the coffee table, rearranging her books. Making space for a self she did not even know existed.

Chapter 14

Maya turned and shouted impatiently over her shoulder. "Come on Mom, *hurry up*. I'm going to be late!" I took a few running steps to catch up and she grabbed my hand, lacing her fingers through mine. She tugged at me so that I would fall into step next to her.

Wasn't it only yesterday that I was a harried young mother rushing her into the daycare center? Late for work, running to reach the next appointment. *Hurry up, hurry up, hurry up!* Now she was a nineteen-year-old college student with more ambition and raw talent than I ever dreamed of having at her age. Since her first acting lessons when she was only nine, we had been moving toward this moment.

The cold January air outside the theater at Santa Barbara City College crackled with her pent-up energy. The Pacific Ocean pounded in the distance under a sparse sprinkling of stars. I squeezed her hand. We headed toward the theater for "Scene Night," the culmination of Maya's second-year acting class. She tightened her grip on my hand when we entered the building and pulled me backstage as if I were one of the crew.

"Mom, I want you to meet my drama professor." She grinned

at her teacher. "This is Rick Mokler." I extended my hand to a smiling, dark-haired man who acted as surrogate parent and mentor to the students swirling around him.

"Rick, this is my Mom." Maya's voice reflected her pride in me.

"Do you have any more at home like her? She's phenomenal!"

I thought of eleven-year-old Meghan, her deep placid eyes and calm, almost Zen-like serenity, and answered, "Yes, but I think she is destined for greatness in other areas."

I patted Maya's shoulder, overflowing with happiness and pride.

"I have to go, Mom." She turned on her heel and vanished. Professor Mokler pointed the way to a small auditorium with the chairs arranged in a horseshoe.

Maya and Melissa, a fellow drama major, had prepared a scene from *Top Girls* by the British playwright Caryl Churchill. I settled into my seat. Butterflies formed in my stomach as I read my daughter's name in the program. The audience of about one hundred people appeared to be a mixture of parents and students.

Maya would be playing the main character, Marlene, an ambitious thirty-something London entrepreneur who has just been named a managing director in a temporary agency, Top Girls. She decides to come home to visit her ill mother and confront her past. She had gotten pregnant at seventeen, given birth, and then left her baby to be raised by her older married sister, Joyce.

The curtain rose and lights framed the small stage. The two actresses faced each other, conflict visible in their tense bodies and frowning faces. Dressed in clinging black top and pants, Maya, as the driven, ambitious Marlene, crosses the stage to a table. She pours herself a drink. She and Joyce begin to argue about their mother who is in a nursing home. I am instantly alert, sitting tall in the darkened theater, hanging on every word. Marlene tells Joyce their mother recognized her when she visited that afternoon.

JOYCE: You were very lucky then.

MARLENE: Fucking awful life she's had.

JOYCE: Don't tell me.

MARLENE: Fucking waste.

JOYCE: Don't talk to me.

MARLENE: Why shouldn't I talk? Why shouldn't I talk to you? / Isn't she my mother too?

JOYCE: Look, you've left, you've gone away, / we can do without you.

Adrenaline seeped through my body and my heart began to race. This could be *me* fighting with Maya. She was always more like my sister than my daughter. We grew up together. I was only twenty-four when Maya was born, lost, afraid, far from home. But unlike Marlene, I kept my baby and married in a hurry so she could have a father, choosing what I thought would be the more predictable safety of family.

MARLENE: I left home, so what, I left home. People do leave home / it is normal.

The rapid-fire barrage of words hypnotizes me. Aside from the two voices you could hear a pin drop. Every time she says "fucking," and it is dozens of times in the scene, Maya spits it out crisp as a corn flake. I want to turn and tell everyone there. *You should have seen her as a high school hell child. I was there—I am her mother!*

MARLENE: Of course I couldn't get out of here fast enough. What was I going to do? Marry a dairyman who'd come home pissed? / Don't you fucking this/

JOYCE: Christ.

MARLENE: /fucking that fucking bitch fucking tell me what to fucking do fucking.

JOYCE: I don't know how you could leave your own child.

MARLENE: You were quick enough to take her.

The drama playing out on stage was way too much like real life.

With one vital difference—I took the opposite path from Marlene. Now, my daughter was acting out the underlying conflict and ambivalence that I could never acknowledge. When the pregnancy test came back positive in a Minneapolis doctor's office in the winter of 1972, I leaped to certainty. This was it, a keeper. I was not going to have a third abortion, and I knew that I would never part with my baby once she was born. Waiting on tables to put myself through journalism school, dating a jazz musician, this was not what I had planned. What about my dreams of becoming a writer? I decided to do an about face and become a mother.

Maya tossed her head defiantly. Her fury made her shine. She was living her life on stage, her emotions raw, pure, tidal in their flow. I believed her as Marlene, but I also *saw* her as Maya, the fierce fighter that she was.

My daughter portrayed the conflict between love and autonomy so realistically I wanted to weep and cheer at the same time. Maya knew the intricate movement of human relationships down to the muddy depths. I submerged her in water before she could walk, in order to teach her to swim. As an actress she dove on her own power into the human soul and brought the pieces back to the surface wet and glittering to lay them at my feet. *Here Mom. Look what I can do.*

I clutched a tissue so tightly that when I opened my fist I was

staring down at a knotted white ball. Tears ran down my cheeks.
I could not foresee that three months from that triumphant night
in January I would be leaning over a hospital bed, that the body
I so admired and identified with would be limp and flaccid, the
voice stilled forever. All I knew at that moment in a darkened
college theater was that my daughter was a bolt of quicksilver.
In my mind, and in the minds of her professor and her peers, she
was already a star.

When Marlene broke down sobbing over the daughter she
had left behind, my heart was wrenched. The determination I
had to keep my child, and all the sadness and anger over what
I had sacrificed in order to hang on, merged with the tears my
daughter cried onstage. I wept for Marlene—and for Maya and
me—for every mother who has ever raised a child alone. For
every mother who has let a child go.

Then the two sisters took a few tentative steps toward peace,
and the house lights dimmed.

When the lights came up again, waves of applause filled the
theater. I clapped until my palms tingled. Two grinning divas
stepped forward to take a bow.

Then the curtain dropped. I stared at a black velvet wall. But I
was still in a kitchen in England in the middle of a fight between
two sisters. The scene's echoes of my life with Maya hypnotized
me. *Top Girls*, and her part in it, became a memory that would
implode in my heart again and again, so that I am still held in the
grasp of Maya at her most pure.

I felt drained and incredibly high at the same time. Maya
changed into her street clothes. When we stepped out of the

theater into the parking lot arm in arm, I shivered from cold and happiness. Maya's achievement as an actress was the goal I had been tunneling toward; now I could see how very far we had come together. Mole-like, I had lived for years by instinct, burrowing toward the future. Blindly I pushed through day-to-day life as a single working mother. Without knowing the precise destination, I put my head down and dug in, and, miraculously, the tunnel I created led inescapably here, to this triumphant moment in Santa Barbara. For the first time, I was finally above ground. The second shift of housework, the stacks of bills, the fights, the worries, and the long silences between us suddenly seemed as insubstantial as the night air. I could *see* Maya's future unfolding. I wanted to dance a jig in the college parking lot.

Maya chattered happily all the way to a little downtown bar. We sat and drank beer with Professor Mokler and the other students, shouting to make ourselves heard above the din. In the midst of the hubbub of Friday night in a college town and raucous kudos for Maya's performance, I was filled with a calm sense of fulfillment—a conviction that the years of sacrifice had been worth it.

Then we drove back to her place. The four-bedroom house sat on a quiet residential street in the middle of the block. It was painted white, nicely furnished, with gleaming wooden floors— very upscale, considering its tenants were four college girls under the age of twenty. From my perch on a sectional sofa in the living room, I gazed around at plants and artwork, marveling at how adult and organized it all was.

"Mom," Maya called to me from her bedroom, "I have this scene I'm working on for my audition at UCLA. Can I read it to you?"

"Sure," I yelled back. Maya could have read me the Oxford English Dictionary that night and I would have thought it was the most brilliant, original thing I had ever heard. Her audition for the prestigious UCLA Theater Arts program was coming up in February. As a community college transfer student, her chances of being accepted at UCLA as a junior were about the same as getting accepted at the Yale School of Drama—slim to none. But Rick Mokler's assessment of her talent, what I had seen earlier that night, as well as Maya's burning ambition, made me believe it was going to happen.

She strode into the living room, boot heels clicking on the wooden floor, clutching a sheaf of pages. Maya had chosen a scene from a play called *Laughing Wild* by Christopher Durang as her audition piece. Durang had appeared on "Saturday Night Live" dressed as the Infant of Prague in elaborate robes and a standup lace collar and was known for wacky, irreverent humor. It was just my daughter's style. She turned her back to me for a moment, took a deep breath, and when she turned to face me again, there was a wild, agitated look on her face. She paced the floor, script in hand, nodding on certain words for emphasis as she read.

WOMAN: I want to talk to you about life. It's just too difficult to be alive, isn't it, and to try to function? There are all these people to deal with.

She looked up and rolled her eyes, gesturing wildly. Then she took a deep breath and rattled on. There was something in her manner that made me laugh, even before the words spilled out in a long breathless riff.

WOMAN: I tried to buy a can of tuna fish in the supermarket and there was this *person* standing right in front of where I wanted to reach out to get the tuna fish, and I waited a while to see if they'd move, and they didn't—they were looking at tuna fish too...

I was suffocating with laughter as she developed the utter madness of this woman through her gestures and facial expressions. There was humor in her elbows, in her thighs, in the odd way she cocked her head, in the slant of her eyebrows.

WOMAN: And so then I started to cry out of frustration, quietly, so as not to disturb anyone, and still, even though I was softly sobbing, this stupid person didn't *grasp* that I needed to get by them to reach the goddamn tuna fish, people are so *insensitive*, I just hate them, and so I reached over with my fist, and I brought it down real hard on his head and I screamed: "Would you kindly move, *asshole!!!*"

She spoke the long run-on sentence in one breath. When she reached the part about pounding the guy on the head, she leaned forward and shouted "asshole" with the demented force of Durang's paranoid woman. I was practically choking, leaning back into her roommate's cream-colored sofa to steady myself. Laughter spilled out along with renewed awe of the young woman standing before me. Maya never cracked a smile. She was *into* this character.

WOMAN: I ran out of the supermarket, and I thought, "I'll take a taxi to the Metropolitan Museum of Art, I need to be surrounded with culture right now, not tuna fish."

At this, Maya raised her left eyebrow into a twitchy arch, and looked around wildly as if the Gestapo were closing in on her.

I knew, then, without a doubt, that my daughter was going to be a successful actress. Whatever mysterious combination of intelligence, creativity, ambition, and pure abandon was called for, she had it.

"I guess you liked it, huh?" A grin spread over her face as she continued pacing in front of the sofa.

"It's great!" I said. "You were fantastic. Let me see that script." Pride filled me like helium.

She handed the pages to me. "You've got this madwoman down," I said. "Should I be worried?"

She threw back her head and laughed. "Well, hey, you taught me everything I know."

Yeah, I thought, *me and our crazy family of actors—my talented and wildly neurotic parents.*

I clasped her shoulders and held her close. I told her she was going to be great at her audition, and that I was so proud of her I could burst. She was quiet then, and a little pensive, and I could see that the adrenaline rush was wearing off. I was bone tired myself.

Maya insisted that I sleep in her bedroom that night. She took an armful of blankets and went to sleep on the sofa. As I lay in my daughter's single bed, still too keyed up to sleep, I thought of my father, the drama professor and actor. I mentally ticked off all the plays he had directed, stage-managed, or acted in. I remembered the time he directed my mother as Queen Gertrude in *Hamlet;* when she fell to the ground after drinking from the beaker of poisoned wine at the end of the play, my three-year-old brother screamed, "Mommy! Mommy!" I clapped my hand over his mouth so that he wouldn't ruin the moment for the audience.

Drama was woven into the daily fabric of our 1950s household. As part of his morning routine, my father would shave and belt out Broadway show tunes in our downstairs bathroom. "You Gotta Have Heart" from *Damn Yankees* filtered out into the kitchen as my mother scooped our Cream of Wheat into wooden bowls. "Miles and miles and miles of heart," in my Dad's baritone voice seeped out from under the crack in the bathroom door, and we kids would have to gesture and mouth at each other to pass the sugar, or pass the milk. Dad was performing.

I could see Mom in my mind's eye, hunched over an old wooden "baby tender" in the back yard, typing her own adaptations of well-known plays so that she could use them as community theater pieces. She cast and directed my sister, my brother, and me in *A Midsummer Night's Dream*. I remembered her feeding us lines when we hesitated in rehearsals, how she moved our bodies around the stage as if she were playing an elaborate game of chess.

I thought of all the Mike Nichols and Elaine May comedy routines I had heard as a child on our monaural record player, and the silly over-the-top Anna Russell monologues that my Dad and I would laugh over. Of course I rebelled against all that drama, and what I dismissively thought of as the narcissistic excesses of theater people. I was too introverted to go on stage, but even as a young child, Maya had no fear of being the center of attention. When she was only four years old she played a convincing Santa Claus in her daycare Christmas pageant. By the time she was in grade school, it was clear that she had the drive and the talent to act. Lying there in her bed in Santa Barbara, I mentally replayed her young life, and realized that my daughter was going to be famous. The acting gene had simply skipped a generation.

I even thought of Maya's lost father—how he growled every time he played a drum solo in the days before pot and booze destroyed his brain and derailed his ambitions. He played like a man in a frenzy, and the jazz fans crowded into the St. Paul club "Take Five" would roar for an encore. Between sets they would buy him drink after drink because he was the young Buddy Rich of the Twin Cities. And here I was spending the weekend with our gorgeous daughter, the daughter with drama talent bigger than my parents', with gifts and heart and mind more solid than her father's, with ambition beyond even my biggest dreams for her. She was *my* child in some primal, fundamental way because I had claimed her before she was even born. I said "Yes" to her birth even though it seemed to contradict my own ambitions. And just three years later, I took her away from her father for both her sake and my own. He was too unreliable, too much like the self-centered actors I had run away from to start a new life in Minnesota. Jeff hadn't set eyes on Maya since she was a skinny nine-year-old girl. She was blossoming for me like a rare orchid I had tended for years. We were a team, and more than most teammates, conspirators in our own survival and success.

On Saturday morning we drove downtown to window shop. In a French boutique where I could not afford so much as a handkerchief, I fingered hand-sewn silk lingerie, letting camisoles slip through my hands like water. We left the store and wandered down the main street to an outdoor café where we ordered café lattes. Maya licked a ridge of foam from her upper lip. As we rose from the table, she grabbed my hand.

"Mom, I just want to tell you what a great mother you are," she said out of the blue. She rushed on, words tumbling out. Traffic noise and people passing on the sidewalk faded into a blurry hum.

"So many girls I know have such messed up relationships with their mothers," she said. "But we can talk, *really* talk. You never gave up on me even when it got so hard." I stood facing her next to the table like a freeze-frame in a movie.

"Maya, that is the sweetest thing you could tell me," I said. We squeezed hands.

"Now, don't let it go to your head," she teased.

Happy and invincible, we strolled arm in arm up the side-walk. Sun poured over us like a blessing. It was one of the hap-piest moments of my life.

Chapter 15

I think I aced my audition, Mom!" Maya was practically shouting into the phone. I held the receiver away from my ear. A Cheshire cat grin broke out on my face. She rushed on. "When I screamed 'asshole' during the monologue, one of the professors cracked up."

"Honey, that's fabulous," I said. It was mid-February of 1992, and Maya had just returned to Santa Barbara from Los Angeles after her audition of the tuna scene at UCLA. She was bubbling over with excitement. Her chances of being accepted as a transfer student at one of the top drama programs in the country looked bright.

Early in March I flew to Los Angeles for the weekend to visit the UCLA campus with her. It was late on a Friday night and the plane hit a violent thunderstorm. Head winds were so strong that we almost turned back. By the time I arrived, I was exhausted.

When I emerged from the jetway into the airport, I spotted my daughter immediately. She was wearing a blue and white crop top and skin-tight jeans. As she walked toward me, her trademark brown suede boots scraped the carpet. She jangled her keys in her hand, casually impatient. She'd been waiting at LAX for almost two hours.

"Mom, what happened? I was so worried."

"I thought we were never going to make it," I said into her mane of blond hair as I wrapped my arms around her back. I ran my hands along the little knobs of her spine, relief flooding my body. "There was a really bad storm."

Businessmen in rumpled suits pulled carry-on luggage around us, staring at my beautiful daughter. I held her at arm's length and took a good look. I hadn't seen her since her performance in *Top Girls* in January. In between, she'd done two auditions, one at UCLA and one at USC. She'd filled out application forms in triplicate. I had wrestled with financial aid forms and hunted down old tax returns. We had both labored over scholarship applications.

Her drama professor wrote a glowing letter of recommendation. "Maya is one of the freshest and most responsive actors we currently have... She is disciplined yet free, confident yet vulnerable in her work... She has all the trappings of a fine young actress."

"You look fabulous," I said.

"You look beat to hell," she shot back.

"Remember that time we were driving around the McDonald's parking lot in Walnut Creek and I almost hit a guy in a Mercedes Benz and I said, 'Mercy upon us,' and you said, 'Don't you mean Mercedes upon us?' We all laughed so hard that Meghan peed her pants!"

"Yeah," she laughed, "what made you think of that?"

"The way you said I look beat to hell..."

"How is the Meggers?"

"She's fine. She sends her love."

She took my arm and grabbed my carry-on bag.

"Come on. I'm parked illegally. Let's get the hell out of here!"

We each had our own queen-sized bed at the Chesterfield Hotel in downtown Westwood. Later, when we were snuggled under matching flowered counterpanes, Maya whispered across the space between us, "Mom, I'm so excited. I really want to get into UCLA. Do you think I will?"

"Honey, yes, I think you will. You wowed them with the tuna scene, didn't you?" I whispered back, as if this achievement required a reticent hush.

She laughed. "Oh right, when I brought my fist down and shouted 'asshole' with that wild look in my eyes, that one professor broke up. But what if I don't make it, Mom?"

"If you don't make it, come back to San Francisco and apply at the American Conservatory Theater. Don't worry. You'll get in."

"Is the alarm set?"

"Yes, and I asked the front desk for a wake-up call. We'll be there on time. Now relax, and get some sleep."

She sighed and turned over. I lay awake imagining the first time I would see her face on a movie screen. What would *that* be like?

At UCLA the next morning we attended a reception and campus tour for "High Achieving Community College Students." There were sweet rolls and orange juice, slices of cantaloupe and honeydew melon, six different varieties of muffins, and a flock of alumni to field questions. Panels of professors and students talked about the university and its programs. We both took notes.

They taught us the UCLA fight song and all the gestures to
go with it as if we were Freemasons. Later, after we toured the
library with its leaded glass windows and checked out the theater and the science lab, we went to the bookstore. Maya wanted
to buy a pair of plaid UCLA boxer shorts and a backpack. She
picked out a mug for me that said, "UCLA Mom."

"Don't you think we ought to wait and be sure you get in?"
I asked.

"What?" she snorted. "You told me I'd get in for sure."

"All the same," I said, "let's wait on the mug. It makes me feel
kind of old."

"Oh, Mom, don't be silly," she said.

The next morning was Sunday, March 8. Her boyfriend Dale,
who had grown up in Los Angeles, arrived from Santa Barbara
to go to brunch with us. Dale drove us out to Manhattan Beach
to a little café he knew of where the food was terrific. There
was a line out the door, but they served coffee on the sidewalk
and everybody was very relaxed, sipping coffee, reading the
Los Angeles Times. Finally, we were seated in a red Naugahyde
booth. Immediately, Maya and I began the ritual of breakfast
negotiations, promising to trade half of a waffle for half a Spanish omelet. Maya and Dale got into a mock fight because she
took sips of his orange juice without asking.

"Didn't your Mom ever teach you any manners?" he challenged.

"Yes," she glanced at me. "Didn't yours teach you to share?"
Her eyes flashed.

Dale's earnest, slightly worried look contrasted with Maya's
mocking, I-know-more-than-all-of-you-combined sass. Her fair
hair next to his dark hair and tanned face looked spectacular.
People turned to stare.

After breakfast, we strolled through town to the beach. I

knew I'd be getting on a plane in an hour, but I didn't want this happiness to end. The future seemed expansive and unlimited. And the present was a kick! Maya was wearing cut-off jeans and her legs flashed as she bounded up the beach ahead of me. We approached some swings near a redwood bench. Dale sat on the bench, and Maya and I began to swing side by side like two hyperactive kids.

"When I'm rich and famous, Mom, I want to buy you a house," she said, pushing her feet deep into the sand for more lift.

"Okay," I said, "but can it be a ranch with some horses?"

"Sure," she said, "whatever you want."

Later, on the plane ride home, I daydreamed about a ranch in Oregon, with a sorrel mare and her colt, and a pasture where the grass danced in the wind and I could take long walks. I imagined going to Los Angeles every few months to visit Maya and, of course, being there for all her opening nights. Life was grand!

And then came Maya's fall. "My life is shit," I told one concerned friend that first summer. We were walking. She stopped and turned to look at me.

"You don't mean that," she said. I just looked straight ahead and kept walking, fighting back the ever-present tears. No one but John and my psychiatrist knew how close to the edge I really was.

Maya's life was *my* life. When her life ended, mine came crashing down too. Suddenly there was no more future. The past was totally transformed by that one stunning moment when she slid from the back of a horse. That past was the only place I could find her now, and for months I ransacked it for clues. Every memory seemed prescient. I wanted to record them all, mining the words for a moment of relived time with my daughter.

When my eye caught a blond head moving through a crowd of people, I would track it, watching obsessively, hoping somehow a miracle had happened and she had come back. It would be many more years before I gave up my search and accepted the truth. Maya was gone.

PART III

Resurfacing

Chapter 16

Several weeks have passed since we buried Maya. My primary occupation, other than grieving, is writing acknowledgments for donations to a scholarship fund for young actors that I set up in her memory. Sitting at the dining room table bent over my task, I hear the mail truck pull up in the lane. When the mail carrier's key scrapes in the lock and the metal boxes clank open, I hurry out to pick up my mail.

Among the stack of bills and magazines I pull from the mailbox is a business envelope from the California Transplant Donor Network. The official return address sends a surge of adrenaline through my body. I walk briskly up to my patio and enter the apartment, tearing open the flap in one motion. I am holding a letter from the young nurse who was our transplant coordinator.

I had treated Shelley badly during the request process, yet she accepted the brunt of my shock and anger with professionalism. Now in spare prose she sets forth the miracles that resulted from donating Maya's organs. I sit down at the dining room table, holding the letter in my hand.

For some reason, I had assumed that the recipients would be on the West Coast, but that turns out not to be true. Scarce organs are allocated according to the severity of the recipient's condition—those who are the sickest get highest priority. Each of Maya's kidneys was an exact tissue match with recipients outside California. One kidney, triple bagged in a special solution and placed in an organ preservation box, was flown to a forty-seven-year-old New England man who had been waiting for several years. The second kidney was given to a young woman from Boston who is only two years older than Maya. The letter says she is twenty-one years old and has chronic kidney disease. Reading the words, I suddenly understand that the recipients could be *anyone*, of any age, anywhere.

"John, come look at this letter. I can't believe this." My voice rises with hopeful energy, something that feels very foreign after weeks of grieving. John joins me at the table, and stands behind me, reading over my shoulder.

A team from the California Pacific Medical Center in San Francisco transplanted Maya's liver. The recipient is the mother of a seven-year-old daughter, and just five years younger than I am. She has a very rare form of liver failure known as Wilson's disease. A new liver is the only cure for this thirty-eight-year-old woman from Arizona. Of course I had realized that some of the recipients might be parents of young children, but I had not thought it through fully until now.

I burst into tears when I reach the paragraph about Maya's heart. I heard it beating when I laid my head on her chest in the hospital to say good-bye; its steady drumming was the last sound of her I would ever hear, the last trace. Shelley's words tell me that this vital part of my daughter is still alive.

"Her heart was recovered by a team from the University of California San Francisco. The recipient is a fifty-four-year-old man originally from Chile." The square black letters on the page blur. I reach up and grasp John's hand and continue reading.

The letter says the heart recipient lives in Burlingame, California. "He is married and has two children and works as an import-export specialist."

When I read about the children, I set the letter down on the dining room table with trembling fingers. My mind travels to Meghan's tear-stained face and the groans of family members in the hospital conference room on the afternoon of Maya's death. How still I had been, frozen in disbelief. I vividly remember the moment when the surgeon told us Maya was brain dead, and immediately said, "Would you consider organ donation?" My first thought, even before he finished his question, was that if it would prevent some other family from feeling the annihilation that we all felt in that moment, then *do it!* Somehow, I had hoped that the other family would have children. My primitive mother self rose up in that moment. *Keep them together.* That is what I meant when I said yes to him.

John squeezes my shoulder. "It's a miracle," he says. Wordless, I pick up the letter again to read more about the man who holds Maya's heart in his chest.

"He had been waiting for some time for this lifesaving gift. He is recovering very well after the surgery. Without this transplant he could not have survived."

But that is not all. Maya's tissue and bone is being processed and placed for transplant and will potentially help dozens of people through bone grafts, middle ear grafts to help restore hearing, tendons and ligaments to restore mobility, and cartilage that can be used for reconstruction following disfiguring injuries. Both of her corneas were placed for transplant locally; one has gone to a thirty-nine-year-old woman from San Francisco, the other to a sixty-six-year-old man from Alameda, restoring their sight.

Suddenly, the entire story seems surreal. I stare at the blocky paragraphs on the page, then gaze out the window. My daughter's body was a cornucopia. Six transplant operations have resulted from her death. Three children still have their parents. A young woman will be able to finish college. Wives and husbands continue to wake up side by side each morning. People can see. They can go on with life.

When I said yes to transplantation, deep in my cocoon of shock and denial, it seemed that giving Maya away in pieces was the only way not to lose her entirely. It was the one act extreme enough to equal my grief. Now I am holding the evidence that supports my spontaneous decision in my hands.

The letter closes with these words, "On behalf of the California Transplant Donor Network and all those whose lives have been changed by your compassionate and heroic decision, thank you. May thoughts of how you have helped so many others comfort you and may you find peace in the days ahead."

John reaches his arms around my chest. I grasp his wrists and sob. For the first time since Maya died, the tears contain joy. Like little joy seeds they rain onto my dining room table, pooling on the surface of the wood.

Because it is the heroic and happy side of our tragedy, I become fixated on organ donation. I spend hours in the graduate writing and literature courses I am taking at Mills College researching transplantation. But my grief does not go away; if anything, it intensifies. Keeping Maya's organs alive comes at a price. Yes, the thought of her recipients and their new lives provides great comfort, but the peace that Shelley wishes for me in her letter is beyond my reach. The mother is at odds with the altruist in me. I feel fulfilled, proud, and even happy that others were saved or helped. At the same time, chilling images of what I allowed high-tech surgeons to do to my child's body torment me in the night. I can find no safe pigeonhole to contain these conflicting feelings.

Compounding my confusion and guilt is an administrative error that should never have happened. Within days of my daughter's death, I received a bill from the local blood bank that provided donated blood for Maya. It shows that she was given several units of blood *after* she was declared brain dead. She was transfused after the death certificate was signed; this took place some hours before the transplant operation (to keep the organs viable, I am told when I inquire). My mind immediately seizes on this as possible evidence that my daughter was not really dead before the organ recovery surgery began and that my decision to donate her organs may have effectively killed her. They said her coma was irreversible, but how did they really *know*? I remember the cerebral blood flow study and Dr. Carr telling us that no blood was flowing to her brain. I call Shelley and ask her to explain brain death to me again. She apologizes in advance for what she is about to say and tells me a terrible thing—Maya's brain was actually riddled with gangrene before she was declared dead that April afternoon.

Still, I can't fully accept the gray status of an organ donor. Further stoking my fears, I also receive a hospital billing summary showing that she had received anesthesia and muscle relaxants during the operation to remove her organs. This ensured that no involuntary movement of her body could spook the operating room staff as they assisted the various organ recovery teams. The dividing line between life and death seems razor thin. "Brain death" means that the person is *virtually* dead—that the brain is unable to orchestrate or sustain life—but that the other organs are still functioning. Absent life support, Maya would certainly have died. But when? That is the question that haunts me. When the transplant recovery teams began their work, she was dead, but not quite. This is a key point that medical ethicists debate unendingly, but as I research organ donation, I am learning about it for the first time. In medical jargon she was a "biomort," and it was this indeterminate state that allowed the miracle of transplantation to unfold.

John tells me that he saw Maya hovering above her comatose body taking in our good-byes as we gathered around her bed on the afternoon of April 6. This gives me some comfort because I think it is entirely possible that her soul witnessed the death of her body. Many people who have had near death experiences describe this phenomenon. I cling to John's account, wanting to believe that she was out of her body by the time the surgeons began their work.

Ultimately, Shelley meets with me to review the sequence of events that took place after we said good-bye to Maya and left the hospital. Once Maya was declared brain dead, Shelley's role became "organ support," as she puts it. Life support was now over, and the machines were unhooked. The focus shifted to doing whatever it took to make sure the organs would be usable. CTDN paid for everything following the declaration of death, including the blood transfusion and surgical fees. Organ donors are never charged (or compensated) for their gifts.

The heart recipient was at the top of the Status One list of the most critically ill patients; he was hospitalized at UCSF Medical Center and near death. When consulted, his transplant coordinator eagerly said yes to Maya's heart. In the early morning hours of April 7, several surgical teams were dispatched to the John Muir Medical Center.

UCSF arrived first. They recovered Maya's heart. Interesting to me is the new knowledge that removing a heart is actually fairly straightforward—it can be done in about an hour. The liver recovery is far more difficult because it involves many more blood vessels that must be meticulously clamped and severed. So after UCSF removed Maya's heart, packed it in ice, and transported it across the Bay Bridge in a plastic picnic cooler, a second team from California Pacific Medical Center removed her liver and her kidneys. The liver, also packed in ice, had to be taken immediately to the waiting recipient; kidneys remain viable for up to seventy-two hours, so they were processed and shipped to the East Coast. Surgeons from Stanford evaluated her lungs, but decided against them because they were filled with fluid and unidentified bacteria—she had been on the venti-lator too long.

The organ recovery surgery began at 3:05 in the morning. An anesthesiologist stood by Maya's draped head monitoring the flow of oxygen, fluids, and muscle relaxant. Using a tool akin to a hacksaw, surgeons opened her chest. They harvested her heart, put it on ice in a picnic cooler, and then removed her liver and kidneys. She had been cut from sternum to pubis. By five o'clock in the morning they were closing the massive incision and leav-ing the hospital with their treasures. Maya's body was then sent to the morgue where a technician performed a "sterile tissue recovery" to remove her corneas, long bone from her thighs, skin tissue, and inner ear bone.

After the organ recovery operation was completed at John Muir Medical Center, Shelley debriefed the operating room nurses, telling them about the successful status of the organs. She then returned to the Intensive Care Unit. There, she told the critical care staff who had labored for four days to save Maya's life that the organs had been successfully recovered and were on their way to the waiting recipients. She had done her job of obtaining consent, safeguarding the organs, facilitating their placement, and helping to orchestrate the complexity of the operation. She went home to bed at 6:30 on the morning of Tuesday, April 7.

Anguish over what I had set in motion for Maya, as well as joy at its outcome, well up in me. I had denied my daughter the repose she so richly deserved after the trauma of her fall, the brain surgery, the long hours on life support, and her declaration of brain death. I did it knowing that it would be violent, and yet, I wanted to keep the many parts of her alive. Yes, to help others, but also to serve my own need for her physical preservation. The image of Maya's radically aged face in the coffin continues to tug at my heart. The letter says my decision is heroic. I am not sure I can agree. Or at least this act of heroism has a shadow side. As the survivor of my daughter's sudden death, and the one who made an impulsive decision about how to dispose of her body, I have become a hero at her expense.

Still, I cry tears of joy for the first time since Maya died. My wild gamble has paid off and now she lives on in the bodies of others. I make copies of the letter and send them to our grieving relatives. John is also immensely buoyed by Shelley's news.

Enclosed with the letter is a note from the wife of the heart recipient. She doesn't sign her name, but that doesn't matter because I can literally hear her voice through her words. Her gratitude lifts my thoughts from what has been sacrificed to what has been saved.

"My two children and I want to express how thankful we are to you for the gift of life you as a family have given us as a family. My husband is getting better every day and the children, eight and twelve years old, have another chance to grow up with a father. This was only possible thanks to the decision you made to become part of the donor program. From our hearts—thank you—we will pray for you and for your daughter every day." She signs it, "The Receiving Family."

Eighty-six words. During the months to come, I will often pull out this ivory card with its neat, spiky letters and reread it, as if I can balance my loss against another family's joy, as if it is ballast enough.

Chapter 17

The painful places in my relationship with Maya draw me like tourist attractions I know I won't have a good time visiting but feel compelled to see anyway. Real and imagined mistakes loom in my memory, tormenting me.

Two months after Maya's death, I find myself doubled over on my bed, clutching the photograph album Meghan made for the memorial service. Pictures encased in plastic are tantalizing reminders of her, but they are flat and silent, and more than anything I want to touch her and talk to her. I long for Maya deep in the pit of my gut.

In desperation, I dial her father's number in Minneapolis. He takes my call without surprise. I tell him over and over how wonderful she was, how proud he would have been of her, about her last months at college, and the incredible triumph of her acceptance at UCLA. It is a rambling monologue broken only by my sobs and his exclamations of "Aye, carumba," at especially poignant moments.

After twenty minutes of this he says, "Well, maybe we should get back together again and have another baby." He is completely serious.

There's a moment of silence. "Wow, Jeff," I stammer, "I don't think so." I set the phone back in its cradle overwhelmed by the turns my life has taken. How could this man, so creative and full of energy when we met twenty years ago, have become someone with such a tenuous grip on reality? More importantly, why had I fallen in love with him?

The night I met Jeff I had worked a full shift as a cocktail waitress in a Minneapolis cabaret theater. The cabaret featured an adaptation of "Jesus Christ Superstar" and the show was packed with out-of-town businessmen. When Jeff played his drum solo that night he bounced up off his stool, dropped his drumsticks, and played with his hands. The crowd cheered. I stood in the back of the room watching as the intense man in the spotlight pounded a snare drum as if it were a Conga.

I was twenty-three years old, affecting a tough persona to disguise how lost and vulnerable I felt. After my shift ended, I sat at the polished wooden bar counting my tips, drinking a scotch and soda, which I ordered only because it sounded hip.

"Want to buy me a drink?" The tall blond drummer slid onto the barstool next to mine. Jeff's eyes were blue and his smile easy. He pointed at the wad of bills I had arranged in neat order with all of the Presidents' faces turned to the ceiling.

"Okay," I said. "I like your playing." This was true. I had watched him and the back-up band for the last three weeks, and his drum solos really ignited the audience.

"I'll take a bourbon and a water back," Jeff said. I slid the money across the bar, but the bartender waved it away. "Jesus Christ Superstar" was a big hit. People kept stopping by the bar to tell Jeff how much they had enjoyed the show.

"Would you like to take a drive with me sometime?" Jeff

asked, taking a long pull on his drink. "Sure," I said, lighting a menthol cigarette, another prop in my tough act. I slipped the wad of bills into my purse.

Early in January, after a punishing snowstorm, the drummer and I cruised down Hennepin Avenue in his olive green Corvette. Bundled in goose down jackets with scarves wrapped under our chins, we walked around Lake of the Isles. The frozen lake gleamed, its islands studded with evergreens whipped sideways by the wind. Our breath escaped in white puffs.

An hour later Jeff helped me jam open the door to my apartment because it was warped from the steam heat that clanked on and off all night long. We fell into my tiny furnished studio and hung our wet jackets over the radiator. A harvest gold foldout couch with a lumpy mattress and a metal bar that cut into my hipbones, a pressboard coffee table, and a matching end table with a lamp stood against the beige walls. When I first moved in I had to use a butter knife to pry open my newly painted kitchen cabinets so that I could stack cans of Campbell's soup and boxes of Hamburger Helper in them. I didn't know one person in my three-story building. I had fled from an abusive boyfriend in Ohio, and the anonymity suited me. I had begun to meet people at the University of Minnesota where I was studying journalism, but I was desperately lonely.

Jeff leaned against the kitchen doorframe while I put on hot water for instant coffee. He asked me what sorts of things I was currently writing.

"Articles for the campus newspaper, book reviews and stuff," I said vaguely, trying to hide how awkward I felt.

"Yeah, that's cool," he said. "So, you like music."

"Yes," I nodded, warming to this topic. "I love it! I love to dance."

"Really... what kind of dancing?"

"Oh, you know, free form, kind of funky. In Cleveland there's a lot of rhythm and blues, rock and roll, that kind of thing."

He followed me around the kitchen with his eyes. He stood back from the doorframe and did a little drum riff on it with his open palms.

When he kissed me, he had to stoop down because of the difference in our heights, and our teeth bumped. I shivered and kissed back. The beige radiator hissed on. We drank our coffee sitting on the sofa, kissing in between sips.

"So, are you seeing anyone?"

"Well, not exactly," I lied. I had been dating one of the relief bartenders because I was wild with loneliness and didn't know anyone else.

Jeff maneuvered his hand under my sweater, and I realized I needed to decide what direction I was going here, but his hand was warm and smooth against my skin. I drifted along. When we pulled open the gold couch, he snapped on the radio and dialed in a jazz station. I lit a candle.

Later, I stumbled up from the fold-out bed to find the contraceptive foam in a built-in dresser outside the bathroom. The black and white diamond tiles of the bathroom floor were icy under my bare feet. I hopped from foot to foot, filling the plunger and then propping my leg on the side of the tub to insert it. The man I barely knew called me back to bed, lifted the covers, and pulled me over to him in breathless haste. The next morning my lips were swollen in the aftermath of his kisses.

By the end of January, I was pregnant. Without much discussion we decided to get married. The night we set a date for our hasty wedding, I stared at the studio's flecked gray carpet with wavy red and turquoise lines and figured it had to turn out okay. At least I was getting out of the barren studio apartment. I would have my own family now.

After Maya was born in October of 1972, I worked part-time as a reporter for *The Minnesota Daily*, the student newspaper at the University of Minnesota, while a woman who operated a small daycare center in her home watched my six-week-old daughter. My tiny income was essential. Jeff's gigs were erratic and we began having money problems and high volume arguments.

By the time we celebrated Maya's first birthday, I was the assistant managing editor at *The Minnesota Daily*, a modestly paid position, and I was writing freelance articles for local magazines to make extra money. Whenever I raised any issue, from why our checking account was overdrawn, to why my husband had not come home until four in the morning when his gig had ended three hours before, Jeff's response was that I was exaggerating the problem.

One of my jobs was to balance our checkbook. During the second year of our marriage, I discovered Jeff hadn't made a mortgage payment on our house in three months. When I questioned him, he admitted that he had transferred money from our personal account to cover bad checks he had written against his jazz band's account. He was too broke to pay our bills. I was so angry that I pounded the cheap wood paneling on our basement walls with my fists until it cracked.

We fumbled through our days in a wary standoff. Sex became a cautious negotiation on the rare occasions we were at home together. I pinned a clipping from *Ms. Magazine* above my desk: "I've been married to a fascist. I've been married to a

Communist. Neither one of them took out the garbage." I was miserable.

One blisteringly hot day in mid-July, the *Minneapolis Tribune* real estate ads tucked under my arm, I walked from building to building in a district near Lake Calhoun. Maya was at daycare. I wore a seersucker suit and high heels on the theory that if I looked professional it would be easier to rent an apartment. All the apartment managers whose doorbells I rang were dressed in shorts and T-shirts with window air conditioners humming in the background. At noon, I crumpled down onto the curb exhausted, but I had filled out a dozen applications. One of them was accepted two days later.

In August of 1975 I left my husband, taking our almost three-year-old daughter with me. A few weeks later, Jeff and his band drove to Huron, South Dakota, for a month-long gig. I was happy not to hear from him.

In the months after we separated, I worked two jobs, but it was not enough to make ends meet. When I went grocery shopping Maya would beg for Cheerios and Oreo cookies, but I barely had enough to cover staples. I heaped the things she wanted in the cart, knowing the check I was about to write would not be good for another two days. Our food stamps had run out a week ago. Even when Jeff was in town, he rarely paid child support. When he was scheduled to visit our daughter, he was always late. Maya would watch for him, clinging to the windowsill for hours. "When is Daddy coming?" she would ask me again and again.

When I review these scenes, I am wracked with guilt. I was such a young, inexperienced mother that I did not know how to create stability for her or for myself. Maya and I had been entirely alone.

The mantra that opens and closes each day is my obsessive, unanswerable question *why?* Why did Maya die? What is the meaning of this chaos and pain? *Why live?* I am forty-four years old, but I feel like a fake. Being a mother is something I taught myself the same way I learned how to swim as a child—I made it up by crawling along the shore of Lake Erie, lifting my hands in a scooping motion to copy the others. I have pieced together a pattern handed down from my grandmother and my mother, but the pattern is tattered and murky. Maya's death rips what I have constructed into shreds.

The routine of work provides some respite. After Maya's funeral, my boss encouraged me to take as much time as I needed away from the office. By mid-May, six weeks after her death, I am ready for a predictable schedule to distract me from the grief.

I leave my apartment at seven o'clock each morning and walk briskly to the commuter train. But by the time I reach San Francisco forty-five minutes later I feel lost. I climb the stairs from the dark tunnel of the New Montgomery BART station up into the light, emerging startled as a mole on the crowded street. Among the busy that summer, I bob aimlessly.

I soon find an anchor. His name is Michael, and he stands on the corner of Market Street and New Montgomery hawking "Street Sheets" to raise money for the homeless, taking a cut for himself. "How are you this morning?" he inquires, shivering in his denim jacket in the shadow of the Palace Hotel.

"Hanging in there," I say, handing him a dollar.

We talk in bursts, gesturing at each other. He tells me about his fight to regain custody of his four-year-old daughter, his one-year anniversary of sobriety, how he might be able to get a job in a local print shop if they'd just give him a chance. A job would mean he could find an apartment and a place where his daughter could stay with him. When he asks if I have any kids, I tell him about Maya and Meghan. Each morning I reveal a little more of the story, so he knows the essential facts of Maya's death, and that Meghan is away for the summer. I share the triumphs of the last two years of Maya's life, as if her accomplishments somehow vindicate my failings as a mother.

With nothing to lose, Michael is completely unthreatened by the story I pour out to him. His dark eyes register genuine sorrow for my loss.

I walk on to my office looking straight through the bodies of approaching people as if I have laser vision and they are transparent ghosts. Bodies have become superfluous to me. If Maya could drop hers so suddenly, couldn't any one of us? Life seems flimsy and tenuous.

When I arrive at my desk on the sixth floor of the Pacific Bell building, and settle myself by my phone and computer, I slip into an identity beyond loss. I know what is expected and how to behave—although I am often not capable of measuring up to my own standards that summer. But my colleague Rosalyn steps in and takes up the slack.

As the associate editor of *Business Digest,* the magazine we publish each month for Pacific Bell managers, Roz has always been a steadying force. In the months after Maya's death, when the grief is most insupportable, she offers me a refuge of reliable sympathy and seemingly unlimited patience.

One afternoon, following a meeting where some colleagues were innocently discussing the deaths of their dogs and how emotionally difficult it is to replace them, I burst into our shared office. Roz studies my face, rises immediately from her desk, and, without asking any questions, closes the door. I am sobbing. She returns to her work area and lifts a box of tissues from the top drawer of her desk and then crosses the room and sets it down gently in front of me.

"Jesus," I sputter, "how can people talk about getting another *dog*? Don't they know I can never replace Maya?"

I drop my head to the desk, hiding my face in my arms.

Roz pulls up a chair next to me and sits down. "I am so sorry," she says, patting my back. "I know how much you miss Maya. She was everything to you. You worked so hard to raise her. This is just so unfair."

"Why? *Why* did this have to happen?" I ask between gusts of weeping.

"I don't know," Roz replies. Her gentle honesty is immensely comforting.

When I look up at my friend, tears are running down her cheeks. She passes me a tissue. We sit at my desk and cry together. Wadded up tissues grow into a pile on my desk blotter. At last I feel empty and peaceful after the storm of tears. Roz's compassion has allowed me to touch bottom.

We go to the restroom to pat our faces with moist paper towels and reapply our makeup. Roz is always impeccable in her clothes and her grooming. She taught me the importance of finding the perfect pair of shoes to set off an outfit and we often joke about asking our boss for a shoe budget for *Business Digest*. That afternoon, the two of us pass from intense grief, to gentle humor, and back to focused work through the filter of Roz's kindness.

When I arrive at the office the next morning I find a greeting card with my name written on a square white envelope. It is Roz's angular handwriting. Sitting next to the card on my desk blotter is a bright blue lapel button. The shiny metal button greets me with this message: "Clinical studies show there are no answers."

I laugh and wince at the same time, because I know it is true. Then I pick up the button and turn it over and over, warming the cold metal in my palm.

Chapter 18

When she returns from her summer in Garberville, Meghan lights up our household with her smile. Eager to restore some sense of normalcy, I host a swim party for her twelfth birthday at our apartment pool. Meghan and her girlfriends bob in the water playing Marco Polo, trying to locate and tag the one who is "it" while keeping their eyes closed.

"Marco," a voice calls.

"Polo," another echoes.

I am sitting by the side of the pool reading *The Courage to Grieve*, closing the book after a few paragraphs because that's all I can absorb. I stare off into space, blindly aware of the children's bodies plunging, surfacing, and stroking across the pool. My entire body feels bruised and there is a suffocating heaviness over my heart. Later, as I light the candles on a three-layer chocolate cake, I bite my lip to hold back tears. A few days later, I host a second gathering for family members.

Meghan's presence buoys the atmosphere at home, and my strategy works—life feels more normal with children's laughter filling our small apartment.

My younger daughter has always been more physically solid

than her sister was. Where Maya was wispy and insubstantial, Meghan's body is ample. She is acutely sensitive about the difference, and although her deep clear eyes and generous grin make her beautiful even as an awkward pre-teen, Meghan believes her sister to be prettier. Their personalities mimic their physical differences. Maya's dramatic flair and fluctuating moods were always tempered by Meghan's phlegmatic, down to earth approach.

Meghan's style of grieving is calmer than mine, more private, and more pragmatic. When she settles back into the routine of school, she quickly picks up where she left off with her friends. Kids are in and out of our apartment every weekend and sometimes on school nights too. Of the many lessons learned while raising Maya, the importance of getting to know my daughters' friends and their parents tops my list. I had been way too naive and ill-informed on that score and it's a mistake I don't plan to repeat.

Now that she's entering junior high school, I am extra watchful of Meghan. Seventh grade with its selection of classes and an increased load of homework provide plenty of structure—and distraction from her grief.

Part of my "new normalcy" campaign involves holidays. Halloween has always been special for my daughters and I am determined to keep the tradition alive. Meghan and I agree to meet at the supermarket to do our Halloween shopping one night after work. A last-minute meeting delays my departure, and I scramble into my coat and run from my office to the BART station. Checking my watch, I see that I am already more than half an hour late to meet her. In the BART train I read to distract myself from my rising panic, but the story only makes me fidget and want to cry.

"A Small, Good Thing" by Raymond Carver is about

bereaved parents—a mom and a dad—whose young son Scotty gets run over by a car on his birthday. In the ensuing turmoil the parents forget to pick up the child's birthday cake. The baker calls repeatedly and the distraught parents think someone is purposely torturing them by continually asking if they have "forgotten about Scotty."

I stare at the blurring paragraphs, knowing so much more than I want to about these fictional parents, their little son, and the sheet cake with the rocket ship and the green lettering that no one will ever eat. I want to jump out of my skin and be next to Meghan that moment.

The train crawls into the station. The train operator's voice booms over the intercom. "Please stand back from the doors while I reposition the train." My held breath is bursting my lungs. *Just get me there!*

At last the train jerks forward. I am first in line as the doors slip open and I dash through them, run across the platform, down the steps of the escalator, slam my ticket into the slot in the machine, race to my parking space, and drive like a maniac to the supermarket.

I am at the entrance by the ice machines when I spot her. Meghan is also at the front of the store but at the opposite end, where I see her bent head rise and scan for me. Even before I call her name, she looks at me.

I raise my arm and wave, calling, "Meghan, Meghan!" I run across the store so focused on reaching my daughter that I can't feel the purse banging against my hip, or hear how the fear in my voice scrapes the air. She just watches me, not moving from her place near the checkout stand. I throw my arms around her neck, crying now, and the story of the little boy and my fear and my *I'm sorries* spill out.

"Mom, don't worry," she says, her voice low and calm. "I promise I won't die before you do."

I stare at her, dumbfounded. Only six months have passed since Maya died, barely time enough for the anesthetic of shock to wear off, but Meghan gets it. My biggest, scariest fear is that I might lose her too.

She doesn't have the power to keep her promise, but it doesn't matter. Our small good thing is the intention behind it. Later, I will see that there are more sides to this—that the promise is also a plea for freedom. Meghan is also saying, *Let me go, don't hover. I promise to be more careful than my sister was. Let me have my life!*

But standing next to the *National Enquirers* and the Snickers bars holding my daughter close, what I hear is bravery and compassion.

Side by side we complete our shopping. We leave Safeway with a Halloween pumpkin for carving and a stash of candy to hand out to the trick or treaters who will come knocking at our front door.

In the photos we take that Halloween, Meghan and her girlfriends stand in our kitchen made up like Madonna wannabes. Meghan is dressed in tight denim jeans and a black leather jacket with silver chains. She's wearing her sister's silver hoop earrings, a heavy layer of eyeliner and mascara, left hip thrust out, affecting a pose of sexual sophistication. At the last minute, she invites me to go with them to trick or treat. "Come on, Mom, you come too," she says. I take a flashlight, pull on my jacket, and follow at a discreet distance as the girls canvass the wide leafy streets in Lafayette. Despite Meghan's assurances that she will outlive me, I don't want to take any chances.

❀ ❀ ❀

One evening after work, I pick Meghan up at a girlfriend's house. I pull into the driveway where my daughter waits for me in the front yard. When I get out of the car, I see that Brooke's father is trimming their hedges. "How are you doing?" He moves toward me.

"Not very well," I say.

He gives me a look that telegraphs profound sympathy and then draws me into a bear hug. When he pats my back, I break into sobs. Embarrassed by this display of raw emotion, Meghan walks to the car and gets in on the passenger side, slamming the door. I realize my mistake. Settling myself behind the wheel, I turn to look at her.

"I'm sorry," I say. "I never knew it was possible to feel this much pain."

"It's okay, Mom," she says, but I know that I have upset her and I redouble my efforts to keep the grief under wraps around her.

That fall, the class I choose at Mills College is "Literature and Medicine." There, I find support for researching and writing about being the parent of an organ donor. I pore over articles on the medical, ethical, and emotional repercussions of transplantation.

Early in 1993, through my contacts at the California Transplant Donor Network, I am invited to speak at a Stanford University symposium on transplantation. It will be held in April, just days after the first anniversary of Maya's death. I eagerly agree to speak as the donor representative on a panel with three organ recipients.

I am unprepared for the intensity of my grief as the first anniversary approaches. Night after night I leave the bed I share with John at two o'clock in the morning and sit alone at the dining room table writing in my journal, never returning to sleep. Each morning, I arrive at my office in San Francisco listless and hollow-eyed.

Nothing I try seems to offset my intense anxiety. Finally, John and I decide to join a support group for recently bereaved parents that meets weekly at the local crisis center. The group is facilitated by a social worker and by a bereaved parent, one of the most empathetic and perceptive people I've ever met. A week before the anniversary, I pour out my feelings to the group.

"I feel like I should be able to do something to stop this—to stop this accident from happening," I say in between gasping sobs. "I mean... I know it has *already* happened, but it seems as if it hasn't, not really. I just can't believe Maya is gone."

Heads nod in understanding, and I plunge on.

"I feel as if I should go back to that field and stop her from getting on the horse. As a mother, that's my job, to protect my child." I cover my face with my hands. John squeezes my shoulder.

"It's painful, isn't it," one of the leaders asks, "to feel that you have failed as a parent?" I can only nod; speech is now impossible. "But you *didn't* fail, Eleanor," she continues. "There was no way to know what was going to happen that day. Maya's accident is not your fault."

As I grow calmer, I listen carefully to other parents pouring out their feelings. A slow glimmer of reason begins to dawn. Stories spill out. Cystic fibrosis, cancer, a bicycling accident, a drug overdose, a teen who flipped out of the back of a Jeep that overturned—there are as many different causes of death as parents sitting in the room. We could not *all* have been bad parents, I reason, looking at their drawn faces.

But my guilt and remorse are acute, raw, and so deeply woven in with my grief. Then another realization dawns. *My guilt is based on a belief that I had control over my daughter's life. But I didn't. Control is a fantasy.* This insight makes me shake with fear because in so many ways my sense of security is based on the illusion of control.

A week later I am on a stage facing an audience of three hundred transplant surgeons, recipients, donor families, and people desperately waiting for scarce organs. Stanford's transplantation program is world-renowned. Several of the top surgeons in the program speak about advances in the science of transplantation before our panel is introduced. Video clips of the three recipients on the panel provide moving introductions about what their lives were like before their transplants, how near death they were, and how their families coped with the stress and disruption of their illnesses. Two of the panelists have received donated hearts, while one is a liver recipient. As I listen to their stories, I feel so moved by what giving someone an organ actually *means* that I choke up. I have read and written about donation extensively, grappling with its aftermath in my life. But this is the first time I've ever sat side by side with three miracles.

Dressed in the same silk suit I wore to Maya's funeral, with a triple strand of pearls at my throat, I am costumed to look very much the professional public relations woman. It is a superb defense against the pain. The moderator introduces me as one of the "unsung heroes" of transplantation, and the audience breaks into applause.

As the moderator asks me questions, I tell our story. The field. The horse. The brain surgery and subsequent brain death. My decision to donate Maya's organs and tissues. I talk about how inspired I am by the note I received from the wife of Maya's heart recipient, and by meeting the recipients here today and hearing about their gratitude. In my mind, Maya is the true hero of our story. When I finish, the audience rises and applauds. I hold up a large framed photograph of Maya.

A young heart recipient on the panel with me has just given birth to her first child. She wraps her arms around me. This young woman, transplanted at the age of twenty, is studying to become a sign language interpreter for the deaf. Any lingering doubts about my decision to donate Maya's organs and tissues are swept away by her presence. In that moment, I make up my mind to share my experiences with an even larger audience. A few weeks later, I revise a piece I wrote for my literature class and send it to the Sunday magazine of the *San Jose Mercury News*. The editors agree to publish it. In June, when the article appears, I go public with our story.

It is customary for donors and recipients to maintain their anonymity; medical personnel and donor coordinators go to great lengths to ensure this barrier of privacy. For me, contact with recipients is uplifting and positive. But it is taxing. The emotions are complex. For recipients, there is guilt that some-one must die in order for them to live, as well as overwhelming gratitude for the donor who makes their new lives possible. And there is still something taboo about an organ being taken from a cadaver and passed on to someone else. My feelings as a grieving mother are intensified by my too sudden and too recent loss.

After my experience at Stanford, I see that the human psyche is not quite in sync with the advances in surgical techniques and drugs to provide immune suppression that make transplantation possible. Because of the emotional complexity of such contact, only about ten percent of donor families ever meet the recipients of their gifts. But something in me nudges me toward a meeting with our *own* recipients, although I don't know how it will happen.

At that moment, Maya's heart recipient is about to return to the Bay Area for his annual check-up at UCSF. Later I will learn that his doctors are amazed by his progress in the year since his transplant. All his symptoms of cardiomyopathy—an enlarged and diseased heart incapable of pumping adequate blood—have vanished. Severe exhaustion, breathing problems, irregular heartbeats that required a defibrillator to shock his heart back into action are gone. He has Maya's young healthy heart and his life has been utterly transformed. Yes, there are a plethora of drugs to take for the rest of his life, but this man was given up for dead. Now he is alive and well. As I wrestle with my grief, the heart recipient regains his strength.

In June of 1993, I attend the Transplant Games, a Special Olympics for organ recipients. The event is held in Palo Alto, not far from the Stanford campus where I spoke two months earlier. Copies of my article, "The Greatest Gift," are prominently placed on a table for attendees to pick up. Someone who happens to know Maya's heart recipient takes one. He realizes from my description of our heart recipient as "a Chilean businessman," that it must be his friend Fernando, and gives his friend a copy.

Until he reads the article, all Fernando knows is that his donor heart came from a nineteen-year-old female college student. Suddenly, through my words, his anonymous donor and her grieving mother become real. He tells his wife that he wants to meet me.

Chapter 19

We are a few weeks away from the New Year—1994—when my psychiatrist quits on me. Dr. Bierbaum has guided me through the depression that followed my mother's death in 1990, and then the seismic shock of Maya.

But I don't feel as if I am getting better; in many ways I'm worse. I still wake at three in the morning. Dread of something happening to Meghan keeps me hyper-alert. My doctor believes that I am high functioning with just some neuroses that are well integrated (these are his words) and a bit of grief. No big deal, he seems to imply.

While I am flattered by the high functioning part, I am furious about his dumping me because of my managed care plan's new forms and fee caps.

With a measured voice and thoughtful manner, he has always been intent on encouraging me to figure out my own solutions. Now, he leans forward and speaks so directly that he catches me off guard.

He reminds me that he has treated many traumatic head injury cases over the years and then bluntly states that death was the best possible outcome in Maya's case. He straightens his lean frame and looks at me gravely.

"They never return to their families as the same person," Dr. Bierbaum continues, scratching his close cropped beard, a mannerism that makes me itch. "They have temper tantrums, speech impediments, uncontrolled spasms, even epilepsy. Their behavior is often unpredictable. Basically, the personality change is total."

Given the severity of her brain damage, I find myself agreeing with his assessment. If Maya had returned to consciousness either mentally stunted or physically crippled, she would have begged me to kill her. I feel the tiniest bit of relief that I am not saddled with a deformed or demented daughter—but it is far outweighed by lingering sorrow and longing, which he doesn't seem to grasp fully.

"She didn't suffer. It's probably for the best in the long run," he says, leaning forward in his expensive ergonomically correct chair to underline his point.

"You'll be fine," he assures me, reading my thoughts. "Let me know if you want to go on antidepressants, and I can supervise that for you."

This is a tempting proposition. I barely have the energy to do my work, let alone live any kind of life. True to my pattern, I hide the full extent of my depression and anxiety from the outside world, including Dr. Bierbaum. I change the subject.

"I'm still feeling really conflicted about my relationship..." I want to cover as much as we can in our final session. As I become stronger and more able to function in the world, I feel increasingly weighed down by John's overprotectiveness.

Dr. Bierbaum pulls no punches. "Here's my strong advice— don't settle. You're going to meet lots of wonderful people through your organ donation contacts and bereaved parent conferences. You are strong enough to resolve this grief. Ultimately, you're going to want someone who is more your equal."

He checks his watch. Our fifty-minute hour is almost up. Okay then, I guess that's it. There's no point in hanging on. "You know," I say, "I think the medication might be worth a try."

He reaches for a prescription pad. Zoloft is best, he says. It's pretty new but he is having good results with his other patients. "Work your way up slowly. You can cut the tablets in half. Call me if there's a problem."

He hands me the scribbled slip of paper. He has treated me for almost three years. I've been through a lot in this little room with its love seats and modern art prints in expensive frames. Its tidy little boxes of tissue on glass end tables.

"Well, good-bye then." I extend my hand.

"Good luck," he says. "You're a terrific person. You will meet a great guy eventually and be very happy."

Like the blessing of Isaac on his son Esau, these parting words are a backhanded curse. I hurry out before I can go too much farther with this Biblical train of thought.

As the Zoloft kicks in I start to feel a bit more energetic, even hopeful, but the holidays with the missing person at the dining room table and the empty second stocking hanging from the mantel are hard to endure. Somehow we open our presents without tears, and Meghan goes off to spend the evening with Dan's extended family.

John and I continue our tradition of going out for Christmas dinner at The Duck Club, a posh Lafayette restaurant located in an upscale hotel. The food is continental, and the décor classic, with deep green leather wing chairs in front of a massive stone fireplace. Carved wooden mallards decorate the mantelpiece.

"John, I have to talk to you." The waiter is clearing the main course.

Bierbaum's frank advice pushed me off the fence.

"What is it, love?" he asks, as if he has no clue that anything is wrong.

I feel suffocated by John's constant hovering and weighed down by his unresolved grief and depression combined with my own, but it's impossible for me to voice these feelings because of my gratitude for his support. "I need to make a change," I blurt. "We're stagnating. We never seem to be able to confront the things that are missing in the relationship..."

"Whoa," he says, raising his hand as if he could block my words. "Have some more wine. Don't you think this is a little heavy for today?" Although he stopped drinking after our first breakup, John still relies heavily on denial as a coping skill.

"I don't want more wine. I want to move on with my life," I say, roiled by his attempt to placate me. The waiter approaches with dessert menus. John waves him off.

"Look, Ellie, I know I sometimes don't focus on us in the way you want me to... but this has been hard for me too. It's brought back a lot of my grief over my son's death. Sometimes, I'm just in another world."

"I know, and I'm sorry for that." I twist the Irish friendship ring he gave me around and around on my finger. John's unresolved grief is a big part of my discontent, but I can't exactly demand that he seek treatment.

"Life goes on—and I need to go with it," I say. "I don't want to become one of those parents whose whole identity gets wrapped up in perpetually grieving."

He knows what I'm talking about. We have both encountered people in our support group whose entire lives revolve around their loss.

"You're probably right... but, I don't know if I can be what you need... I'm not even sure *you* know what you need." He purses his lips like a disapproving nun.

"Damn it," I say, but I feel a surge of affection for him. We have been through so much in the last six years. "This time I need to make it stick. I can't stay with you, John, whatever the reason. I'm just not happy."

He reaches for my hand under the table and squeezes it.

"Do you want some dessert," he asks, "or maybe some hot tea?"

This is the man who watched over me in the night when I didn't think I could live until morning. He has been more of a husband to me than either of my ex-husbands ever were. He is kind, generous, loyal—and the most considerate lover I've ever had. Part of me can't believe I am about to leave him. But a stronger part wants to move on.

We drive home without speaking. My heart is incredibly heavy. I love him. But I just don't know how to bridge our differences.

We go in the house and John hangs up my coat for me, then climbs the stairs in silence. I trail after him.

He has a habit of stripping off his clothes and getting straight under the covers. He usually watches me as I undress, clearly eager for me to join him. That night, I feel too self-conscious, so I take my nightgown into the bathroom to change. I dawdle over brushing my teeth. "Woman, what are you doing in there?" When I crawl in next to him, I am close to tears.

"John," I whisper, "I just need to live alone now, can you understand?"

"Not really." He reaches across the sheet that covers us both and cups his hand around my right breast. I place my hand on top of his. We stay like this for a long time without speaking, tears rolling down my cheeks and into my ears.

"I love you," he says at last.

"I know," I reply, "I love you too, but it's not enough."

When I tell Meghan that John is moving out, she responds that she will miss him, but that she is not surprised by my decision. Unlike Maya, she has a father who is close and affectionate, and although she is close to John, her real attachment is to her own father. She studies me calmly.

"I understand, Mom," she says. "He's nice, but you need someone who gets it." She makes quote marks in the air with her fingers. I speculate that she might mean someone like her father who is facile, well-educated, and even more verbally inclined than I am. That didn't work out so well.

Stifling my amazement, I say, "I'm glad you see it that way, honey. I hope it isn't too disruptive for you."

"I'll be fine, Mom," she says. "Besides, what choice do I have?"

A pang shoots through me for imposing this loss on Meghan. "This is absolutely the last time," I swear to myself under my breath.

John packs his things and moves to an apartment in Lafayette that he shares with his middle son. A couple of months later he calls to chat. He tells me that he is playing golf now and has joined a singles group. He sounds upbeat. I'm dating again too, but I am still too distracted with grief, work, parenting, and graduate school to figure out what I really want in a relationship. John was right on that score. Bierbaum's prediction about meeting Mr. Right seems like a bad joke.

Chapter 20

The silver bumper gleams in my headlights. My foot teases the accelerator and the little sedan speeds forward, boxed in between a pickup truck and a tailgating car. The bumper holds my attention as if it were a hypnotist's watch. *I could just slide into him.* It would be so easy. Then seemingly of its own accord, my foot taps the brakes. The pickup speeds away on Highway 13 toward Berkeley. Jolts of adrenaline make my heart pound so insistently that I feel my aliveness. *I am still here.* And then the corollary thought—*Maya isn't.* A cry bubbles up and escapes into the empty air.

It's costly to keep functioning, to contain my despair and keep it away from others. I'm exhausted. A day of ringing phones, clicking computer keys, parsing out deadlines and assignments, and then the seminar at Mills College. Rafts of poems with their arrow-tipped words. I fell though the gap in those words, out of my numbness, into the space where Maya is still missing.

The car speeds though the Caldecott tunnel, a hollowed out mountain, and travels through the Orinda hills, looping around a curve. Mt. Diablo rises into view. To others it is only mountain as backdrop, but to me it is a knife cutting through the moonlit clouds. I gaze at the highway, blocking out the mountain, then thread across a lane of traffic and guide the car off on the exit, looping under the freeway and past the high school.

I unlock my front door and fall into the house. Music wafts downstairs from Meghan's room. "I'm home," I yell up to her and dump my briefcase on the chair. By the phone there's a stack of papers. I dig out The Compassionate Friends call list, scanning quickly. I dial and miraculously another member picks up.

"I'm falling apart." Words about the truck, wanting to die, my perpetual heaviness tumble into the receiver. There's silence on the other end, then an audible exhale. Frank's son committed suicide five years ago. He and his wife have been through hell.

"I almost killed myself," I repeat.

"I understand," he says, "but you didn't."

"No, but I was out of control."

"Are you in therapy?"

I explain about having to end sessions with Dr. Bierbaum. Frank suggests that I consider seeing Lou Ann Kary, one of the facilitators of the support group John and I attended for almost a year.

"Lou Ann? I didn't realize that she's a therapist."

"Yeah, and a damn good one—although I guess I'm somewhat biased." They are old friends, he says. I know Lou Ann's teenage daughter was killed when she was thrown from a pickup truck she was driving without her parents' permission. Lou Ann had decided to help others once she resolved her own grief, and she was an exceptionally compassionate facilitator. But I'm surprised to learn she is also a therapist. "Give her a call," he suggests. "She really gets it."

I scribble her number on a piece of paper. Twenty-four hours later I have an appointment. At our first session I am instantly at ease, partly because I already know her, but mostly because she is so down to earth. If she is taking a psychological history I never notice it; we are just having a conversation.

"I don't seem to be getting better—in some ways I feel worse," I confess.

"Tell me about that," she says.

I describe the incident on the freeway. She asks if I often have suicidal thoughts. They have diminished during the past year, but the suddenness and intensity of the other night frightens me, I tell her. I mention the antidepressant.

"Your previous therapist prescribed that for you?

"Yes, he was a psychiatrist actually."

She asks why I am no longer seeing him. I try to explain.

"He didn't get it. He kept pointing out how well I was doing, which was partly true, but then I'd have these relapses."

She pauses. "So how does it feel to be abandoned by someone who's supposed to be helping you?" Her voice is so calm that it almost deflects the sting of her question.

"Lousy." I hang my head. Tears materialize out of nowhere.

"I have the sense that you think you owe it to people to be strong, to 'get over it,' and that you are working really hard to protect other people from your grief."

She's right. I've been hiding the depth of my grief from anyone who has children, from most of my colleagues, from the men I date, from my own daughter, and even from my psychiatrist. One place I can't hide is in my writing. The only other place where I feel safe enough to tell the truth is in the safety zone of a Compassionate Friends meeting. Grieving parents are the only ones I can't contaminate with my sorrow or despair—they already know. Fortunately for me, Lou Ann is one of us.

I spend so much time rerunning mental movies about Maya that I am shocked when I discover that my younger daughter is finally at an age to defy me. Now going on fourteen, my normally placid girl battles with me over my plans to send her to Catholic school.

"If you make me go, I will run away," she threatens. Meghan is now as tall as I am. Her thick reddish brown hair flows over her shoulders. She has begun to slim down and the beauty of her eyes and strong bone structure is evident.

"Catholic school will have smaller classes," I point out.

"With only other girls in the classroom, you'll feel more comfortable about speaking out," I coax. "Don't you think that would be better?"

She widens her eyes. "No! Well, maybe it would be, but I don't care. All my friends are going to Acalanes."

Meghan is amazingly bright, but she is also shy and reserved. Around the time of the first anniversary of Maya's death, she began to show symptoms of depression. I convinced her to attend a support group for grieving teens. She reluctantly agreed. About six months into it, she came to me one afternoon.

"Mom, I'm tired of talking about death now. I want to leave the group."

"Okay," I said. "Do you think it helped you?"

"Oh yeah," she said, "just seeing that there are lots of other kids with the same kind of problem helped a lot."

The life and death questions she has already faced make her far more mature than her peers. But I still worry that the mark the grief has made might dampen her self-confidence in the rough and tumble atmosphere of a competitive school. I explore several options, including getting a transfer out of our Walnut Creek school district to Lafayette's Acalanes High School, a public school with an excellent reputation. But when I go there to visit, it seems cold and impersonal. The administrators I interview seem more focused on high SAT scores and prestigious colleges than on the kids.

My unspoken fear is that public school is too dangerous for Meghan—and more than anything I fear that I could lose her. What I can't bring myself to admit, but what she knows perfectly well, is that I still blame peer pressure at Maya's high school, the freedom of an open campus, the testosterone factor, and readily available alcohol for her sister's acting out, and ultimately, for her death.

Her father is doubtful about my plans at first. But after we visit the school together and meet several of the faculty and staff, Dan agrees that the smaller, more individualized classes at Carondelet High School are best for Meghan. She relents. Early that spring she takes the entrance exam.

At my next therapy session, I tell Lou Ann how conflicted I am as a mother. I overprotect Meghan, but I underprotected Maya. I am constantly second-guessing myself about just how closely to monitor my growing teenager.

"You don't have that inner margin of safety that most parents do. Can you acknowledge that extra vulnerability without getting paralyzed by it?"

Typically, I either run as fast as I can from feeling emotionally exposed, or I don my emotional armor and fight back.

Lou Ann already knows the outlines of my family history, and because of our work in the support group, she understands how deeply attached I was to Maya. She urges me to look at the multiple roles Maya played for me. "She was your parent replacement, surrogate spouse, best friend, and your companion—and you played multiple roles in her life too."

I was mother, father, confidante, mentor, cheerleader, and

way too late, disciplinarian for Maya. "But maybe that wasn't good for her," I sob.

"Attaching was not a choice for you, it was a matter of survival," she says. "Because your feelings for Maya run so deep, you won't recover quickly."

I feel as if an invisible billboard has been staring me in the face and now I can read its message in stark relief.

"So what am I supposed to do?"

"Grieve," she says. "You can survive on your own. And now you can explore that for yourself."

She warns me that until I am done grieving a successful intimate relationship is not really possible. I let that sink in. Being celibate until I'm fully healed seems a lengthy and unpleasant prospect. Sex is one of the ways I find comfort. I give her a doubtful look. "Just keep asking yourself, 'What do I want?,' and then put that out there."

In my family I had been drilled to believe that such choices weren't possible. Either I had to give in to the demands of others or take the consequences. There was no middle ground. I could never enforce a limit with my father, for instance. He considered such behavior selfish, disrespectful, and grounds for punishment.

"Give yourself some credit, Eleanor," she says. "You gave Maya so much. You helped her to blossom in a way that your own parents never helped you. They weren't capable of that."

As if I am unpacking an old trunk stuffed with beloved but long lost items, I let her words tap a primal sorrow. Beneath the surface of the successful persona, and even of the grief-stricken mother, is a girl I set aside in order to play a role. It's a role that girl hoped would allow her to be in charge and make her feel safe. But the burden of disguise has become too heavy. And besides, my pretense never really worked. Now I see that my daughter's death shattered my illusion of invulnerability. It is finally time to face all the other losses, the ones that drove me to become a mother in order to be mothered myself.

Chapter 21

Finally ready to contact the heart recipient I have spent so much time speculating and writing about, I call our donor coordinator to request a meeting. It is May of 1994, a little more than two years after Maya's death. Shelley phones back to tell me that several days earlier Fernando did the same. When we give our consents, a meeting is quickly arranged for the end of the month.

Memorial Day is unseasonably warm. I drive to the cemetery with a new bunch of flowers and a head swirling with questions. What will he be like? What will we say to each other? Will I feel Maya's presence?

Sprawling over a broad ridge, Oakmont Memorial Park has a direct view of Mt. Diablo. As I kneel above my daughter's grave, I look at the jagged face of the mountain. It towers above the suburban valleys east of San Francisco, its saw-toothed outline a sharp, cobalt blue. Almost four thousand feet tall, and many miles around, this place was considered sacred by the native peoples who once lived at its base. I regard it with awe. To me, it is a temple of the gods, of doom, of wild horses—a mysterious place that swallowed my daughter in one sudden gulp.

Soaking a rag with polish, I apply it to the granite headstone, bringing up the luster of the gray and black flecks in the stone by rubbing in small, concentric circles. As I work, I begin to speak to Maya.

"I need you with me today," I whisper. "Help me to be strong."

The permanent smile of her picture flashes up at me from its brass mounting on the headstone. Sometimes her smile supports my fantasy that nothing as dire as her death could possibly have happened and that she is just away; but today, that brilliant grin underlines the reality of her absence.

My words drift away on the wind. I settle back on my heels looking at her image, knowing that what I am asking will have to come from within me. Yet something makes me trust that she will help me.

One of my treasured mementos is a card Maya wrote to me less than six weeks before she died, about how much my support meant to her. Up until her death, she fueled my hopes for the future and motivated me to become a better parent. Her triumphs as an actress in the last months of her life brought me tremendous joy. Caring for her, planning a future with her, helping her to achieve it—that was my total focus. Now, there is only empty space where the future should be. My sidekick is gone. Perhaps meeting her heart recipient will help me to accept the raw newness of my life. But, at the same time, I dread facing it in this new, more tangible way.

All I know about the family is what Shelley has told me. They have lived in the United States for many years, and their children were born here, but now they divide their time between their native Chile and the Bay Area where Fernando comes each year to see his doctors.

Flushed with sun and exertion, I tuck the last of the flowers in place, and hurry home to shower and dress for my meeting with Fernando. In the months after Maya died, I broke one of the cardinal rules of early grief. Virtually every grief book I read advised against moving. But with Maya gone, the money I had saved to send her to UCLA was a painful reminder of the future that had imploded so suddenly. I acted on a long-deferred dream. Using her tuition money, I made a down payment on a townhouse-style condominium. It nestled against a green hillside a few miles north of Highway 24, one of the East Bay's major arteries. Hoping that I could build a new life, and provide a fresh start for Meghan in our own home, I packed and prepared to move. With John's help, Meghan and I left the apartment where we had spent the most painful hours of our lives to begin again in a corner of neighboring Walnut Creek.

In anticipation of meeting my "transplantation kin," I riffle through my closet searching for an outfit. Then I lay the clothes out on the bed, dress, and get into the car for the forty-minute drive through the hills, across the Bay Bridge, and into the city.

Without full awareness of how I arrive there, I find myself in a conference room in the San Francisco headquarters of the California Transplant Donor Network. Celia, Fernando's donor coordinator from UCSF is there, as well as our coordinator, Shelley. They keep up a constant stream of small talk as we wait for the family to arrive. I fumble nervously with the edge of the conference table, trying to join the conversation but feeling hopelessly out of my element. When Shelley signals to me that they are coming, I stand in the doorway to greet them and she and Celia hover behind me. Four figures walk toward us down a long corridor.

When Fernando is about ten feet away, I see that his eyes are beaming. He has salt-and-pepper-hair, wire-rimmed glasses, and he is dressed in wrinkled khaki chinos and a blue sports jacket. Before he even speaks, warmth emanates from him. His eyes meet mine, and I am overwhelmed with tongue-tied shyness. I really do not know how to greet this man, so I simply extend my hand. He takes it and then pulls me into an embrace that lasts several long moments. As my head rests against his jacket I find myself weeping, and through that sound, I hear the steady beat of Maya's heart in his chest.

His wife Penny, a stylishly dressed blond with a kind smile, stands silently at his side. Ten-year-old Evelyn, as blond and fair as her mother, holds Penny's hand, watching openmouthed. Christopher, fourteen, stands behind his father, obviously ill at ease, but curious, his almond-shaped eyes darting from face to face.

"You have given me a part of yourself," Fernando says, stroking my hair. "The child who lived in you is living in me. I have so much respect for what you have done."

I absorb his words and I am grateful for them, but at the same time it is intensely confusing to know that Maya's presence is just inches away, yet unreachable. A middle-aged man stands before me vital and alive while my daughter's bones are buried thirty miles away. My hands shake as I grip his shoulders. I have a powerful urge to hold my daughter instead.

When Fernando and I end our embrace, Penny takes me in her arms. "If it weren't for you, I wouldn't have a husband," she says. "There are no words to thank you." I hug her also, feeling happy that my fervent wish to keep another family together as mine disintegrated has come true. At the same time, I feel ill at ease, as if my decision in a moment of crisis cannot possibly be the reason Fernando is still alive.

All of the grownups cry, including the two donor coordinators. One of the coordinators gestures to the cluster of metal folding chairs around the table, and we sit down and begin what turns into a two-hour conversation.

I had asked Meghan if she would like to come with me, but she was firm in her response—she was not prepared to meet this family. But she urged me to bring the photo album she had created in honor of Maya to display at the memorial service. So, using the album as a prop, I narrate significant events of Maya's life to Penny, Fernando, the children, and the donor coordinators. On the first page, the infant Maya sits wide-eyed with her father's stereo headphones dwarfing her ears and cheeks, only six months old, but already listening to jazz. By the final pages of the photo album, she has become a young adult with a model's bravado, vamping for the camera at a Christmas party just months before her death.

Penny and Fernando ask me for a copy of one of the photos.

"I'll have it enlarged," Fernando says, "and put it in my study with the other family photos. She will always be a part of our family."

The transplant has made a profound impact on Fernando's energy. During the ten years of his illness, his damaged heart ballooned in size and could not pump enough blood through his body, making his breathing labored and tenuous. He could barely move from the sofa, and climbing stairs became impossible in the months before his operation. Now, he is overflowing with vitality, and Penny says she can't keep him off the treadmill or the tennis court.

"I can't keep up with him," she teases.

"Oh, that's Maya for sure," I respond. "She was a fitness freak."

"I feel her," Fernando laughs. "She won't let me sit still."

Fortuitously, Maya's healthy heart is almost an exact tissue match with Fernando's diseased one. Four of their six antigens— a protein that determines tissue compatibility—match.

Normally, a match of one or two is considered good. Fernando has had no episodes of rejection, a life-threatening condition most organ recipients struggle with in the early years post-transplant.

Fernando sees the compatibility of the two hearts as a sign of fate. As I drive home that afternoon, I am consumed by this mystery.

During the weeks that follow our meeting, I ask myself if I think it really is fate, or just a stupid, cruel accident. Or are they the same? The stark contrast between the future I lost and the one Fernando and his family gained confounds my ability to accept this so-called fate. I plummet back down into tearful pacing, the eternal tape loop in my brain insistently demanding *why, why, why?* Maya should be graduating from UCLA, but instead she lies buried on a hillside in the "Garden of Remembrance." Her heart makes it possible for Fernando to play tennis, make love with Penny, and go to the movies with his kids. But my daughter's life has been snuffed out. In grief-driven frustration, I hurl a box of tissues at my living room wall.

"God must have a very odd concept of justice," I write in my journal, wondering why Maya's fate was to lose a life so full of promise and why my fate is to be forever separated from my daughter. I miss her quirky humor and mercurial intelligence with fierce, stabbing jolts.

Fernando sends me a photograph taken on the afternoon of our meeting. In it, his arm surrounds my shoulders. His smile is sweet and glowing, centered in his grateful face, and he appears to me as I imagine Lazarus might have looked after Jesus raised him from the dead—surprised, happy to see everyone, slightly dazed. I'm smiling too, turning in towards this man who almost looks as if he could be related to me. We have the same dark brown eyes, sharp cheekbones, and prominent noses. I frame the photo and set it on my writing desk. As I wrestle with the meaning of what has happened, I begin to think of Fernando as my daughter's adopted father, a kind of benign benefactor. A place where she can rest and be safe at last. Perhaps as a way of offsetting my loss, I give Fernando an intimate role in our lives.

Without telling anyone, or even fully acknowledging it to myself, I appoint Fernando the titular head of my family—a family that has shattered on the physical plane but one that I reconstitute in the ghost realm of my imagination. Seeing Maya's continuing life through transplantation offers me a spiritual replacement for the searing physical absence of my daughter. She is dead, yes, but not entirely. Fernando experiences her vitality. As the home of Maya's heart, he becomes a father figure for my daughter. As long as I see it this way, I don't have to conduct the tug of war between my pain and his healing all alone.

Chapter 22

Hearing Maya's heartbeat in someone else's chest feels like returning to the womb, almost as if I am a child again, not a mother. Confronting the complexity of donation nudges me to reexamine what it means to raise a child, and how blurry the role of mother sometimes became. In the oblong white room where my therapist Lou Ann and I meet, I bend my thoughts toward a corridor of magic mirrors where nothing can be taken at face value.

"Tell me about your earliest memory of your mother," Lou Ann urges. I try to push away the image that rises inside me, but the terror and rage are still too real even decades later. Breaking through Mom's wall required all of my three-year-old inventiveness.

"Bring me that pail," my mother said, pointing across our goat shed. "Hurry up!"

She smelled of damp earth, stale coffee, and compost. The milk hissed as it hit the side of the aluminum pail. My mother bent to her task, her head grazing the flank of the goat. I lifted the animal's long ear, fingering its velvety underside. Out of curiosity, I blew into its curving passages. The goat bucked wildly, knocking over the pail and spilling milk across the floor. Mom jumped up from her stool.

"God damn it! Get out! Go, go, *go*..." she shouted.

She swept me towards the door in a rush. I teetered on the threshold of the goat shed, grasping at her shirt. With the flat of her hand against my chest, she pushed me away. I flew down three cement block steps to the ground. When I picked myself up, she had already turned back to her work.

I stumbled along the path with bloodied shins and cheeks hot with shame. I hated her! I hated the drafty farmhouse with its gray shingles and tilting cement porch. I wanted my father to come home in his green Jeep with his loud laugh and dark, slicked-back hair. I limped to our driveway, picked up a handful of gravel and turned toward the house, throwing pieces of stone one by one as hard as I could at our cracked porch steps.

Lou Ann tracks every word. "What comes up now as you remember this?"

"Fear, mainly, and anger." My jaw is clenched so tightly it begins to ache. "I thought she hated me. I figured she pushed me away because I was bad."

"It had nothing to do with you," Lou Ann says. "She was terrified by how much you needed her."

The truth of these words lies on my chest like an anvil. Mom was afraid to love, afraid to touch. Sorrow for a frightened little girl and her even more frightened mother pulls more grief to the surface. Fear cost us both so much. I can't even imagine not cuddling with my daughters; it was one of the best parts of being a mother. But when I look back, it was my father who bathed me, who brushed my hair, who played games with the three of us kids, even if they were sometimes brutal. Part of me wants to defend Mom.

"Lots of people thought my mother was a saint," I say. "She

attended Mass and took communion every day. She told me she wished she could be a twelfth-century mystic. Maybe that's why being a mother was so hard for her."

Lou Ann says that the aim of spiritual transcendence, while noble, may have masked something else. "We've talked about the possibility that your Mom was sexually abused before. That may be one reason why she shut down and avoided touch." As I look back, I have to admit that Mom was never comfortable with physical affection. She pushed me away if my hugs lasted longer than a few seconds. I grew up with a touch deficit that made me hungry for physical contact and unable to sort out who could safely provide it. When Maya was born, and I held her in my arms, finally I had someone to love whom I did not also fear.

"From what you've told me about your parents' marriage, it's not surprising you leaned on Maya. They were so caught up in their own conflict, there was no room for them to focus on you."

"You're right, it was a pretty amazing power struggle."

When I was in my teens, Mom insisted that she had married in order to have children, so I grew up believing my parents' unhappiness was my fault. But later my Dad painted a very different picture. Mom was adamant about *not* wanting children. When she refused to use a diaphragm and insisted my father take care of the birth control, they spent an entire summer fighting about it. Dad finally forced the issue by refusing to use a condom. Mom got pregnant in the fall of 1947, and I was born the following May.

Becoming a mother changed her. She began to rethink her decision to leave the Catholic Church and become an agnostic. With the fervor of a convert, she studied Catholic doctrine. Several months before my sister was born in the winter of 1950, Mom announced that she was leaving him unless Dad would agree to remarry her in a Catholic ceremony and raise their children as Catholics. She took me and left the apartment they shared in downtown Cleveland to move back in with her parents. My mother was seven months pregnant, and I was just eighteen months old.

My father was furious. But there was a major plus for him. At thirty, he was suddenly free to pursue his real love interest, a young actor he had met the previous summer. Their relationship grew so intense during my parents' separation that the young man proposed that they enter a committed relationship. This provoked a crisis of conscience in my father. He ultimately decided, even though he was actively homosexual, that he should save the marriage. He convinced Mom to return to him, but waffled about marrying her again in a Catholic ceremony.

When Mom was in labor with my sister Tess, a nun took my father aside in the hospital corridor and warned him that his coming child would be illegitimate. "If you don't remarry in the Catholic Church, you'll never be with your family in heaven," she warned.

On Easter weekend of 1950, when their new baby was a month old, my parents were married for a second time in a simple Catholic ceremony at the church rectory. Not to be outdone, my father had elected to be baptized Episcopalian the week before. As it turned out, there would be a lot more hell on earth before anyone had to worry about who they'd be seeing in heaven.

Mom left Dad four more times by the time I entered first grade. By then, my brother had been born. She always took the three of us with her—first to a neighboring farm, then to California and Mexico, later to Washington, D.C., and finally to live with her mother. Our departures were furtive and sudden, and my father would make frantic calls to my grandmother to try to find out where we were.

I can't help but wonder if my own nomadic twenties and thirties were shaped by my mother's restive escapes, made when I was too young to remember them clearly. Maya once counted up our moves—seventeen by the time she left for college. Coincidence or pattern? Perhaps unknowingly I was copying my mother, never content to stay in one place, chafing against the constraints of my unhappy marriages.

All the times I goaded Maya—to succeed, to take risks in the world, even to leave home—rise into my consciousness. Pushing in all its forms is a theme I can no longer ignore, especially since I now believe my daughter pushed herself beyond her own limits. Transcending limits was a way of life for my mother, for Maya, and for me.

When I was about to enter grade school we moved so that my father would not have such a long drive to his job as a professor of speech and drama at the local college. Our new house in town had real heat from a coal furnace, running water, and indoor plumbing, a big step up from the farm. But it was still modest by the standards of the 1950s, when sleek ranch houses sprang up everywhere. My sister and I shared a drafty upstairs room, sleeping together in a double bed. My parents had purchased the furniture from the previous owners, and those children had scratched their initials on the bed's wooden headboard.

At bedtime, Mom started a fire and jammed the potbellied stove in the upstairs hallway with wood until the cast iron glowed, but by morning our breath hung in the air in foggy puffs. On cold nights, Tess and I put our bare feet on the

window by our bed to see who could keep them there the longest. Our footprints would be etched in frost each morning.
Heat drifted capriciously into some rooms and stayed entirely
out of others.

As I had on the farm, I still looked to Dad for the energy and
attention I craved, but it came at a price. When my father put his
lips next to my ponytail at the dinner table and threatened to cut
off my ears if I spilled my milk, no one seemed to hear, or even
notice. When his spankings tilted into beatings, and he screamed
invectives, Mom was always mysteriously absent. I already knew
it was useless to ask for her protection. Until I became a mother
myself, and hovered over my daughters' first steps, or cried on
their first day of school, I didn't comprehend the impact of my
mother's neglect.

Too impatient for us to walk with her, Mom would pull us on
an ancient wooden sled in the winter. Yanking the frayed rope
attached to the sled's frame, she focused on her destination. The
three of us had to cling together to keep from falling off as our
mother dragged us over the icy streets so she could go to confes-
sion or attend Mass at our church.

Crucifixes with yellowing palm fronds tucked behind them
decorated the walls of our living and dining rooms. A ceramic
Infant of Prague in lace collar and starched robe stretched out his
dimpled fingers above a little desk. A picture of the martyrdom
of Saint Sebastian, each wound dripping blood, hung in a frame
above my brother's bed. There was also a small holy water font
next to the front door. Mom crossed herself and mumbled, "In
the name of the Father, Son, and Holy Ghost," each time she
entered or left the house.

A portrait of Joan of Arc painted by one of my father's students hung on our living room wall. Joan's oil-painted face was
knobby, a series of tiny crosshatches and bumps. Brilliant orange

tongues of fire lashed her cheeks and shoulders. Her eyes rolled upward to gaze beyond the borders of her death by fire. Her hair was brown; close cropped, with short, jagged bangs, the identical style in which my mother wore her hair. The portrait hung above our green Naugahyde couch, dominating the room. I felt a mixture of feelings toward Joan—horror at her graphic suffering, admiration for her courage, curiosity about how she came to be a saint. Why did God talk to *her*? Was she crazy? Truly a saint? Both?

These questions echo the ones I have about my mother, the same ones Lou Ann and I try to fit into the riddle we're decoding. My mother's struggle to survive in a culture and a marriage that punished her for being a maverick—and perhaps caused her so much anguish that she became mentally unstable—shaped me as a mother in ways I am only now confronting. Although she grew up thousands of miles from my parents, Maya lived in their immense shadow.

Mom spent her spare time creating adaptations of plays with religious themes and producing and directing them at our church. A wooden chest filled with costumes sat in our upstairs hallway. One Saturday morning I was rummaging there for a dress-up outfit. My parents were in the kitchen. Their voices rose and fell in waves, and my father's was growing heated. I began to eavesdrop.

"You can't just take things out of the house," Dad argued.

"They don't belong to *you*," Mom flashed back.

"I work to support this family," he was shouting now. "The least you could do is ask permission."

"Ask you for permission to use my own shawl..." Mom laughed derisively.

My parents' acting and directing careers had diverged wildly since their days together as staff actors for a regional theater company. My mother favored religious morality plays. Dad chose Broadway shows like *Damn Yankees* or *Oklahoma,* or Shakespearean classics for the college productions he directed. Mom often appropriated household items for costumes or props. A silk paisley shawl that had once covered the top of our second-hand piano had recently appeared on one of the three kings in a Nativity play she produced at our church.

I crept down the stairs and peered around the corner into the kitchen. Dad was leaning over Mom, blocking her into a corner by the kitchen sink. She crossed her arms over her chest, staring him down. Without warning, he struck her hard across the face. She fell back from the force of the blow. I heard this more than saw it—first the smack of his hand on her cheek, then a startled gasp, then her hip hitting the cupboard door beneath the sink as she lost her balance.

"Don't you dare use that tone of voice with me," my father shouted, arm still cocked.

Mom leaned against the sink and grasped the edge with both hands. Her knuckles were as white as the porcelain. I half expected her to turn and hit him back. My mother was incredibly strong, and I knew she could physically overpower my father. But she bent her head and tears slipped down her cheeks.

I backed up the stair treads until I was out of earshot. Then I turned and ran up the last three steps and into my bedroom. I leaned my full weight against the door until I heard my father's Plymouth station wagon gun out of the gravel driveway.

When I relive these scenes with my therapist, even four decades after they happened, I quake with fear. The rifts in my parents' marriage, their hopelessly confused hearts, the lies they told to keep the family intact, and their inability to parent three children wisely make me question everything about my life. My struggle to keep my daughter close and yet let her go seems like a perilous journey that only leads deeper into more grief and pain. I grew up in a madhouse. One minute we were singing Broadway show tunes and in the next moment a tsunami of rage was smashing us all to bits.

Chapter 23

Dressed in a black gown with a velvet hood, I stride across an outdoor stage framed by towering eucalyptus trees. In the audience, my fourteen-year-old daughter watches as I extend my hand to the Mills College president. No one could be more thrilled to be reaching for a diploma at the age of forty-seven. Most of my classmates are in their twenties, the same age Maya would be if she were still alive. In May of 1995, I finally realize a dream I had set aside when she was born.

After the ceremony, Meghan snaps photos of me like a proud mother. We drop plump California strawberries in our plastic glasses to sweeten the champagne and toast my accomplishment. Maya's sassy charm and affection inhabit my inner being, missed on the physical plane, but very much with me. I wear a photo of her I had made into a pin-on button on my lapel to keep her close for the celebration.

I miss Mom's presence, too, because she would have understood what earning an MFA in creative writing means to me at this stage of my life. In my mind's eye, her man's shirt and muscular arms will forever contrast with the self-effacing curve of her shoulders as she bends over a used typewriter tapping out her plays. She worked alone, with no support and little recognition. Today I look around and see that I have a rich community of writers beyond anything my mother could have hoped for. I'm moving beyond the limits she set for herself—and by extension for me—a scary and wonderful prospect.

Meanwhile, Lou Ann and I are hacking through the tangle of my past in weekly therapy sessions. Every time I touch the raw nerve of how much I longed to be mothered and how little mothering I actually had, I break into sobs. It's a chain of losses with one leading inexorably to the next.

"Grief is like that," she reassures me. "Whatever is unhealed comes up again."

While my mother labored over writing for no money, when she did work for pay it was frequently at menial jobs. She once worked as a nurse's aide for several months, but she could never keep a job long because she hated to have anyone exert authority over her. Mom had a master's degree in theater arts from a prestigious university, and her mother scoffed at her forays into employment far beneath her abilities. That changed when my father faced a professional crisis that forced my mother back to work.

One day when I came home from school, I went to look for Mom in her usual spot in her room by the window reading a book. But that day, when I entered the room, I quickly saw that something had changed. The leather manicure case that always sat on top of Dad's dresser was gone. His collection of silk ties and crisp white shirts had vanished from the closet. His neat row of shoes—all gone.

When I asked Mom where he was, she said he planned to pursue his acting career in New York City, and was going to be staying there with friends. She put the best face on things. But that wasn't the real reason he left so abruptly. When police arrested two male students for lewd behavior, one of them bargained for his release by accusing my father and another professor of running a homosexual ring. The accusation, although false, caused college officials to deliver an ultimatum—quit or face legal consequences. Dad resigned in the fall of 1962, the year that I entered high school.

That year, Mom found a job teaching English literature part time at a college in a neighboring town. She rode her bicycle eight miles one way for her afternoon class. When she wasn't teaching or gardening, she often lapsed into despair.

My mother had a habit of pulling out her eyebrow hairs with her fingers while she was reading. The jagged gaps in her eyebrows sometimes bled. Because of calcium deficiency, she lost her teeth shortly after my brother's birth, and her five-foot-six-inch frame carried forty extra pounds. She cut her own hair with a pair of sewing scissors. At home, she dressed in baggy men's clothing and often went without her false teeth.

One afternoon I found her pacing in the kitchen before an open cupboard door. It contained one jar of Skippy peanut butter and a box of Saltine crackers. "There isn't enough money for groceries this week," she said, wringing her hands.

I was fourteen years old. I hardly knew what to say. But I knew we needed to eat.

"Call Dad," I coached her. "Tell him we need food." She looked at me blankly. Tears rolled down her cheeks.

"He'll just laugh at me," she said.

"Tell Grandma," I suggested.

"No, no! I get paid on Friday, we can make it until then."

The supermarket in town delivered groceries to our door and extended credit. We never went hungry. But I was terrified my mother would have a breakdown. When she made a new friend at the college, Serena, an eccentric twenty-seven-year-old art teacher, I was relieved.

Serena's offbeat humor lightened my mother's mood. She was short and stocky, with straight hair that hung to her waist and the longest fingernails I had ever seen. The nail on her little finger was so long that it curled like a Chinese Mandarin's. She was a painter and sculptor who had spent a year in Paris and spoke French with a southern accent. She introduced me to the music of Jacques Brel and Edith Piaf and showed me how to play the bongo drums, treating me like a kid sister.

That spring, Mom said we were going to move to Cleveland to live with my grandmother. This seemed like a good plan to me. I looked forward to attending a larger high school and getting out of our little town where people had always treated us as outsiders. Besides, the house was too gloomy without my voluble father. I missed his energy and his humor. Grandma sent my uncle to pick us up because Mom had no car. Later, my uncle said that his mother told him to pick us up at night because she wanted to hide our family situation from public view. To my grandmother, image was everything.

That summer, my father returned from New York and moved into his mother-in-law's home as if we could all pick up our lives as a family. But my mother had now lived independently from him and she had a trump card.

Serena settled in at Grandma's as if she belonged there. I will never know how she did it, but Mom persuaded my grandmother to let her new friend stay in the rambling house along with her estranged husband and the three of us kids. Seven of us gathered for the nightly ritual of dinner—three confused teenagers side by side with hostile adults in various states of denial.

"Pass the bread," Serena would ask politely, a veneer of disdain in her voice.

My father would give her a withering stare and shove the gold and white bread plate across the table towards her. "Thanks, Leonard," she would respond as if they were playing by Robert's Rules of Order.

Dad would snort and press his knife violently into a rare slice of roast beef. Ever the shy one, my sister Tess looked down at her plate. Tim nervously fingered the edge of his napkin. Mom fumed in stony silence. My grandmother would hold a bright string of irrelevant conversation aloft as if she could somehow keep our minds off the simmering hostility. The tension in the air was so thick it made my jaws ache.

Once, I overheard my grandmother tell my mother, who was sobbing at the kitchen sink after a particularly difficult dinner hour, "Janet, get a grip on yourself. You have to think of the children."

One night I woke with a severe toothache. I searched the upstairs bathroom for aspirin, but found none. In desperation, I went downstairs to wake my mother. Mom and Serena slept on my grandmother's glassed-in front porch facing the lake. It was dark on the landing that led out to the porch, so I turned on the kitchen light.

In its reflected glow I saw my mother and Serena lying side by side, sleeping in a tangle of sheets. The sight was peaceful but unmistakable in its implications. My mind churned with questions. I knew our living situation was odd, but it had never occurred to me that Serena, who was only twelve years older than I, could be my mother's bed partner. At fifteen, I was still grappling with the mysteries of sex, and my mother's routines—daily attendance at Mass, gardening, reading Theillard de Chardin and the collected works of St. Teresa of Avila—seemed asexual, even holy.

Suddenly, the truth walloped me. I turned and raced up the stairs two at a time. By the time I reached my room, I was sobbing.

My father heard me and came out of his room to investigate. I blurted out what I had seen. "I don't get it," I said. "What's going on?"

He brought me into his room and shut the door. His normally well-groomed black hair was rumpled, but he seemed instantly alert—and ready to tell his version. "Your mother is out of her mind," he began. I stared at the white plaster wall behind him and tried to quell the hot pit of nausea in my stomach. Then he said the L word as if it were the meanest epithet he could think of. "She's a *lesbian*."

I half expected police to come and take my mother away. "What... you mean she loves women?" I stammered.

"She has sex with them, however they do *that*." My father curled his lip in disgust. I wanted to run from the room and hide. But he barreled on.

He said that some of Mom's women friends we kids had always thought of as kindly pseudo-aunts had, in reality, been her lovers.

"Even Aunt Vanessa?" I asked, not wanting to hear his answer.

"Especially Vanessa," he said. "She seduced your mother when she was only fifteen, a student in her theater program." I thought I would vomit. I had traveled with Vanessa to New England alone when I was twelve. I adored her.

"Dad, I don't get it," I repeated.

He launched into a speech about his own orientation. He believed that homosexuality was a noble tradition passed down by ancient Greeks and Romans. I listened to him rant, shriveling inside. Suddenly, pieces of my life fit together in a new way, yet none of it made any sense to me.

At last, I crept back to my room and spent the rest of the night writing in my journal. I told no one, not even my sister and brother, although shortly afterward the neighborhood boys clued my brother in. The subject was never openly discussed in my grandmother's house. Tess and Tim and I put the pieces together on our own.

Weeks later, in a private moment with Mom, I asked her the most difficult question I could imagine. I was terrified she would haul off and slap me. "Are you and Serena lovers?" I asked.

There was a long pause. My mother pulled herself up to her full height. "I don't ask you about your personal life, and I don't care to discuss mine," she said. And she never did, even when I was old enough to talk to her with more wisdom and compassion.

One Friday night my sister Tess and I went to a fancy downtown hotel to pick up score cards at a bridge tournament where my grandmother was officiating. She had gotten us jobs assisting at the tournament. We served as couriers, taking the results of each round up to the judges who were scoring the event.

Somehow we missed our opportunity to ride home with my aunt and uncle who played bridge with religious fervor and often chauffeured my grandmother. The tournament was winding down and we had no way to get home. It was past eleven o'clock at night and much too late for the bus. I phoned my father.

"Dad, can you pick us up?"

He huffed and puffed but finally agreed. I relayed this to my sister. We stayed in the ballroom where the officials were still tallying the scores. Meanwhile, my father and brother had driven downtown to pick us up and were waiting in the hotel lobby. By the time I went to check, more than half an hour had passed, and my father was furious with me.

We had been in the car less than thirty seconds when he started. "Do you think I'm a taxi service? Why can't you be responsible enough to get yourself home?"

"Dad," I said, "we didn't do it on purpose."

"You are the most selfish, self-centered..." he slammed on the brakes for a red light. I lurched forward in the passenger seat.

"Dad," my sister chimed in from the back seat. "It's not Ellie's fault."

"God damn it! I didn't ask for your opinion," he sputtered.

I sprang to Tess's defense and full-scale verbal war broke out. The argument raged during the fifteen-minute freeway ride. Tires squealed as my father pulled the car in next to the sycamore tree at the foot of my grandmother's driveway.

"Nobody move," he ordered.

I unbuckled my seat belt. He reached across the bench seat and cuffed the side of my face. I leaped out.

My sister sat frozen in the back seat. My father slammed his door so hard that the car shook. He marched around to the passenger side.

"Get out! Get out!" he screamed at my sister.

He yanked open the door, reached in, and dragged Tess from the car.

"Leave her alone, you animal," I shouted.

With lightning speed, not letting go of my sister, he grabbed me by the arm and hauled us screaming into the house. My brother trailed silently behind.

By the time we got inside I was hysterical. I accused him of being so cold he would kill his own mother if she asked him for a favor.

He slapped me again. "You always hit me when I tell the truth," I screamed. My sister cowered behind me.

He stalked away through the kitchen and up the stairs toward his bedroom. At that moment, my mother appeared on the upstairs landing. "Len, what's going on?"

He stood in the hall leaning over the banister. We stared up at him from the stairwell below. His face was red and his eyes bulged.

"I am the captain of this ship," he bellowed, "and don't you ever forget it."

"Oh, Len," my mother began.

"You," he snapped. "Shut up. Just shut up!"

Then he turned and vanished behind the closed door of his room. My mother looked as if someone had poured shellac over her. Hatred for both of them burned in me.

My parents divorced when I was twenty-one. Grandma hired a posh divorce lawyer for my mother. Dad moved to the other side of the city to be near the college where he taught in the drama department. He was later named chair of the humanities department, a position he held until his retirement. Serena moved into a duplex up the street and lived there until my grandmother died in the winter of 1974. Then she moved back into the old house, purchasing a half interest. She and Mom were together for twenty-six years, longer than my parents had been married.

From the time Maya was a baby into her grade school years, we went home to visit my mother almost every year. One Christmas Mom dressed up as Santa Claus and four-year-old Maya was completely enchanted with the long white beard and the red stocking cap. Mom read her stories and helped her stage puppet plays. She was an odd sort of grandmother, even a young child could see that, but she was fun. By the time Meghan came along, I went home less often. The ghosts of my girlhood faded.

When Mom died in 1990, she left Serena her half of my grandmother's house. We three kids got the contents. My brother hired an appraiser to evaluate the Oriental rugs, paintings, silver, china, and furniture. When everything was said and done, we each sold our one-third interest in the furnishings to Serena. The home on the lake passed out of our family. But it was never mine in any case. As I search for the deeper meaning of my daughter's death, my mother's legacy leaves tantalizing clues. Mom had handed me a Rubik's cube made up of her courage, her passion for words, and the tangled pieces of her complex life. That was my true inheritance.

Chapter 24

On Saturdays, when the buzz of the workweek wears off, sadness and fatigue set in. Snuggled on the couch with my two cats, I flip on public television to lose myself in home improvement shows where practical, clear-eyed people rehabilitate old houses.

My favorites are Dean and Robin on the *Hometime* show. When Robin dons her safety glasses and drills raw lumber, I am deeply satisfied. Room additions go up, backyards are torn apart and re-landscaped, basements remodeled—crisp new construction replaces dilapidation. It will be several more years before I realize that my home repair idols mirror the interior work I am doing.

Part of the rebuilding process involves my father. Now in his seventies and living in Manhattan, he has pursued his acting career after retiring from teaching. Despite growing physical limitations, he is as buoyantly energetic as ever, and I admire his tenacity and drive. The more I review the past, the more I see that Dad's energy was largely responsible for keeping our family together. Having an absent father had so tragically influenced Maya's life that I begin to understand that even a deeply flawed parent is better than a missing one. My father and I reconstruct our relationship through heart to heart phone conversations. In time, I come to rely on his support and advice.

After my TV shows are over, I dial his number. I can imagine the book-lined shelves of his study, the hundreds of videotaped concerts and plays he has collected neatly stacked in the living room.

"Hi, Pops," I say when he picks up the phone.

"Eleanorrrra," he replies, his jovial voice several decibels louder than necessary. I hold the phone away from my ear. He rolls the "r" with operatic theatricality, jabbing at my imperious personality. "What's up, Doc?"

"Oh same old, working way too much. Missing Maya. Looking forward to taking Meghan to Canada in June."

"How lovely," he says, not pausing to ask about the vacation I have planned with my daughter. He rattles off anecdotes about his latest trips to the theater and the symphony, made possible by former students who give him complimentary tickets. He relishes traveling to the theater district by subway, even though he has been mugged at knifepoint.

When the conversation turns my way, I lament the difficulty of relating to people who are impatient with my grief, believing he will tell me to snap out of it. My father typically doesn't tolerate whiners, but now he springs to my defense.

"Of course you're sad," he says. "Your daughter was torn away from you. This is not something you 'get over.' You just have to go on."

"I know, Dad. I'm trying."

He is proud of my accomplishments at work, and of my academic achievements at Mills. When I tell him about an award I received for my poetry, he is ecstatic. Although he doesn't know Meghan very well, he always asks about her and seems genuinely concerned about her well-being.

"You're being nibbled to death by ducks," he quips when I tell him about some difficult issues I'm facing at work. Dad's humor has always been one of his better traits. Charmed by our virtual contact on the phone, I decide to give my father a present I know he will love.

To celebrate my graduation from Mills and his seventy-fifth birthday, I invite him to go on a trip to the Grand Tetons. Dad has always wanted to visit these mountains in Wyoming that he's only seen in photographs. Now, to make his dream a reality, he requires help (although he won't admit that) and companionship. My boyfriend Bob, a passionate outdoorsman, agrees to go with me the last week of May in 1995.

We fly to Salt Lake City and meet Dad at the gate when his plane arrives. Lulled into a false sense of camaraderie by years of telephone conversations, I am in for a splash of cold reality. Dad is witty and full of spunk, but he is also difficult and self-absorbed with little realistic grasp of his physical limitations or their impact on others. He appears in the jetway in a wheelchair being pushed by a flight attendant. As I approach, she rolls her eyes as if to say, "This guy is a handful!" When we load his bags into the trunk of our rented car, I note that he has more luggage than I do, and I am a notorious over-packer.

As cattle and sagebrush whirl by outside the window on the drive to Jackson Hole, my father holds forth. His stories often reveal new information about my mother and her family, information that helps me put my difficult relationship with her into perspective. I ask him about her father, an alcoholic who was confined to a mental hospital for the final years of his life.

"He was out in cloud cuckoo land." Dad laughs at his own wisecrack. "Once, at your grandmother's, I went upstairs and found him in the bathroom. He was trying to strangle himself with a towel." Dad raises his arms and wraps an imaginary towel around his own neck to demonstrate this pitiable suicide attempt. His eyes bulge as if he were really choking. I know my grandfather was often suicidal, but I'm not sure I entirely believe my father's version of these events.

There are huge gaps in his stories, spaces where his cruelty is conspicuously absent or minimized with humor. "Your mother and I were doing dishes together," he recalls. "She would wash the plates slap dash and then hand them to me to dry—but they were still dirty!" He looks at me, expecting a reaction of distaste, knowing that I am as fastidious as he is. "When I handed them to her to do over, she got so mad that she hit me on the elbow with a pot!"

He laughs uproariously, recounting stories about Mom leaving him as if they were made-for-TV movies with no lasting impact on anyone. In his world, memories can be stripped of pain if told with enough drama and gusto. I'm dumbfounded by his ability to distance himself from reality.

During a week in the Tetons, we ascend a mountain in a gondola, hike in the forests surrounding Jackson Hole, and visit Yellowstone National Park. It is beautiful but exhausting. I take my father's elbow and attempt to guide him or, more frighteningly, keep him from falling when the terrain is uneven. He usually refuses my help and is soon breathless from the exertion of walking without his cane, a prop he leaves in the car.

Bob endears himself to me by deflecting my father's demands. I could never have coped with Dad by myself. He complains in loud hyperbole about the noise in the hotel, the distance from his room to the dining area, the food, and the service. To keep my emotional equilibrium, I relax by the hotel pool, letting the sun bake the tension out of my shoulders. The Jacuzzi-style hot tub with its humming bubbles becomes a private refuge where I wash away my frustration with the gap between fantasy Dad and the real McCoy. On the plane home, I marvel that I kept my patience and that we are still on speaking terms. But then much of my relationship with my father these days seems like a miracle.

Three weeks later, Meghan and I fly to Canada. Pacific Bell's employee newspaper *Connections* has won a prestigious Gold Quill award from the International Association of Business Communicators. I began editing the paper six months earlier, turning *Business Digest* over to my colleague Roz. The award will be presented at IABC's annual conference in Toronto. It seems like the perfect opportunity to combine business with pleasure.

Meghan is a trooper, attending most of the conference events with me, including the awards banquet. One night we go to dinner in a restaurant called "The Lighthouse," located on the top floor of our high rise hotel. It has a rotating dining room designed to showcase a panoramic view of Lake Ontario and the lights of Toronto. The lake gleams like a polished nickel below a horizon streaked with orange. I remember many evenings perched on a picnic table behind my grandmother's house, gazing out at Lake Erie.

When I snap out of my reverie, Meghan is nervously moving silverware around on the tablecloth, staring down at her plate.

"Honey, what's wrong?"

"I don't like looking out there," she says, gesturing at the glass windows with trembling hands.

"Do you feel dizzy?" Perhaps she has vertigo.

"I don't like the emptiness over the lake. It scares me." Tears squeeze from her downcast eyes and run down her cheeks.

Meghan has expressed fear about large bodies of water before, so I take this seriously. But I'm not sure what to do. Our waiter has already taken our orders.

"All right." I keep my voice low and even. "Would you like to leave now? We can take our food back to the room."

Relief floods her face. "Yes, let's do that."

I motion for our waiter.

She is beginning to hyperventilate.

I suggest that we move away from the windows and go to the hostess station to wait. The food arrives in two Styrofoam containers. As soon as we leave the restaurant, Meghan relaxes.

I'm unsure what to make of this. After all, she's only fourteen, but I'm concerned about her free-floating anxiety. Our genetic heritage is shaky in the mental health department, and the grief over the loss of her sister isn't helping any.

On the flight to Cleveland our little propeller plane flies from the Toronto airport across a spit of land and then above Lake Erie the entire way. I am none too calm myself, but I take the window seat and gaze out at the water below us stretching for miles in every direction as the engines sputter and the wings rattle. It occurs to me that unlike Maya, Meghan voices her fears. Her sister, on the other hand, had exhibited a bravado I now see as dangerous, even though I had admired it when she was alive.

Mercifully, the flight is brief. My sister and her husband pick us up at the airport. Her aunt's warm hugs and familiar smile put Meghan at ease. During our week in Ohio we go to the beach at Mentor Headlands, on family picnics with Tim and his children, and spend an afternoon at a Cleveland Indians' game. Each evening we watch old black and white movies in my sister's living room. The energy is calm and nurturing, quite different from the intensity of my time with my father. My sister and I fall into a rhythm of easy conversations, sharing family memories. By the time we return to California, I am sated with ten days of mother-daughter bonding. Meghan exhibits no fears about flying home, and I don't revisit her reaction to the open water.

When we return from Ohio, there is a message on my answering machine from Fernando. We have exchanged several letters since our first meeting the previous spring. Now, he says that he will be in the Bay Area in July and wants to see me again. He leaves the number of his office in Delaware and asks me to call him back to make plans. Since we are now in direct contact, there is no need to involve the two donor coordinators. But with that buffer gone, I feel unsure of exactly how to form a deeper relationship with him.

My relationship with Fernando is more than a friendship, but not quite family. I think of us as transplantation kin, a sort of social hybrid about which little has been written. I am intensely curious about how Fernando perceives our relationship and how he feels about carrying my daughter's heart in his chest. My desire to learn more about him outweighs my reservations. I phone Fernando and agree on a date and time for our second meeting.

Chapter 25

I jump when the phone rings, then pick up quickly. "Eleanor, I am on Taylor Boulevard in Pleasant Hill." Fernando missed the turn to my house and now he's lost. "Where is your street from here?" His voice sounds breathless and rushed, and his accented words strike me in bursts.

After I give directions to my house, my heart begins to race. I flutter around dusting and discarding clutter, hopping from a pile of old newspapers to a stack of unopened mail like a modern day Henny Penny. He's in town for his annual medical evaluation. We had planned this meeting weeks ago. Why didn't I focus on preparing?

I have many unanswered questions about what Fernando's life was like before the transplant, and I want to know more about how he has been affected by my daughter's heart. I am intensely curious about who he is as a person—and who I am in relation to him. Now it occurs to me that my deeper motive for initiating this meeting was simply to sit next to my daughter's heart for a few hours. Despite the intensity of our bond, I barely know this man. It's Maya I am longing to see.

When I hear a car pull into the driveway, I step out the front door. Flustered and sweaty, he emerges from the tangle of his seat belt, but I notice that his crisp cotton shirt looks as if it has just come off the rack at the dry-cleaners. We embrace, and then I guide him up the steps to my home.

As Fernando is about to enter my modest condominium, it dawns on me that the gap between our two lives is cavernous— he is a wealthy international businessman while I scratched my way into home ownership with my daughter's unused tuition money. Suddenly, the plush surroundings of his home in Santiago arise in my mind's eye with alarming clarity. "Come in," I say, holding the door open for him. "It must be ninety-five degrees out there."

"I don't mind the heat." He stares at the walls of my front room, his eyes flicking over the framed prints and the photographs of my daughters. We walk through my galley kitchen to the dining area. "Please sit down."

He reaches into a canvas satchel and sets a gift box wrapped in tissue paper on the table. "Here, I brought you something. I hope you like it."

At our first meeting, he and Penny had presented me with a beautiful lapis lazuli necklace. The beads were edged in gold, and there was a gold and blue heart at the center.

"Fernando, this is very sweet of you, but you shouldn't have."

"Open it," he says, the same warm smile spreading across his face that I remember from our first meeting.

Fumbling with the paper, I open the box to find a perfectly crafted pottery bell. Terra cotta with a green band at the bottom, it is engraved with the word "Chile." There's also a little matching pitcher. "It's lovely. Thank you so much."

A pleased look spreads across his face. "Tell me about your book," he says.

I tell him that I've drafted a dozen chapters, but that I'm

eager for more information in order to focus the book on the aftereffects of donation.

"When I read your article about Maya it made me cry. You have a way of describing feelings that is so real."

"Thank you." I feel honored—and uncomfortable.

"I'm jealous of your ability," he says, explaining that his family had owned one of the major daily newspapers in Santiago. He began his career there as a reporter. "I didn't have your kind of talent, so I moved over to the business side of the paper."

Scrambling to find a way to put us both more at ease, I suggest that we sit on the couch. It faces a sliding glass door that leads out to a patio and a hillside covered in ivy. It will be pleasant to have some visual distraction. He settles in and turns to me again.

I had asked his permission to tape-record our conversation. Now, I prop my tape recorder on the coffee table and turn my gaze to him.

I am curious about his background and about how he had managed to get a transplant in the United States as a foreign national. He must have had access to the best doctors because he had moved quickly up the list of waiting transplant candidates. By checking statistics from the United Network for Organ Sharing, I had learned that only thirteen non-resident aliens had made it onto the list in 1992, the year of his transplant.

As he describes his family, I struggle to hide my discomfort. They are exceedingly rich and politically conservative. I am horrified to learn that they had supported Augusto Pinochet's violent coup. But I bite my lip and let him continue.

After his father's premature death from heart disease in the late 1960s, Fernando took over the family import/export business, while other family members continued to run the newspaper. He exported fish to North America, and brought motors and other automotive goods into Chile.

He and Penny and their children had lived in the United States for extended periods, both in New England and California. Penny's family was originally from England, and as he tells me about meeting and marrying her, Fernando mentions that he has always been attracted to blond, fair-skinned women. My antennae go up—Maya fits this description perfectly.

When he awoke from the transplant operation, all that he was told about his new heart was that his donor was nineteen years old, that she was female, and that she had been a college student from the Bay Area. As he looks at me, I sense that he is bursting with questions about Maya. Now I realize how important our initial meeting must have been for him, and how difficult. In an effort to put him at ease, I offer him a glass of water.

"Do you have any diet soda?"

"I'm so sorry, I don't have any soda."

"Is there a store nearby?"

He seems set on going to get his favorite brand of soda, so I offer to go with him. I switch off the tape recorder and grab my purse.

He guides the rented car down the hill and into the shopping center parking lot, and our conversation grows more relaxed and natural. He asks about Meghan's feelings regarding the amount of time I spend reliving Maya's life in my book.

"She doesn't say much about it." I'm not entirely sure how Meghan *does* feel about the book. She is always supportive of my writing, but his question implies that I might somehow be unfairly focusing on Maya at Meghan's expense. I have no easy answers to this. Instead, I tell him about taking Meghan to Toronto and about her interest in Latin American culture.

When we get home, I pour two tall glasses of soda and we settle down on the couch again. Fernando tells me about his recovery in the spring and summer of 1992 right after he received Maya's heart. He felt a new energy inside his body that was palpable and very foreign. "It was strange," he remembers, "because I felt this young female inside me, and I kept trying to imagine who she was." He fumbles with his glass, then continues.

To solve the riddle of this feminine presence, he made up an identity for his anonymous donor. He called her "Lolita," which translates from Spanish to English as a vivacious young woman.

When he first says the word "Lolita," I recoil. He immediately says, "No, no," and explains that this way of using the term Lolita means something entirely different from the sexually precocious heroine of Nabokov's novel. "Maya's heart became my Lolita," he insists. Increasingly ill at ease, I shift my body back into the sofa. This is my daughter he is talking about.

"I knew the sex, the age, but I did not know her name, so that's why I just gave her a name," he offers. "Then something began to change in me in the sense of... some relationship there, as strange as it sounds. I have talked with my wife about it. I got scared sometimes."

His voice trails off. I stare out the sliding glass door, losing myself in the glossy shapes of the ivy leaves. I've heard of transplant recipients undergoing mysterious personality changes. They crave food they have never liked before. Sometimes they become obsessive about activities that had never interested them prior to their transplants.

But this? I don't know what to say to him.

"The Lolita inside of me is so *real*," he says, clearly torn by this complex riddle.

I am equally confused. Proud of my daughter's vitality, I also feel sorry for Fernando as I try to imagine what it must feel like to receive a new heart. Now, after years of debilitating illness, he has a healthy heart, but it is not entirely his. Within a year after his transplant, Fernando says, he could ski and play tennis, activities he couldn't do for more than a decade. Then, when we met last Memorial Day and I showed him Maya's picture, his Lolita suddenly had a name, a face, and a family.

"I hid my sentiments a lot," he confesses. I ask why. He hesitates for a moment and his brow contracts.

"If you put a photograph of Maya and a photograph of my wife when she was eighteen side by side, they are very similar. Why? I cried so much after our meeting."

I am awestruck. It is almost as if he were in love with Maya. He owes his life to her, and he knows a part of her intimately, but he doesn't really know *her*. He gives me a pleading look and I feel as if my heart will break. I know now that I have to write the book for Fernando—he needs this story almost more than I do. It's the only way for him to learn more about Maya because there is no way I can tell him everything now. Besides, sitting face to face with him I am getting drawn in by his emotional conflicts, and I am in danger of losing touch with my own feelings. Writing the story down is the only way for me to preserve my daughter on my own terms.

"Did you talk to anyone besides Penny about this?" My voice is barely louder than a whisper. Suddenly, I feel like a voyeur.

"Oh yes," he says, "but they couldn't understand." He waves his arm as if he were swatting a mosquito. "They told me this feeling of being overtaken by a new soul showed why you shouldn't donate organs."

"That must have been so hard for you..."

In a deeply Catholic culture like Chile's, where the resurrection of the dead and the reconstitution of their mortal forms are very real for believers, some people thought that what he had done was morally suspect. This only caused him to seek more deeply for answers within himself.

"There is a prayer that says, 'Love God, Our Lord with all your strength, with all your heart, and with all your soul.' Except to complete it you need a soul. The soul in Spanish is *alma*. *Alma* is physical. It shook me a lot because I thought of it almost as an invasion of Maya's soul in my body." He pauses and lowers his voice. "Sometimes as I go to sleep, I actually tuck her inside of me."

I suppress a gasp. I do this too, but he actually has a physical piece of her. A pang of envy shoots through me. We stare at each other, and our silence hangs in the air. It almost seems that Fernando and I must learn to share Maya. I am her mother, but I lost her. Now he has her. This riddle will vex me for a very long time.

I try to imagine how difficult it would be to have someone else's heart beating in your chest. No wonder he often seems confused. Perhaps it's partly due to the medication he has to take, but it must also be because of the complexities of carrying the cellular intelligence of another being in his chest. I am learning more about transplantation on this July afternoon than I had bargained for.

"Wow, Fernando, that must be really difficult for you." I'm searching for a way to connect with him.

He smiles, and his lips form a little half-moon.

"You are a courageous person," he says. "I wonder what I would do if I had to make the decision you did..."

"Hopefully, you never will." I fumble with the hem of my skirt.

He says he must get back to his friends on the Peninsula and asks directions to the freeway. I clear away our glasses and then walk to the car with him, pointing the way down the hill, giving him landmarks and street names. We embrace. "Write to me," he says.

"I will," I promise.

The car glides away, carrying Maya's heart and its new home. I still want my daughter back. But I also want Fernando alive. Our connection as donor mother and heart recipient hinges on resurrection, and we both know that is gray territory.

Perhaps Maya is becoming more real for Fernando than she is for me. He depends on her heart for his every bodily function. Without Maya's physical presence, all I now possess of her is in my memory. I can no longer hear the sound of her voice, or remember her scent with precision. I'm terrified of losing my daughter at an even deeper level than the physical. What if she continues to fade from my mind? I root myself in a vow that this will never happen. Then I turn and walk back into my empty house.

Chapter 26

The his time, Fernando's call is completely unexpected. He phones my office and invites me to dinner. "I am eager to see you," he says. "I have good news."

We agree to meet at a San Francisco restaurant near my office. It's early August of 1996, and he's again being evaluated at the UCSF Medical Center. I set down the phone and stare out my office window at the San Francisco Bay Bridge. It drapes across the water, held in place by scallops of steel suspension. Little toy cars snake across.

I wonder if I am really strong enough for this.

I turn back to my desk, straighten the papers, and grab my coat. In the elevator I panic, imagining awkward gaps in our conversation. The slick granite floors of the lobby echo with each footfall. I make my way into the Galleria, a pedestrian mall filled with expensive boutiques. There, I take an escalator to the restaurant.

"I'm meeting someone," I tell the maître d', attempting to describe Fernando. "Your party is already seated." He leads me to a corner table. My friend rises to greet me, his face beaming.

"It is so good to see you, Eleanor. How are you?"

"Well, Fernando. Busy, as always, but very well."

"And your daughter?"

"Meghan is growing up—she just turned sixteen."

"Ah, sweet sixteen, that is the expression, isn't it?"

I nod at this vigorous and seemingly healthy man, his tanned face serene, his eyes untroubled. He tells me his good news. Tests of his heart tissue still show no episodes of rejection; he is the first of more than seventy-five heart recipients at UCSF never to have rejected a donor heart, he says proudly, as if he has just received a perfect grade on an important test paper. The doctors have reduced his immunosuppressant medication to the lowest possible dose.

He's been spending the Chilean winter in Delaware where he maintains an office to consult with clients on their financial affairs; he gave up the import/export business after his operation. For relaxation he visits his condominium on Florida's Sanibel Island, where he plays tennis.

As he describes this to me, I glance up at the noisy cocktail hour drinkers at the bar, annoyed that I must struggle to make out his heavily accented words. I redouble my efforts to concentrate. All at once, he leans over his bread plate. His voice fills with urgency as he tells me about his sixteen-year-old son. Chris is drinking too much, experimenting with drugs, and has been expelled from school, he says with rapid-fire words and gestures. Fernando's hands begin to tremble as he speaks.

"Penny was supposed to call me today with the results of his drug test, but she hasn't called..." his voice trails off.

I study Fernando's face. What I see there is a mixture of anger, fear, and guilt—the emotions I remember from my difficult days with Maya. They are all too familiar.

"If he wants to throw his life away, I can't stop him," he is saying.

No, you must stop him any way you can! I want to shout them, but the words stick in my throat. I push my fork away, trying to find the best way to respond. "Does Christopher realize that you are alive today because my daughter threw her life away? Because she was careless, a little drunk... Does he realize that?"

Fernando shakes his head. "He knows nothing... he doesn't think..."

Then he brings two white tablets to his mouth and gulps them down with a goblet of water.

"Part of the problem may be too much time—and money," I offer.

Fernando waves his hand in front of his face. "Money, no. I'll cut him off!"

"Yes, but his friends have money, and there's so much peer pressure."

He looks pale and his hands begin to tremble violently. I sense that his agitation is rooted in more than concern for his son. It has become physical.

"You don't look well... are you okay?" I try to stay calm.

"No! I'm feeling much worse." He glances nervously around the room, then puts his hand to his heart, pressing against the black fabric of his shirt. My own heart pounds. *What if Fernando is having a heart attack?*

In slow motion I rise and tell Fernando that I am going to call a taxi. We must get to the hospital. As I walk toward the bar the salmon-colored plaster walls seem to enclose the space too tightly. The vases with their large, elaborate cut flowers seem elephantine and out of place.

"My friend is ill. Can you please call a cab?" The bartender picks up the phone.

Within moments we are on the corner of Sutter and Kearny Streets, shivering as the wind flattens Fernando's pant legs.

Deserted office buildings loom above us, blocking the sky. The moments seem to lengthen, just as they had while I waited for Maya to come out of brain surgery four years ago.

When the cab arrives, Fernando gives the driver the address of the UCSF Medical Center. We climb in. Union Square, Civic Center, the Opera House pass in a blur. We sit shoulder to shoulder in the back seat holding hands. "Quickly," I urge the driver. "This is an emergency!"

"Maya won't let me down!" Fernando's hoarse words hang in the air between us. Beads of sweat appear on his forehead and his entire body shakes. He presses my hand to his chest. Through the fabric of his shirt, the wild beats of my daughter's heart fire the nerve endings in my skin. I cannot bear the thought that Maya's heart might stop beating. It would be a second and even more dreadful death to lose Fernando and this remnant of my daughter at the same moment.

The taxi speeds up Stanyan Street to Parnassus, and careens into the entrance of the UCSF emergency room. I pray with obsessive focus. "Please keep Fernando alive." Then out of nowhere a new sense of detachment descends, as if in answer to my prayer. For the first time I understand at a gut level that it is not *her* anymore. These tissues, these cells, are Fernando's now. His biochemical reactions are orchestrating this discordant symphony.

When we go in, they immediately bring a gurney and rush Fernando into an examining room. I sign in, bearing down on a triplicate form with a ballpoint pen, answering the clerk's questions, then presenting the insurance card Fernando presses into my hand. My fingers still tingle from his grip. Below the line where I sign my name, the clerk has typed, "Wife."

Let them think we are family, because in so many ways, we are.

The clerk points to a waiting room. Gray, sterile, linoleum

tiled, with the usual regulation television bolted to a corner of the wall, it yawns open before me. I yearn to be somewhere else. This barren place reverberates with memories of Maya's accident.

As vividly as if it were a scene in a movie, I see Maya and me out on our front patio when she learned about her acceptance at UCLA, that one pure moment on the night before her accident. I had gone to buy cake for the celebration, leaving the banner "UCLA SAYS YES" taped to the bookshelf. When I returned, Maya was home. She greeted me at the door with a big grin. Our eyes met and then she leaped through the doorway and threw her arms around my shoulders. We clung together, jumping up and down, screaming. Arm in arm, we went inside, Maya's rapid-fire exclamations ringing in my ears. "I can't believe this! Mommy, Mommy! Oh my God!" We cut huge hunks from the chocolate cake, licking icing from our fingers.

When I recall this joy, I see myself as if I were a child. I was so happy for Maya. So confident about the future. Still so naive. For Meghan and me this was the last moment of innocence. After years of believing that enough inner work could repair any wound, I now understand that some things cannot be fixed.

The waiting room smells of stale coffee and disinfectant. Some primitive center in my brain recognizes danger in the sound of clanking gurneys, the whoosh of elevator doors, the shuffling of sterile coverings on doctors' and nurses' feet.

In the far corner of the room there are a few straight-backed chairs. I sit and begin mindlessly thumbing through magazines, pondering the irony of it all. It is the dinner hour, and I am quite alone. Is this some kind of weird synchronous cosmic joke? Four years ago when I was called to the John Muir Medical Center it was also a Thursday evening at dinnertime.

A new set of questions begins gnawing at the edges of my consciousness. I see how vulnerable and bound to Fernando I am. What kind of an attachment is this, exactly? Am I just hanging on to Maya through Fernando, prolonging my grief by trying to experience her as if she were still partly alive? Is this why more donors and recipients don't become friends? Only ten percent of donor families ever meet the recipients of their loved ones' gifts. Why?

My thoughts are interrupted when a nurse comes in to let me know I can see Fernando. Suddenly bone tired, I walk down a long corridor. A doctor meets me outside of the examining room. "We understand that you have a pretty special relationship to this patient," he says.

I shoot him a doubtful look and he quickly continues.

"You'll be glad to know that he is fine. His heart is perfectly normal. He forgot to take his tranquilizer and he had an anxiety attack."

The knot at the back of my neck softens. When I enter the room, Fernando smiles at me in his beatific way. We clasp hands.

"I am so embarrassed," he says. "It was stupid and careless of me to forget my pill. I'm sorry."

I wave his apology away.

"No," he insists, "I ruined your evening and I want to make it up to you."

His statement is so far removed from my level of grief and confusion that I fumble for words. Every time Fernando looks at me he is reminded of his new life. But when I look at him, loss stabs me again and I have to fight to acknowledge and celebrate his reality. When I am with him, my heart seesaws between joy and grief.

"You didn't ruin my evening." This is my weak attempt to spare him the embarrassment. "I'm just glad that you're okay."

When Fernando grips my hand, I squeeze his fingers in mine. I would have given anything for Maya to squeeze my hand like this, just once, in all those hours while she was in intensive care. Just to see a flicker of life on her face, any little sign that she could hear me whispering to her.

Fernando and I continue talking until we are calm enough to say good-bye. Back in the lobby, I phone a cab and then stand alone in the entrance to the emergency room. I don't cry, although the return journey by taxi, and then BART, and then car from the train station to home—almost two hours—affords ample opportunity.

The kickback comes the next night. I feel shaky and weak, and then my vision blurs. The signs of migraine are unmistakable. Once the vomiting begins, I know I have to get help. Carol has been a warm and supportive friend, and when she hears how ill I am, she immediately agrees to drive me to the hospital. The John Muir Medical Center is a place I would do almost anything to avoid. It is here that my daughter's life ended, and now I find myself in a curtained cubicle only steps away from where the trauma team frantically tried to resuscitate her.

Carol holds my hand as we wait for a doctor, and her warm fingers help ease my trembling. When the drugs they give me take hold and the nausea finally ebbs, I look up at my friend and realize that I have been asking way too much of myself. I can no longer stand next to the man with my daughter's heart beating in his chest and comfort him, when I am the one whose heart is breaking.

"You've been so brave," Carol says. "We all admire you for going on without Maya. But you don't have to be brave forever. Now you can do it differently."

I soak in my friend's permission to be my true self—a wildly grief-stricken mother. Four years after my daughter's death, I let myself fall apart again. In the months to come, the grief is more powerful because this time I will agree that it can win. This time, I will let the undertow of loss take me where it wants to go.

Chapter 27

Crouched in the closet of the room I shared with my sister, I drew my knees up in a ball and rocked back and forth. My father had hit me so hard that he left bright red handprints on my bare flesh. Cowering in the dark, I spun elaborate fantasies to transcend this humiliation, longing to emerge from hiding as a different girl, lovable and whole.

"I really thought what happened in my family could never touch my kids," I tell Lou Ann. Moving to the opposite end of the country where my daughters were safely insulated from people and scenes from my childhood always seemed like good camouflage. Now, it appears I brought the past with me.

"All these years I believed it would be different for them."

"It *was* different for them—you broke the cycle of abuse," she says. "But Maya's death is inviting you to resolve what happened to you at an even deeper level."

What frightens me even more than my childhood memories are the new associations I make between my experiences as a young woman and Maya's accident. After two years of therapy with Lou Ann, I've reached the scariest point—looking back at my life when I was Maya's age, a troubled college student.

✿ ✿ ✿

Jake was an adjunct professor who taught the urban studies seminar I enrolled in for my final academic term. It was 1970 and the Black Power movement was at its height. He wore brightly colored dashikis and lectured from personal experience about the urban renewal program he ran in Cleveland. Handsome, charismatic, and articulate, a man much like my father, he never mentioned that he had a wife and two children when we began dating.

One night after we had been together for several months, we were driving on the freeway when a car pulled level with us and the white driver and his passenger began shouting racial epithets through the open window. Jake reached in the glove box, pulled out a pistol, and aimed it at the driver. The car sped away. I couldn't figure out if I was more terrified by the fierce hatred in the eyes of those strangers, or by the fact that my lover carried a concealed weapon wherever he went.

After I had graduated and moved home, I often spent weekends with Jake at his apartment in a large suburban complex about a half-hour's drive from my grandmother's. His wife had recently moved in with her boyfriend, taking the kids with her.

I did not lie to my mother about my whereabouts. On some level I was proud of defying the race taboo, and I knew that she knew I was having sex, so there was no point in deception. One weekend, out of the blue, an ex-boyfriend phoned my grandmother's asking to speak to me because his father had died, and he needed someone to talk to. My mother gave him Jake's phone number.

He picked up the call and handed me the receiver with a strange look in his eyes. I overrode his signals and spoke to my grieving ex-boyfriend.

After I hung up the phone twenty minutes later, Jake called me into the bedroom. "Come here, baby," he crooned. When I stood in front of him, he put his hands around my waist and I let myself be drawn close to his body. With athletic swiftness he grabbed me and stood in one motion, cocked his arm, and back-handed my face with his fist. I flew into the corner next to the dresser and hit my head against the wall. "Bitch, don't you *ever* talk to another man when you're with me."

"I'm sorry, I'm sorry." I was cowering. He was right in front of me yelling into my face.

"I'll kill you," he shouted. "You hear me?"

He gripped my arm and dragged me across the room. When he reached the bedroom door, he slammed it shut and locked it.

"We are going to have a little heart to heart talk," he hissed.

He grabbed my hair and yanked my head back, dragging me toward the bed. My hair was long and thick, tangled in his fist. I could not break free.

"Don't hit me," I begged. He began to shake me.

"Shut up, you lying bitch." My head snapped back and forth until I thought my neck would break. Just as suddenly as he had begun, he stopped. The window air conditioner hummed in the background.

"Jake," I said, "look at me." He stared into my eyes. His were glassy and vacant. I realized then that the odds of my coming out of that bedroom alive depended entirely on my ability to break through his trance.

I began to talk to him very softly, very slowly. I wasn't even aware of what I was saying but I knew that I needed to keep making contact. Finally, he looked up and I could tell that this time he actually *saw* me. By then my eye was swelling shut.

"My God, what have I done?" He covered his face with his

hands, then abruptly stared at me again. "You stay here," he instructed, and started for the door.

I did not want to be locked in that room. I followed him out to the kitchen, and he didn't try to stop me. He removed a handful of ice cubes from the freezer, wrapped the ice in a clean dishtowel, and told me to put it on my eye.

I begged him to take me home. I was so desperate to break free of him that I considered jumping from his second story balcony. Finally, a friend of his buzzed him from the entrance of the building, and I saw my chance. Jake wouldn't let him come up, but I knew that if this man heard my voice there would be a witness, so I spoke to him over the intercom.

Jake yanked me away from the speaker. But half an hour later, he agreed to take me home. He dropped me at the door and drove away.

Mom asked few questions about what had happened to me. I could not believe she had given out the number, thereby setting up a beating. Didn't she realize how jealous guys were of other guys? She snapped at me when I asked why she had done it. "Because he asked for it," she said.

Confused and angry, I sensed that there was a thread in this tangle that led back to my father. Somehow I had become a lightning rod standing between my parents. My role was to take the hits, and my mother knew how to set them up.

Jake kept phoning me, but whenever Mom or Grandma picked up the phone he would hang up. One night I answered. He asked me what I was doing, and I mentioned that I had an appointment for a job interview with a well-known public relations firm in the city, but I did not tell him when I would be there. It didn't occur to me until too late that with his connections—and his charm—he could easily find out.

At the interview, the black businessman who owned the firm

sized up my sunglasses and fading bruises. Frightened and inexperienced, I thought I had to tell this stranger the truth when he
began quizzing me. When I described what had happened, he
laughed. "You white girls are all the same—you always go for
the animals."

His secretary buzzed him, interrupting him in mid-sentence.
"A Mr. Robertson is here for Miss Vincent," she said. I froze.

The man raised his eyebrows. "Is that him?"

"Yes," I nodded, sitting rigidly in my chair. "He's going to kill
me."

The man brushed the lapel of his expensive suit. He leaned
back in his chair and studied me. "The brother is not going to
kill you. This is a game. Don't you get it?"

When I returned to the waiting room, Jake put his arm
around me and forcibly walked me out of the office. Never
relaxing his grip, he escorted me to his car, opened the door, and
shoved me into the passenger seat. With every fiber of my being,
I was determined to convince him to take me home.

It was late afternoon and many people saw us leaving the
office, so when I insisted that we go straight to my grandmother's house, Jake agreed. But once we arrived, he refused to leave
until I promised to go out with him again. We argued for an
hour on my grandmother's porch facing Lake Erie. Like a broken record I repeated over and over that I did not want to see
him ever again. But he kept at me.

Numb with exhaustion, I was completely unprepared for the
coup de grace. My mother came out to the porch, entered the
discussion, and urged me to give him another chance. "You can't
just cut him off like this, Ellie," she said.

He looked at me triumphantly. I felt completely bulldozed,
ashamed, and confused. I agreed to see him one last time. Mom
had tipped the scales just enough.

She was so scrupulous in her attempt to be fair, in her willingness to sacrifice me to some concept of justice she carried in her head, so blind to the consequences of what she was doing. As her oldest child, I had tried to do the impossible—protect myself and my siblings from my father, and prop her up, force her to respond, make her be a fully functioning mother. I would show her how to do it and then surely my mother would love and protect me. What I had believed at age three still ruled my imagination.

On the night of our date, I told my mother to call the police if I had not returned by eleven o'clock. Shaking, I left the house. We went to a movie and afterwards Jake invited me back to his place. I declined, insisting that he take me home. Instead he drove to his apartment complex, fifteen miles from the movie theater. By the time we got there, my hands and feet felt like ice, and I was barely breathing.

He pulled the car into the covered parking structure. When he cut the engine, he turned to me and smiled. "I want to make love to you one last time," he said.

A chill ran up my spine. If I went into his apartment I knew that I would be beaten, certainly raped, and then possibly killed. At that moment, I felt a conviction beyond anything I had ever known that I would never again let a man hit me. I had to confront him now and take the consequences rather than risk being trapped and humiliated in secret. I knew from my experience as a child that capitulation was only a temporary out, and that home was the most dangerous place to be.

"No," I said. "I'm not going in."

He got out of the car and walked to the passenger side. When he tried to lift me out, I flopped from side to side like a rag doll. It was a little after nine o'clock on a balmy Friday evening and there were people coming and going in the complex. His behavior was too obvious. He got back in the driver's seat and took his gun from the glove box. He rested it on his lap and began driving slowly around the complex, threatening to kill me if I did not have sex with him.

He drove to the far end of the complex and parked the car next to a pond where we had often gone to feed the birds on sunny afternoons. "I want you to look at the ducks one last time," he said. As we sat in silence staring at the pond, I remembered the PR man's words. This was a game, and the person pulling the strings offered only two choices—forcible sex or death. Like a cat toying with its prey, he was trying to buy time and compliance. "Come with me, baby," he cajoled. I shook my head from side to side.

He removed a bullet from the chamber, clicked it in place, and spun it around. In that instant, my thoughts slowed. The clicking of the gun barrel reminded me of the sound clothespinned playing cards used to make on my bike wheel when I was a kid. Sensuous and distinct. He put the gun to my left temple, softly coaxing. I could save my life if I would have sex with him, he promised.

"You will have to shoot me," I replied, "because I am not going in with you."

He steadied the gun against my head. The words *I am going home now* flowed through my brain, and peace flooded my entire being. Then my thoughts turned to my mother. Always her protector and her helper, I did not want her to see me with my head blown off.

He pulled the trigger. The gun barrel made an empty click. The PR man had been right, and I understood then that Jake was not going to kill me. It *was* a game. To survive it and win I had to play my part to the end.

He put the gun back in the glove box and shut it with a sharp crack that echoed as if he had just closed the door to a vault. Then he maneuvered the car back to his parking space. Again, he tried to lift me out. Again, I went limp. After he got back in the car, he turned to me in a rage and put both hands around my neck. He squeezed down on my windpipe. As I lost oxygen, I drifted into the calm place again. Blue and white rings floated behind my closed eyes. Suddenly, the pressure of his hands on my neck released. I heard sobs. At first, I thought they were mine. But then I saw he had put his head down on the steering wheel and was weeping into his hands.

"What am I doing? What am I doing?" he spoke into the air.

I sensed that I could not break out of being his victim too abruptly or he might snap again. I began feeling the upholstered ceiling of the car, then touching the seats and the inside door, mumbling nonsense words. I babbled partly as a ploy to frighten him and partly out of crazed relief, letting myself come undone.

He stared at me. "What's the matter with you?" I smiled and mumbled as I ran my hands over the dashboard. By now he was trembling and I knew my ruse was working.

For the thirty minutes it took to drive home, I never stopped babbling. When we arrived in my grandmother's driveway, I did the most counterintuitive thing I could think of. When Jake reached my side of the car, I pushed the lock button on the passenger door. He stood there bewildered, pleading with me to open it, so focused on me that he did not hear the front door open behind him. My mother came out on the porch and descended the stairs. She saw me babbling in the car.

"What's the matter with her?" she asked him.

"I don't know," he lied. "She just started acting really strange."

My mother called my name. "Unlock the door," she commanded.

I stared at her blankly. "Ellie, unlock this door right now."

At last, I lifted the button and the door swung open. Mom helped me up the porch steps and into the house. Jake drove away.

I went straight up the stairs to my room and collapsed into a chair by my bed, shivering with fear and exhaustion. When Mom came upstairs I told her the entire story, so frozen that I could not cry, although I wanted to. When I had finished, she looked at me and said, "Well, now you have something to write about."

Her words made no sense to me, as if I had just come home from some sort of madcap adventure, not an attempt on my life. Was she implying that only beatings and near-death experiences were worth writing about? Or, as she had when I was a child, was she telling me, "You made your bed, now lie in it?" Did she really believe I deserved this? She stood up, said goodnight, and left the room.

As a child hiding in my closet, I used to dream that somehow Mom would stand up and defend me, that she loved me. The odd thing is, I knew she did love me, but at the same time she set me up—first and foremost, with my father, pretending she didn't see the beatings or the violent games, or hear the shouted insults. Then she repeated the pattern with Jake. How much more evidence did I need that my mother was never going to acknowledge that I was being abused and step in to protect me?

Years later, shivering on a couch in Lou Ann's office as I relived these scenes, I began to believe that my mother suffered from such profound despair that she was like the woman who drove her kids off a pier into the lake. She couldn't kill herself, but she was driven to the closest alternative—sacrifice a daughter.

I didn't get the job at the PR firm. Instead, I became a docent at the Cleveland Museum of Art where I led school classes on tours of the collection.

"Dear Miss Vincent," their thank you letters always began, "I really enjoyed the Egyptian mummies you showed us..." I saved the blocky penciled words on lined school paper as evidence that I made a difference to someone.

Mom, Grandma, and I rattled around in the house that autumn. By then, just walking in front of a darkened window in my own bedroom provoked panic attacks. Jake still phoned the house. Sometimes I thought I saw him cruising our street late at night. I knew I had to find a way out, but I was paralyzed by anxiety.

I sought help from a therapist who was an intern in a residency program at University Hospital and took patients on a sliding scale. She asked a lot of questions about my abusive relationship and about my family background. Over the months I saw her, she helped me make a plan.

"If you establish an independent life you can turn this around," she urged. "Maybe your parents will help you."

Just asking my father for money to buy schoolbooks led to shouting matches, or worse, so I had paid my college tuition with scholarship money and loans. My mother was directing community theater for no pay. Asking for help was out of the question.

By making my mother swear never to divulge my whereabouts, I was able to disappear to the relative safety of an upstate Michigan college. In June of 1971 I enrolled in a summer teacher-training program where I made a friend who was from Minnesota. After we completed the program, she invited me to come home with her. I knew I could never go back to Ohio, and I had nowhere else to go, so I agreed. Her parents loaned me money to buy a used car and gave me enough kitchen and bathroom supplies to set up housekeeping in my own apartment in Minneapolis. At twenty-three, I started my life over in a strange city, just as the therapist and I had planned.

Six months later, I quit the teaching job I had found and returned to school to study journalism, working at two waitress jobs to support myself. By day, I served lunches to businessmen in polyester suits who bantered with me and left me generous tips. At night, I carried mixed drinks to patrons watching *Jesus Christ Superstar* in a cabaret theater. It was there that I met Jeff, my husband to be.

I left home in fear for my life, walking straight into another shaky relationship and a classic way out, an unplanned pregnancy. Motherhood offered me a chance to forge bonds I had missed as a child. I could have had an abortion, but I had already experienced too much loss in my young life. I wanted this baby.

When Maya was born, joy welled up in me. And cocky self-confidence. Year by year I moved farther away from that young woman who made a vow never again to be a victim. I forgot about her. I submerged her in work and achievement. I had another baby. The men I married were never physically violent, and that felt like progress.

Like Houdini, I thought I could break free from any trap. The past was only a construct, and I had wriggled out from most of its ill effects. Until my daughter was killed. Then my history crashed around me, pulling me into a rip current of delayed grief and guilt. I flailed and cursed, prayed and wept, until the stark truth stood up and demanded I take notice—*I was the one who should have died, not Maya*. She was only out having fun on a spring afternoon; I had had a gun to my head. She was just playing, while I was literally courting my own destruction, aided and abetted by my mother.

I wanted my daughter to grow up and become the Wonder Woman we played at being as we glided with make-believe capes through our apartment in Minneapolis. In my mind, she could be shaped into an all-powerful girl who would never be harmed, always in total control, the polar opposite of the girl I had been. With the best of intentions I had pushed Maya to be fearless and self-confident, but had I unwittingly set her up for what happened in the field on that April afternoon?

The blow to her head that killed Maya was a random accident. But to my guilt-ridden psyche it seemed that it had somehow materialized out of the death I had evaded. Along with my brown eyes and sharp tongue, Maya had inherited far more from me than I had intended. The undertow of my past swept her away.

Or maybe this was just a phantom rising from the fog of grief, and my determination to die rather than live as a victim had lifted me and my daughters into some feminist heaven I simply could no longer believe in.

I had changed from the child who hid among her own skirts and blouses into a defiant young woman who stood up to power, but at a price. I ran away to save myself, and in the process put two thousand miles between my family and me. I attempted to create a zone of safety for my children that I never had. Now, I can ask, what did I wall out? What price did we all pay for the safety of the virtual closet I built for us?

Chapter 28

Fernando telephones from Santiago to invite me to travel to Chile for the Christmas holidays at his expense. "Please come! And bring your daughter with you. I would love to show you my country."

Clutching the portable phone to my ear, I pace the length of my narrow kitchen. It is mid-October of 1996, but our frenetic taxi ride to the emergency room in August is still fresh in my mind.

He insists that we come for two weeks and describes the many sights that he will show us, including La Serena, a beach town on the northern coast where he owns a vacation home. I don't want to lose contact with him or my daughter's heart, but his overwhelming gratitude and our class and cultural differences are unnerving. When I try to express my reservations, he begins to cajole.

"But you *must* accept. Wouldn't Meghan enjoy seeing Santiago?"

"Yes, I'm sure she would. But Christmas is still so difficult for me... it would be best if I didn't." It's one thing to spend an hour or two in his company, but to be under his roof for two weeks?

"Eleanor, are you sure?" He pronounces each syllable of my name, trilling the "r" at the end. It's impossible to make him understand how difficult it is for me to balance Maya's death with his life, but in the end we make a bargain. I will ask Meghan if she wants to go without me, as long as she can bring a friend with her. I promise to phone him back shortly with an answer.

Later, I explain to Meghan why I don't want to go, warning that if she decides to make the trip she will face the complexity of being not quite a family member but more than a houseguest.

I ask her if she is prepared to handle the feelings that will surface.

She acknowledges that it might be difficult, but she is unmoved by my concerns. "I want to see Chile and meet Fernando. I'll be okay, Mom. This is the chance of a lifetime. Please let me go."

I tell her that I want to talk it over with her father. "I know Dad will let me go, Mom," she says.

In another phone conversation, Dan listens to my concerns but agrees with Meghan that this is an offer she should not refuse. I phone Fernando back to confirm that Meghan and her friend Sarah want to make the trip. "Good," he says, "they won't be disappointed."

Ten days later, two airline tickets arrive in an express mail envelope. Penny faxes me details about what Meghan should bring and outlines the family's sightseeing plans. Dan and I work with the Chilean consulate in San Francisco to sign the necessary documents that will permit our minor daughter to travel to Chile for two weeks. Meghan and I go together to have her passport photos taken.

We take out the atlas and run our fingers over the narrow rib of land where she is going. If she is apprehensive, Meghan doesn't show it. As the time draws nearer, I begin to awaken hours before dawn with a pounding heart. Chile is so far away, and she is only sixteen—why did I ever suggest this trip to her? My every instinct is to protect her, yet I don't want to smother her. Supporting her growing independence and sense of adventure costs me sleep and peace of mind, but I rationalize the tradeoff by thinking of how wonderful this will be for Meghan.

On the morning of her departure on December 26, I hold her close. "Call me the moment you get there."

"I will, Mom. Don't worry about me!"

The following afternoon, I grab the phone before it can ring for a second time. Meghan's voice instantly reassures me. Yes, she is fine. Yes, she is settling in.

"The city is beautiful," she says.

"What's the house like?"

"Big. It's up on a hill. It has a swimming pool and a great view of Santiago." Her voice is tinny and hollow, as if she were in a tunnel. "They have two maids. They *live* here in their own quarters."

"Wow."

"Well, Mom, I better go. I'll send you some postcards."

"Tell Fernando and Penny hello from me. Have a great time, sweetheart."

I set the phone back in its cradle. She is really half a world away and there is nothing I can do to change that now.

The days pass slowly without Meghan in the house. Again, a wave of grief pulls me under as I imagine her with Fernando and his family. I wrap myself in Maya's old comforter and lie down on my couch. My survival kit is nearby—a box of tissue on the coffee table and plenty of bottled water for rehydration after crying spells.

I gaze out at the back patio where ivy trails over the fence in shiny ribbons. The oleander bushes are still green, their buds wrapped in tight little fists that will burst into Technicolor pink blossoms in the spring. Above the patio, a tall pine rains down needles each time the wind blows. I should sweep them up, but I don't move; simply watching the undulating branches captures and holds my attention. The natural world gleams effortlessly, more beautiful to me than ever before. Fragile and transient, it caresses my senses. Every shimmering leaf is an answer to a prayer I have yet to formulate.

The tears feel good and they don't last long. I wipe them away, take a swallow of water, and then go to the kitchen to get something to eat. Afterward I unplug the phone so that I can read in peace and write in my journal, filling the lined pages with memories of the girl Lou Ann and I have uncovered, giving her a safe place in the pool of sunlight that falls on my living room floor. Sleeping on my sofa, I dream of that other Eleanor.

Sunday arrives in a lazy haze of newspaper pages. A Beethoven sonata anchors my floating mind to its cascade of notes.

Late that morning, I dress and leave home for services at the Unity Center of Walnut Creek, only a five-minute drive from my house. It will save gas and time, I reason, but really it has become too painful for me to spend time at my old church. Maya's memorial service and those early months of frozen grieving hang in the sanctuary at First Church. There, every sound and sight triggers my longing for her.

Today there is a guest speaker, a Unity minister from Alabama named Edwene Gaines. She has big hair and a sonorous southern drawl. Dressed in a colorful Hawaiian muumuu, she steps away from the podium and speaks into her lavaliere microphone. "Dontcha just feel like God is messin' with ya sometimes?"

She regales us with stories to illustrate her point. The time she traveled to London for a speaking engagement but couldn't get her hot rollers to work on British electricity and had to go out looking like a fright. Her experience of being slathered with mud at a Mexican spa and then escorted outside to be rinsed off by the attendant in full view of the other spa guests. She even mines her failed marriages for laughs. "My friends say, 'Poor Edwene. Always a bride, never a bridesmaid.'"

Beneath the humor I latch on to the deeper truths about my old nemesis, control, and about learning to let go. When she talks about her brother's death, the laughter subsides. She describes how she sat by his bed in the hospital and listened to him for hours. A Bible-thumping Christian at odds with the New Thought philosophy his sister embraced, he told her all the ways he thought he had failed, confessing his sins.

"I didn't try to convince him that they were really 'learning experiences.'" She holds up her fingers to make quote marks in the air. "I just let him keep talking." By the time he passed he was peaceful, emptying out his secrets to a sister who could hold them without judgment or alarm.

A willingness to forgive and an ability to surrender to a higher power are key, she says. After four years of mourning, this message rings true for me. I have learned a few home truths and one of them is not to take disaster personally. I've finally figured out that Maya's death, ultimately, was not about me—it was an accident. The same combination of poor judgment and bad luck could make it happen to anyone.

Laughter opens a space in my grief. Through that small window I see that I am getting better; ever so slowly I am thinking about Maya's death in a new way. Even though it often feels like a devastating calamity, I can now see that, in reality, it is just a part of life. Apparently cruel and random tragedies happen by the thousands every day. No one is immune. I thought my love would protect *my* child. I was wrong. Death happens. It happens to children. It doesn't take into account how good you are, or how hard you've worked, or how much you loved the lost ones.

Maya's death shattered my precious illusion of control. It broke my China figurine ego and my hard-won sense of safety into a million pieces. Under the hurt and devastation, anger roiled. I thought God had made a dreadful mistake, and I yelled and screamed about the injustice of Maya's death for months. Once that intensity diminished, I still held a grudge against life for something that seemed so unfair.

I had been groping for an answer to the "Why?" ever since Maya's accident. The God I had encountered just days after her birth definitely seemed to be "messin' with me," as Rev. Gaines had said. Maybe I would be less hurt and angry if I let go of my insistence on ultimate justice. Could I actually release my grip on the illusion of control, and if I did, who would I be?

As I sip a cup of coffee on the patio after the service, I realize that Maya's death belongs to *her*. It isn't a punishment directed at me, even when the pain feels very punishing indeed. My destiny and my daughter's are separate. She is her own person. We hadn't finished letting go of each other in life—she was yanked away—so now there is no other sane choice than to finish the process on my own. Finally, I am willing to let Maya have her own life and her own death.

Sun streams down on the patio behind the center. Several people I have met at previous services greet me and we exchange pleasantries. But I am bursting with my sudden epiphany.

When I get home, I immediately sit down at the computer to write.

> God is a probability specialist constantly shuffling multiple alternate realities. There are an infinite number of possibilities for the outcome of any given event. Every outcome depends on human choice because we have free will. We move our little piece of the vast kaleidoscope and the many-colored pieces shift, the probabilities meet and collide, and infinite intelligence learns more about itself. Its drive to experience itself completely is beyond any ego-based human concept. We finite beings may label the outcome "good" or "bad" but we never see the beauty and harmony of the entire kaleidoscope—only God can see entirely through God's eyes.

When Meghan returns from Chile, she brings me a carved wooden statue of a tiny indigenous god with a huge penis that emerges when you pull a lever in his tummy. She wears new silver jewelry, and she is deeply tanned. I discover that she has developed a taste for a Chilean liqueur called Pisco, a popular national drink. Her entire manner and appearance seem far older than the teenager I sent to the airport two weeks ago, and her sudden veneer of sophistication brings me a new set of worries.

Meghan is captivated by her intimate window into the new life on the other side of Maya's death. She describes her trip to me as she unpacks her suitcases. For the moment, I set aside my concerns to listen to her story.

Weary from the long flight to Chile, which included a layover in Texas, Meghan was in a near panic about finding Fernando and his son Christopher in a foreign airport. After the girls deplaned in the bustling terminal, she could not see anyone matching Fernando's description waiting for her at the gate. They waited for some time, feeling helpless and lost. Finally, they set off through the crowded terminal, dragging their bags and scanning every stranger's face.

Chilean men are not shy about staring at young foreign women. She could feel eyes scanning her light hair and complexion, and every inch of her body. She and Sarah quickened their pace.

There was a powerful scent of aftershave on a sea of men's faces mingling with cigarette smoke in a nauseating haze. Eventually she spotted a confused looking man scanning the terminal. With him was a handsome teenage boy about her age. Taking a chance, she approached them, "Excuse me, are you Christopher and Fernando?"

Christopher said "yes" in a perfect American accent and they exchanged an awkward hug. Then Meghan's eyes moved to Fernando. He had a sweet, welcoming countenance that calmed her immediately. Laughing joyously, he gathered her in his arms. Just as I had, she could hear Maya's heart beating in his chest. It seemed surreal and miraculous.

She spent much of her holiday nightclubbing in Santiago. Like most upper-class Chilean young people, she and her new friends came and went as they pleased; she often got in at four or five in the morning. This is not what I had imagined at all but her "get over it, Mom" attitude warns me to tread carefully.

She shows me her photos. In one series of pictures, there is a sun-washed lake and my eye is drawn to a diving platform. Chris and his friends hang out there. I study their handsome faces, lean arms, and brown chests. There is my smiling daughter surrounded by teenage boys, their nonchalance and wealth, their careless faces.

Meghan and Chris quickly became friends. Only months apart in age, and united by the unusual bond shared by their families, the two teenagers began sharing their experiences. They would sit outside in the Santiago evenings looking at the stars. Chris asked questions about Maya—what was she like, were she and Meghan close, did she have boyfriends? Meghan asked him to describe his father's heart problems and the difficulty of his life before the transplant. He told vivid stories of his father's ten years as an invalid, and of his own mixed feelings about Fernando's sudden resurrection and new vitality. Perhaps this explained, at least partially, some of Christopher's drug and alcohol problems that Fernando had been so worried about. The parallels with Maya's feverish acting out were startling.

During Meghan's stay with the family, Christopher's drinking got completely out of control. One night he passed out fully clothed in his bathtub. His parents sent him to a recovery center for an indefinite period. This marred the visit and made her feel awkward and worried about her new friend. But she and Sarah continued their travels with friends of the family who showed them the sights during a car trip to the coast and into the mountains of the country's interior.

Meghan was surprised by the amount of pills Fernando took each day—more than a dozen medications, some designed to ensure that his body would not reject his new heart. Fernando was grateful to be alive and his joy and warmth were contagious, but she saw firsthand that the life of a transplant recipient included a mixture of miraculous healing as well as ongoing health concerns. Fernando was curious about her life, and eager to befriend her.

The family's home in Santiago was filled with expensive artwork and furniture; a huge expanse of windows in the living room looked out over the city. Fernando's office was on the lower level of the house. One day Meghan went into the office to retrieve something for him. As she entered the room, a black and white image on the wall above his desk caught her eye. Fernando had enlarged the photo of Maya I had given him at our first meeting to the size of a poster. Meghan was standing face to face with a larger-than-life portrait of her sister. She backed out of the office and closed the door, never mentioning her encounter with Maya's image to Penny or Fernando.

I remember Fernando's words about the intense relationship he had with his "Lolita" before he even knew her name. Meghan's description of his life now makes the gap between Fernando and me yawn wider than ever, and I feel compelled to back away. In a letter, I thank him and Penny for their generosity and hospitality to my daughter. When Fernando writes back, he mentions that he will be getting ongoing care in the United States from the medical center at Yale University, and will no longer make annual trips to San Francisco. At this, I breathe a profound sigh of relief, knowing that our contact will now become infrequent.

As our life together settles into a routine that winter, one of Meghan's activities brings me satisfaction as well as more worry. She is training with Amigos de Las Americas, a group of teens who serve in seven Latin American countries as volunteer public health workers. One weekend a month she packs a bag and goes off to learn about digging latrines, giving health talks in Spanish, or building outdoor stoves made of straw and mud. When her assignment arrives in the spring of 1997, we learn that she will live and work with another volunteer in a small rural village in the state of Guanajuato, Mexico. Her assignment will last for eight weeks during the coming summer. Her trip to Chile opened the door to a very different world; now she will have an experience at the opposite end of the economic and social spectrum.

The positive shadow of my mother's commitment to social justice lights my daughter's eyes as she speaks about this new adventure. So noble impulses cross the generations too, it seems. Mom would have loved the way Meghan faces the world determined to do good, to be part of a community that helps others to live more humanely, so like the nuns and community organizers she tried to emulate. My mother's flight to Mexico when I was five years old floods back. The children of Nogales ran between shanties, mud caking their bare feet, chasing chickens as I stood in knock-kneed amazement watching them.

Meghan will get to Mexico on her own power, not caught in a frantic escape attempt as I was, but there is no scripted agenda for her days—she'll have to make it up as she goes. This trip offers her a chance to experience her independence in a way her sister never could. Maya's attempts to break free of me centered on our relationship and her attempts to test its limits with her risky behavior. With Meghan, the adventures are carefully planned and the road far smoother. I still miss my older daughter terribly, but the difference in these two is not lost on me. I am grateful for relative peace.

Chapter 29

From the doorway of her bedroom, I watch my daughter gather her things. She hefts her backpack stuffed with jeans, skirts, and a polar fleece jacket I convinced her to pack "just in case," and then reaches for her portable cot. Her blue Amigos T-shirt shows off her figure—small high breasts and muscular arms. Training with her Amigos group has toughened her muscles as well as her determination.

"I can do it, Mom," she says when I offer to help her. "I have to be able to carry this stuff on my own." Six months after her return from Chile, my daughter is about to leave for eight weeks in rural Mexico on a Sunday evening in mid-June of 1997.

Five years after Maya's death, I am being asked to let Meghan go, trusting that, unlike her sister, she will return to me. With one side of my heart I want to help and protect her, but the other side tells me to support her freedom. My job description as a mother has radically changed—I have to let her test her own wings.

Her father and I help stow her gear in the trunk of my little Nissan sedan. Dan hovers over Meghan too, and it reminds me again of how close they are. He's been with us this weekend helping to prepare for the trip and talking to Meghan about her last minute doubts. At last, we all pile into my car. As we head down the hill, Mt. Diablo rises into view, reminding me again of Maya and that other, wrenching good-bye.

Our destination is a restaurant in the Mission district of San Francisco, where we will meet Mark, Dan's son from his first marriage. When we arrive, Mark gathers Meghan into a bear hug. Since her sister's death, he has become her best friend and protector. The four of us drink Mexican beer and eat spicy enchiladas. During the meal, I attempt to memorize every feature of my daughter's smooth but troubled face.

Throughout the meal, Meghan's agitation grows. The realization that she will be on her own in an undeveloped region of Mexico for two months hits home. Her face crumples, and she pushes her plate away. Her brother and father move their chairs closer to hers, and Dan puts his arm around her shoulders. "It's natural to be scared about such a big adventure," Dan says.

I chime in. "Of course it is, sweetheart. We're all so proud of you." She nods and leans her head on her father's shoulder, fighting back tears.

Walking out of the restaurant, she turns to me and lets the floodgates open. I take her hand, "I'll miss you so much, honey." She wipes away tears with the back of her hand and sends me a look of apprehension mixed with resolve. "I know this is going to be a great experience for you. Stay safe and write to me, okay?"

A teary scene of farewell at the airport is now impossible—it would be too much for Meghan to bear. I determine to be as upbeat as possible.

"I'll be okay Mom," she reassures me. "It's just hard to say good-bye."

"I know," I say, pushing away my own fears. Endless

unsavory possibilities fill my head from dysentery, rape, and acute homesickness to violence in the state of Chiapas, hundreds of miles away from her assigned area in Mexico. I smile at her and shoo away my imaginings.

More than a hundred kids in identical blue Amigos T-shirts pack the departure area at the airport. Families are everywhere. Volunteers from around the Bay Area will all depart on the same flight. As we make our way to the check-in line, a mother and daughter are sobbing in each other's arms, and I have to struggle for composure. Meghan presents her ticket and the gate attendant hands her a boarding pass. Our little group huddles together, talking. Then the boarding call comes.

Her father wraps her in his arms, and her brother tells her to stay safe as he gives her a final hug. I embrace her too. "This is hard," she says and turns away from us. She hikes up her backpack and merges into the line snaking toward the gate.

The volunteers move toward the ramp in twos and threes, waving good-bye to tearful moms and dads. Suddenly, I need to break free from the emotional intensity. An image of Steve Martin wearing a ridiculous Mexican sombrero in the movie *The Three Amigos* pops into my mind. When my daughter and two of her friends turn to wave, I yell, "Adios, Amigos!"

My final image of Meghan is of her grin. I wave and crane my neck to watch her blue T-shirt and green backpack disappear into the jetway. I am getting good at airport farewells, but they aren't getting any easier.

The hunger for family gnaws at me that summer. For the first time ever, I am truly alone in my house—no kids and no live-in man. When I unlock my front door each night, Oliver, the gray tabby cat, ambles up and rubs my legs, begging for food. I spoon mixed grill dinner into his bowl. Saffron, a feisty orange tiger cat, is a dry food man and goes straight for the crunchies when I pour them into his dish. For more than two decades I have prided myself on my ability to tie on an apron and put a nutritious meal on the table in less than thirty minutes, even after a ten-hour workday. Like my grandmother Eleanor, cooking is a passion I fuel with efficiency. I can transform a pile of leftovers into a three-course meal without breaking a sweat. Now, it feels very odd to have no one to cook for.

After I feed the cats, I scan the contents of the refrigerator, but nothing looks appealing. In the cupboard I discover a box of broccoli soup, so I pour some into a mug and punch on the microwave oven. Then I open a bag of Hawaiian-style potato chips, and voilà, dinner. The house is too quiet so I flip on the TV and listen to Jim Lehrer's familiar voice read the day's news just for me.

When I look around my little home, I am stunned by the amount of stuff I have accumulated—a collection of novels and self-help books, stacks of CDs, thousands of words crammed into file folders or living in digital limbo. Photos of the girls decorate almost every surface. Maya at twelve months, three jagged pearly teeth in the center of an impish grin, wisps of hair framing her face. The dimples in her elbows make me want to reach into the photo and squeeze her chubby baby arms, or run my fingers over her velvety cheeks. There is baby Meghan too, her head drooping to the side like the stem of a spent flower, asleep in her infant swing. That photo tears at me with each glance.

Photos of me as a young mother, a baby in my lap, a seven-year-old at my shoulder provoke puzzlement. *Who is that woman?* How on earth had I managed to raise two kids?

"Those days are long gone," I say aloud to the empty room. With my fiftieth birthday looming, I am truly middle aged. I study myself in the mirror above the mantel. The face looking back at me has the same eyes and bone structure as the photo, but my skin is less buoyant, marked with fine lines. Grief has aged me.

My professional life is shifting too. I have transferred from my old job in San Francisco to Pacific Bell's administrative facility in San Ramon, a suburb south of Walnut Creek. My new job is at risk because of a planned merger with another company, and days after Meghan leaves for Mexico, the pink slip lands on my desk. My old department is cut from more than a hundred positions to six, and my new department will be completely eliminated. My boss is beside herself when we discuss the change.

"I'm in shock," I tell my car pool partner as we walk across the sprawling parking lot after work that evening. "I knew this might happen, but now that it actually has, I'm about to panic."

"Getting laid off is a big deal," Kris says, putting her arm around me. On the way home we discuss various options as she weaves through commuter traffic on the freeway. Her suggestions are creative and helpful, and I begin to feel a trace of confidence return. When we reach her place, she invites me to dinner.

"You need a drink and a hot meal, woman," she tells me.

Her husband retired early from his job, and divides his time between his consulting business and keeping their domestic scene together. Kenny had once famously waxed their washer and dryer to protect the finish, so I have nothing but admiration for his house husbandry. One of his margaritas and a home-cooked meal sound like great medicine.

Minutes later I am settled on a stool at their kitchen counter drinking tequila laced with tangy fresh lime. Kris takes a sip of her trademark bourbon and lemon—with a teaspoon of sugar—and begins to collect ingredients for chocolate chip cookies.

As Kris and I cream butter and sugar, we quickly get the giggles. Kenny is a generous bartender. He grills steaks, and we heap steaming baked beans and corn bread on our plates. When I arrive home in a great mood later that night, I realize that I am handling difficult transitions better than I have in the past— hugs, hot food, and good friends make all the difference. I'll think about finding a new job in the morning.

"Mom? Hi! It's me."

"Meghan! Oh thank God, where are you?"

"In a village outside of San Miguel de Allende."

This is the first time I've heard my daughter's voice in more than a month. I press the phone to my ear and walk from the kitchen into the living room.

"Honey, I've been so worried about you." I haven't received any letters from her since she left home for Mexico, although she tells me she sent one several weeks ago. I've managed to keep my sanity by reading weekly updates on the Amigos website, and phoning other parents who have kids in the program and have also heard nothing.

"Sorry, Mom. I'm fine now. They had to move us from our first village to here, so it's been kind of hectic."

The first village couldn't afford to house and feed the Amigos volunteers for two months so her field supervisor transferred them. She and a fellow volunteer are now living with a family where the father works in Texas six months a year, so the family has income to supplement the subsistence farming they do on the outskirts of the village.

"We have an indoor bathroom," a luxury, because in the first village they didn't even have a latrine—it was out to the fields with a roll of toilet paper.

"Thank heavens," I say. "Are you sure you're okay?"

She assures me that she is fine. Her biggest challenge is convincing village families to pick up baby trees for a reforestation project. She has a hundred and fifty seedlings in pots, and if they aren't planted soon they are going to die. I launch into a brainstorming session with her about ways to encourage the villagers to pick up the trees.

I could have kept talking for hours—I want to know everything she does from the moment she gets up each day. She seems happy and excited about her projects, despite her frustration with the trees. She will celebrate her seventeenth birthday on August 1, and for the first time ever, I won't be with her on that day. But she seems much older than her years to me. Meghan already has her own life—and she is living it now in another country.

"I have to go Mom," she says. The mayor of the village owns a *tienda*, a small store, and she is calling me from the pay phone there.

"Okay, honey. Phone me again as soon as you can."

"I will," she says, "I love you."

"Love you too." She clicks off the line.

I pace for ten minutes after her call, crumpling a tissue in my fist. Oliver comes to me, begging for food. I lift him against my chest. He stretches his paws around my neck and we snuggle together in the kitchen. Later, we go outside to weed the garden. He rolls over in a patch of sun and lifts a paw lazily in the air while I pull knotweed in the shade of the pine tree. The twenty-minute glimpse into my daughter's life in Mexico rattles around in my brain.

At least she's okay and she's doing a wonderful thing. She is conducting her daily life in Spanish and doing hard physical labor that makes a difference in the lives of others, something I did not have the self-confidence to do at her age. I spent my junior year abroad in Switzerland where it was safe and orderly and I could get by in English. Meghan's choices are bolder and more adventurous. Like her sister, she is a risk taker, but with more structure and safety than Maya was capable of. Perhaps I've done a few things right as a mother after all. I remember Lou Ann's words about breaking the family patterns and realize again that there are positive things to pass on as well as hurtful ones. The trick is sorting out the difference, and making the wisest choices. Meghan is thriving, and that more than makes up for the pain of her absence.

Unpacking boxes on the September morning after I leave Pacific Bell, my head is spinning with the rapid-fire changes in my life. I set up framed photos of my daughters on the laminated desktop in my new cubicle, located in the back corner of a Walnut Creek office complex. I pin the button Roz gave me to my bulletin board. "Clinical studies show there are no answers."

After her return from Mexico in August, Meghan spent the final weeks of summer preparing for her senior year in high school. Now that she's old enough for distance to matter less, my office is only a mile from her school. To me, this aspect of my move seems a paradoxical form of comfort.

With college tuition looming, I can't afford to spend a penny of my severance pay. As a contract editor for the health plan giant Kaiser Permanente, a major employer in the Bay Area, I'll be able to maintain my cash flow. But I feel lost and disoriented in my little gray cubicle, and I can barely find my way to the ladies' room.

Loose patches of frayed carpet and dented mental filing cabinets along the aisles between cubicles vex my sense of order. I am used to long open corridors, light-filled spaces, manicured plants, and expensive paintings on the walls. Pacific Bell was flush with hard cash. Kaiser is socially conscious and frugal.

Dispirited after my first day on the job, I phone my sister in Ohio. When she answers, I burst into tears. "I don't know what's wrong with me—this is so difficult."

"You've just done a 'Henry.' Be patient with yourself," Tess says.

"What's a 'Henry'?"

"Remember Mom's old cat?"

"Oh, him. Yeah, he was huge."

One afternoon Henry jumped, or fell, from Grandma's bedroom window and tumbled thirty feet to the grass below. My mother was outside gardening. She watched as he plummeted down, landed on all fours, shook himself, and walked off to sit in the sun. He must have been rattled as hell, but he never let it show.

"Well, you've just done a Henry," Tess continues. "You need to celebrate the landing and move on slowly. This is big."

She advises a hot bubble bath and a good book.

She's right, of course. On top of adjusting to a new job, Maya's birthday—it would have been her twenty-fifth—is less than a week away. No wonder I feel like an orphan. I am whirling to earth from a leap whose height I have vastly underestimated.

The months pass in a blur, and before I know it, two major events loom—my fiftieth birthday and Meghan's graduation from high school.

Although baby boomers are entering their fifties by the thousands each day, to me it feels like a great personal triumph to meet a new decade. I still can't believe I have survived the loss of Maya. It hits me with renewed force that she was the love of my life, and my best friend.

With little time to reflect on this May milestone, I plunge into plans for Meghan's graduation. More than thirty people will be at our home after the ceremony. Between the invitations, the food, the decorations, and the housecleaning, I am distracted enough to let the flashbacks of Maya's high school graduation eight years earlier come and go. But when the day of Meghan's commencement arrives, I can hardly pull myself out of bed.

Watching Meghan's class process to their seats in the Carondelet High School auditorium, I feel Maya with me. She must be so proud of her sister. When Meghan marches across the stage in her cap and gown, I weep openly. This achievement signals a new, freer time for both of us, but also another loss—I can't even contemplate how much I will miss her. She has grown up so fast. That afternoon, it is Meghan who orchestrates the photos after the ceremony, gives directions to friends, and welcomes them to our home for her celebration.

She will be going to the University of California at Santa Cruz in the fall. It is her top—and only—choice of college. Now that my work hours are more flexible, I'm able to spend leisurely mornings with her, sipping coffee under the shade of a giant podocarpus tree that grows all the way up to her second story bedroom window. We sit together on the patio talking before

I leave for work. I have purchased a small wrought iron glider, and I love to rock back and forth and study my daughter's face in the morning light. We talk about little things—my work, her friends, the novel she is reading, her plans for the coming weekend. Neither of us speaks about her impending move away from home.

Chapter 30

On a rainy September day in 1998, Meghan leaves for UC Santa Cruz. We've planned and shopped and packed, but I awake still unprepared.

One of Meghan's best friends offers to drive with her. That morning, we cram Katie's family station wagon with Meghan's clothes, a stereo, her computer, and other personal belongings. The girls get on the road before I do. Like my mother, I am a reluctant leave taker and something always seems to crop up right before any departure. I dash around my kitchen doing endless unnecessary tasks, cleaning the stovetop, emptying the dishwasher. At last, I leave with one of my closest friends at the wheel of her car. Launa is a former colleague from Pacific Bell who has agreed to go with me; I need some support with this difficult good-bye.

As we wind over the Santa Cruz Mountains, everything I see reminds me of the times when I took my daughters camping on the beaches below. The twists of the road are treacherous, slick with the season's first downpour. Highway 17 knifes through towering redwoods that cast long shadows over the traffic. At the summit, four thousand feet above sea level, drivers get a panoramic view of the Monterey Bay.

When I check the radio for a traffic report, the news is bad. There's been a fatal accident at the summit and suddenly sirens are wailing. Ambulances and police cars attempt to bypass miles of stopped vehicles to reach the wreck. In some dark place in my heart, I am afraid that Meghan might be involved.

Somehow we make it through the jam and get over the hill. When we arrive in the parking lot closest to her dorm, there is no sign of Meghan or of Katie's car. I panic. What if something has happened to them? My palms sweat as I dial my daughter's cell phone number, terrified that there will be no answer.

When she picks up, I let out a slow breath. Clutching the phone to my ear, I pace back and forth in the parking lot listening to Meghan's explanation of how they got delayed. They stopped for bagels and coffee, and by the time they got back on the road, they faced a wall of cars. "We're fine, Mom," she reassures me.

It's still drizzling, but I barely notice drops of water from the oak trees above pelting my head. "Come on, let's get some coffee," Launa urges, taking my arm.

A group of low-rise dorms are arranged around a quadrangle with a central cafeteria and a small library and study area. Stevenson College, one of eight at UC Santa Cruz, is woodsy and feels more like summer camp than a major university campus. With Launa to distract me from my fears, I begin to explore my daughter's new home, pleased to find a little café only steps from the quadrangle. We order espresso drinks and sit down to people-watch and chat while we wait.

At last, the girls arrive. After hellos and hugs, we begin to unpack. Kate and Meghan lug suitcases and computer boxes into the dorm. Launa grabs a cardboard box labeled "Tapes and CDs" while I unload a laundry basket packed with towels and blankets. We carry the gear up two flights of stairs to Meghan's room, brushing past excited coeds and weary parents in the stairwell.

Meghan introduces us to her new roommate, a petite Los Angelino with fawn-colored hair. They begin to negotiate about the placement of posters, the best spot for the stereo, and how to soften the overhead lighting. I watch my daughter and marvel at her maturity. I can still see her as a chubby two-year-old at a campground just a few miles from this campus. She is running away from the waves and back to the safety of her mommy's arms. Now, the prospect of living by the ocean she used to fear doesn't seem to upset her in the least.

The room is cramped, and with all of us unpacking, it quickly becomes warm and chaotic. Once the suitcases are emptied, I am suddenly drained, so I look around for a place to take a break. Finding none, I crawl under my daughter's high, institutional bed and lie there on my back like a little kid playing hide-and-seek.

Her bed creaks above me as she stands on it pinning posters of Tori Amos and John Lennon to the wall. The rim of her duvet cover makes an uneven sight line toward the horizon of gray carpet. "Mom, what are you doing under there?"

"Trying to get out of the way," I reply.

What I can't say chokes me—how unspeakably difficult this good-bye will be—and that getting out of *her* way is my task now. I have to step back so she can step forward. My mind floods with memories of her sister. An image of Maya's chic blond bob and willowy figure in tight jeans on that last trip I took with her to visit UCLA engulfs me. Our whispered conversations filled with so much hope for her future seem unspeakably tender, full of naive and yet achievable dreams.

Then my mind travels to the fall afternoon more than thirty years ago when Dad dropped me off at college. Mom didn't come, and our good-bye was perfunctory, but it must have been wrenching for her. At eighteen, I was so self-involved that I didn't even consider what my parents might have felt. My father helped me carry the suitcases to my second story dorm room, then said good-bye. I found myself alone with two sets of wooden bunk beds, a table that would serve as my desk, and a gaggle of women I didn't know shouting at each other up and down the hallway outside my door. None of my three roommates had arrived yet. I hung my clothes in a closet I would share with a stranger. As I remember myself as a college freshman, my daughters seem far more grown up than I was at their age, when the idea that I could live a life separate from my parents seemed like a danger-ous heresy.

Meghan's voice interrupts my thoughts. "Hand me a push pin, Katie," she says, cursing loudly when she drops it among the heap of posters spread out on her bed. Launa helps decide on poster placement while my eighteen-year-old wobbles above me, creating her new nest. She's already a person in her own right, something that took me years of therapy and decades of experi-mentation to achieve.

Meghan's CD player infuses the room with Ella Fitzgerald's cool rhythms. I tap my foot and sing along, *Hates California, it's cold and it's damp, that's why the lady is a tramp...* and restrain myself from worrying aloud that Meghan has not brought enough warm clothing.

I imagine the ocean fog folding into the meadows outside the dorm. Then I mentally embrace my daughters. The first born who had the audacity to live large and then leave home forever. The child above me who grew up in a storm of grief and sur-vived it better than I could have hoped.

When I emerge from under the bed, I dispense crisp twenty-dollar bills into my daughter's outstretched palm and offer advice on nonperishable snacks that are nourishing and low in fat. Meghan rolls her eyes when I urge her to separate her bathing suits from her underwear and put them in a lower drawer. We unpack her portable coffee maker. She goes with me to the recycling bins to dispose of the used cardboard boxes.

"You won't be too lonely without me, will you?" She studies my face.

"I'll try to soldier on," I say, only partly flippantly.

We go to dinner in the college cafeteria, and conversation turns to Meghan's classes, buying her books, and whether a bicycle makes any sense on a campus this hilly. At last, it's time to go. I hold Meghan a long time as we say good-bye. She embraces me in a way she hasn't in ages. We have a real, sustained hug, like the kind we had when she was a little girl. I stroke her hair, then hold her by both shoulder blades, and let myself sink into her warmth. We hold one another close in the dark and our beating hearts meet as mother and daughter, but also as respected friends. It would be pointless to hover or try to offer any parting words of wisdom. I trust Meghan to do the right things.

As Launa and I link arms and walk toward the car, the sharp gunmetal smell of rain overpowers my resolve. I make a sudden veer back toward the rectangle of light in Meghan's second floor window.

Standing below in the darkness, I shout, "Meghan, Meghan!"

She leans out the open window over the bed pillows, the top of the wooden closet just visible behind her head.

"Good-bye," she calls, waving.

"Good-bye," I echo, walking backward along the path gazing up at her. At last I turn toward the parking lot.

I ride home dry-eyed, making small talk with Launa, letting my thoughts wander. When I enter my empty house, pieces of my life are spread out on the dining room table. There are stacks of receipts from the final shopping for dorm room supplies, my grossly unbalanced checkbook, and a pile of unread magazines.

On the bookshelf is a photo of Maya. Her intense eyes drill into mine. Meghan's picture displays her unforced grin and more placid face.

This is *my* home now, filled with images of little girls who no longer live sheltered by my wings. Being a day-to-day mother is over. But the transition to a new kind of life beyond the role that has consumed and nourished me is only beginning.

A few days later Meghan calls me at the office and leaves a message. "Hi, Mommy," she says in a higher, more childlike voice than usual. In her "Introduction to Feminism" class they talked about mothers, and she thought about me. "I miss you, Mommy."

She misses me! I imagined that my college freshman was too busy to miss me, or if she did miss me, so determined to be independent that she wouldn't tell me. I smile and push the save key on my phone pad.

To be missed feels like a victory.

Meghan and I have lost so much, and yet our relationship feels more solid and abundant than ever before.

That Sunday night on the Stevenson College quadrangle I sent her an important message—all I had to leave with her was my love. Now she is telling me that she understood my unspoken words. I listen to her recorded voice again, basking in its comfort. The daughter who swam in an ocean of grief with me, who faced and overcame her fears, is on her own now. I learned so much from raising her sister; in some fundamental way my struggles with Maya—as well as the joys that remain so vivid— brought me into being. Fighting my way toward freeing Maya made me see how delicate the child's job of truly leaving home can be, a process that only death forced me to finish. First my mother and then my daughter left this world, while I remain between the generations of women in my family with only Meghan for company. But what a solid and comforting fellow pilgrim my daughter has been.

Some might see the long shadow Maya cast over Meghan as a curse, but she has used the gifts of her sister's life and death to grow stronger. In the end, the lessons Maya taught me are her legacy to Meghan. I became a better mother because of my first born, and I grew in understanding of my own mother's trials in a way that helped me free myself from the strictures of being her daughter. Here I am, setting my own child free, claiming my life at last.

Epilogue

On a spring evening, I drive to the Mills College campus for a reunion with the professors and former students who harbored me in the months after Maya was killed. After the evening's lecture, we gather to sip our wine and gossip. I leave the library at twilight, stopping to listen to the murmuring creek that runs through the campus. In a literary frame of mind, I think of Virginia Woolf and of the River Ouse, the place where she drowned herself. This creek might have become such a place for me. For many years, grief made collecting the fragments of my life seem impossible. Back then, each breath brought fresh pain. I remember late afternoons when I came to class with a canvas bag crammed with manuscript pages, and how one by one the semesters passed and gradually I recovered. When I wanted to give up, the words I wrote here kept me alive.

I feel Maya with me tonight as I gaze at the little bridge that crosses the creek. Her tongue-in-cheek voice reminds me that this creek can hardly be more than four feet at its deepest, and thus impossible for me to drown in no matter how many rocks I might have stuffed in my pocket. Perhaps she has always known that her death wouldn't kill me. More than I did, she respected my inner resources. Of course I can only speculate about her life now, but I often sense it deeply, its ongoing current and the way it interlaces with mine, sometimes submerged, then flowing close to my heart, jolting me awake—again—with fierce love.

A few months after Maya died, I had a vivid dream. In it, she is swimming underwater, gliding from end to end of a swimming pool. Smoothly she rises above the surface of the water, her face ghostly white, her lips blue. She smiles at me. I feel happy to see her. I start to move toward her yet something in her manner tells me I cannot touch her body. Her face glows with innocence and pride. She looks surprised and pleased to be alive. Then she vanishes under the calm surface of the water.

She tries to tell me something important in the dream, something she wants me to understand, but each time I approach comprehension, a terrible static drowns out her words. I think her message is about moving between the worlds of what we call life and death. Maya is showing me how good she is at operating in this alternate reality—a metaphysical diver, every bit as graceful as she had always been. My role is to stand aside and watch. I struggle to let Maya go, to be the observer of her new life in another element, as I did all those years ago when her father and I plunged her under the water to teach her to swim.

Maya swims eternally back and forth in me. Although she was my child, now she seems to have become my elder, far wiser in the ways of life and death than I am. She moves between the anchors of her lost life on earth, in an element so fluid, so encompassing, so diaphanous, I cannot see it with earthly eyes. But in my soul I know it is so. And as she moves, I move back and forth between life and afterlife in my dreams, swimming with Maya.

Afterword

May 2012—The Garden of Remembrance

The leaves pinwheel above, casting shadows on the grass. An American flag whips and clanks against its metal pole. I didn't visit on Memorial Day—yesterday—so I'm alone in this section of the cemetery. I sit on a granite bench beneath a California oak, staring at Mount Diablo in the distance, remembering my daughter Maya.

Two minutes ago I was kneeling on the ground below her headstone, arranging a bouquet of flowers, speaking aloud to her.

The conversation is always the same. "I miss you, honey." The wind whips at me. "We all miss you."

By "all," I mean her sister, Meghan, and Meghan's husband, Todd, and their two-year-old, Lucia. Already Lucia talks about her aunt, pointing at the picture on the cover of my book, saying "Maya" over and over.

It's been twenty years since the April afternoon in the hospital when I held Maya's hand and whispered in her ear, "If you need to go, Maya, go. I'll be okay." It was a monstrous, necessary lie.

Her fingers lay warm and pliant in mine, her face utterly still. Despite her coma, I believed she could hear me so I spoke those fierce words so that she could die in peace—as if the fates, or God, or Maya, for that matter, needed my permission.

I trace the outline of her tiny photo on the headstone. "Beautiful girl," I say, and make my way to the bench.

Translucent as a piece of gauze, a full moon rises over Mt. Diablo. The sight of the moon on a bright California afternoon always amazes me. Today, it seems like a miracle that I am still here when my daughter isn't.

February 2012—Meeting Fernando's daughter

She sits across from me in the dim light, the restaurant's noontime bustle a hum behind our voices. The last time I saw Olivia she was eight years old, holding her mother's hand, staring up at me. Now she's twenty-seven, and about to become a mother herself. The child she carries, a girl, will be named Maya.

Walking to the restaurant together I felt dwarfed by her— she's half a head taller, big-boned, blonde like her mother, but with her father's crinkly smile and kind eyes. As I look at her now, I remember Fernando, looking at me with the same half-pleading, half-questioning eyes as his daughter. For fourteen years, my daughter's heart beat in Fernando's chest, keeping him alive. Olivia wrote to me saying her father died in 2006. Not heart disease, but cancer.

"The last time we met, I didn't understand what it meant," she says, "you giving Maya's heart to my Dad."

It meant so many things to me. I tell her some of them: saving another family from the grief tearing mine apart; making something hopeful out of something tragic; and then the selfish part: saving some piece of my child, a piece that would stay here on this earth and cause another human being to think of Maya as much as I did. Every hour. Every day. Fernando was that person.

"You'll never know how many lives you changed," Olivia says, tears sliding down her cheeks. "I don't know how you did that," she says, looking into my eyes, stroking her belly, comforting her baby and herself.

She hands me a picture of her high school graduation—Fernando with his arm around her shoulders, beaming with pride. "He was there with me because of you," she says. "Thank you."

I begin to cry. I have the same high school graduation photo; only it's me with my arm around Maya, her devilish smile, the happiness, and balloons. I'm crying for Fernando who let me put my ear against his chest and listen to the steady "whomp, whomp" of Maya's heartbeat.

I'm crying happy tears too, for little unborn Maya, the namesake, and for Lucia, my granddaughter, and for the whole mysterious cycle of birth and death, for the passage of time, for my own Maya and for myself. I look into Olivia's eyes and think there is nowhere I'd rather be but here with this woman who is kin, not by blood, but kin nonetheless. She's come all the way across the country to meet me, to show me that life goes on, to share her grief and her gratitude.

I smile at her.

Our eyes meet and hold across the table. "You're welcome," I say.

July 2011—Family vacation

I wake with the spacious feeling of having nothing to do just like summers when I was a kid. Sunlight slants across the quilt, making the bedroom walls glow, and I snuggle under the covers.

Then I hear Lucia's cry from her room across the hall in the house we've rented for a week in Madison on the Lake, Ohio.

When I come in, she sits up in the Portacrib, babbling to her green monkey, holding him nose to nose. She looks up and I see a different, brighter light. She is my sun, reaching her arms up. "Mimi, Mimi," she says, and I take her in my arms feeling her curls tickle my nose.

"Lulu," I whisper. "Did you have a good sleep?"

She nods into my neck. I gather a diaper and clean clothes. Her parents are still sleeping in the adjoining room, the fan humming, their bodies mounding the sheets.

I steal down the hall and into the living room with my precious cargo. She rubs her eyes when I set her down, gives me a mischievous look, and races from the sofa to the kitchen door, where I nab her.

"Look, Lake Erie," I say, opening the door and walking out on the patio with Lucia in my arms. I repeat the magic words and point at the lake. She points too and forgets she's been corralled. Flat and shining, the lake is becalmed, signaling that the day will be hot.

"Down, down," she begs, and I let her bare feet touch the concrete and she takes off running. I marvel—wasn't she just a baby a few short months ago?—and watch her legs churn over the wet grass. She's heading for the road and so I run after her.

"Lucia Maya," I shout. "Stop!"

She pauses. I sprint up behind her. "You little imp," I say, grabbing her hand.

She looks up with a bold grin and for a moment I see Maya, blonde curls bobbing. For one second I'm treading water in the past, happy to be there, but happier still to float forward in time, suspended between worlds, living with the tremendous risk of loving. I hoist Lucia up and stand holding her against my heart, our faces turned to watch sunlight glinting on water.

April 2011—The girl on the horse

I pull the car into my usual spot by the water spigot nearest Maya's grave. The sun dashes behind a cloud. The grass dances in the spring wind.

Today is April 6, the day my internal clock stopped nineteen years ago. Maya's been dead almost as long as she was alive.

Ahead of me, a woman looks for the loved one she lost, circling around headstones until she moves deliberately toward a grave. As I get closer I realize she is at *Maya's* grave, kneeling in front of the bronze plaque with the inscription, "Dearly loved, deeply missed."

The stranger grasps a bouquet of yellow roses close to her chest. When I approach, she looks up, clutching her flowers as if she'd like to hide behind them.

I study her face and see that she is not young—the mouth and eyes are etched with lines—but her body is trim, the arms muscular. She has long hair and the well-scrubbed look of a Midwesterner.

"Hello," I say. "This is my daughter Maya's grave."

I pause, unsure what to say next. Then I blurt, "Who are you?"

With the tiniest hesitation she replies, "I'm Julie—the girl who was on the horse with Maya that afternoon." She sucks in her breath. I do the same.

There is an awkward pause before she begins to cry. "I've always been afraid I would bump into you one day," she sobs.

"Oh my God," I breathe. "And I have always *wanted* to see you again." I had met Julie only briefly at the hospital after the accident, but everything was such a blur that I barely remembered her.

"Really?" She looks like a frightened child. "I figured you

must be so angry with me, and so... bitter," she says, brushing away tears.

I sink to my knees on the ground above the headstone, staring at this apparition. "Angry with you?" I had been furious with Maya, and briefly with her ex-boyfriend, Alex, once the shock wore off.

"How could I be angry with you? It was a freak accident—it was no one's fault." There was a time when I blamed God, or fate, or Maya's daredevil nature. But I never blamed the other girl on the horse.

Julie stares at me, not quite believing my words. I gaze into her eyes, the face no longer fresh but still echoing youthful good looks. I need to know what only Julie can reveal about Maya's last moments of consciousness.

"I'll go now," she says, "you must want time alone with Maya."

My heart leaps at the sound of my daughter's name.

I wrestle the bent metal rim of the vase loose from its holder. "You stay. Have a private moment with Maya," I say, glancing at the roses in her hand, willing her not to run away.

She follows my gaze. "They didn't have anything very nice," she apologizes.

"They're lovely," I say, hoping she hears my appreciation. Something akin to tenderness wells up inside me. I give a little wave and head to the water spigot.

When I come back, Julie is sitting next to the grave, shading her face with an open palm. The clouds have blown over. The sun is strong now. I coax the vase back in place and sit on the grass above the headstone.

I ask about her life, and while she talks, time spools backwards.

She will turn forty in a few months—she was a year older than Maya and went to a different high school. They met for the first time just hours before climbing up on the horse's back together. Julie had a crush on Alex, so he was the connection that initiated their meeting that afternoon in 1992.

"I have an eight-year-old daughter," Julie says. She tells me her daughter's name and that she and her ex-husband care for their child together.

"What can you tell me about that day?" I ask, knowing this may cause her pain, but I've wondered about it for almost two decades. All I knew is what Alex told me afterwards when we were both still in shock.

When Julie describes the accident, how the horse reared without warning and threw them to the ground, how quickly it happened, how she sat up dazed and saw Maya lying inert on the ground and began shaking her shoulder calling out, then begging, then demanding, "Wake up! Wake up!" it all closes over my head. I'm drowning in Julie's bad memory—a prank gone horribly wrong.

"I've had survivor guilt for years," Julie says, crying quietly again.

I nod. I have too, so I understand perfectly.

The sun beats down and I take off my sweater. The wind feels good, and I breathe in its freshness, glorying for the umpteenth time in the pure, strange magic of being alive.

"I was never angry at you," I repeat. "I was jealous of you—and of your parents."

Truth—for months after Maya died, I was beside myself with envy of intact families. I almost ran over a family crossing the street in downtown Lafayette because life seemed murderously unfair. I held myself back from gunning the accelerator and crushing two gorgeous little blonde kids and their parents. That's how crazed I was. I toy with telling her this, but decide it's too much.

"I'm sorry," Julie says. "I'm so sorry."

"I'm sorry too," I say. Meaning, I have some idea of what you've lived with these last nineteen years.

"I made a promise to Maya," Julie says, "that I would come every year on the anniversary. For the first five years I couldn't—it was too awful. But then I talked to her and decided I needed to come, and I've been here every year since."

For years I've wondered who was leaving the mysterious flowers—usually yellow, always bespeaking cheerful spring afternoons—and thought possibly Alex, or one of Maya's girlfriends still living in the area. All this time Julie has come to this spot knowing I might be here, or might arrive as she lingered, and yet keeping her promise to Maya.

"I should be going," she says, brushing grass from her jeans.

I ask for her e-mail address. She scribbles it on a scrap of paper and I ease it into my pocket, and then pat it to be sure it's really there, feeling the crinkled paper through the fabric of my jeans.

I watch her walk to her car and then I turn back to Maya's headstone and get to work. Julie's engine surges and fades as she drives away.

Just days after Maya died, her eleven-year-old sister Meghan had said, "I wouldn't want to be any of the kids who were with Maya that afternoon." At the time I agreed, thinking that, yes, their lives are ruined.

It was Alex I felt sorry for, his defeated face looking down at his tennis shoes every time we talked. The girl on the horse was not part of Maya's world and therefore not part of mine. She was a cipher, a missing piece I didn't realize how much I missed until now.

"Can you believe it baby? Nineteen years," I say. "I miss you, honey."

I polish the letters of Maya's name, the bronze curlicues around the plaque, the granite headstone. I fuss with the flowers, making them perfect, the yellow of Julie's roses setting off the bright centers of the mums I brought, making the pussy willow catkins glow.

I pull out my phone, realizing I want Julie to know her flowers are mixed with mine, not separate as in the past. I snap photos, experimenting to get the right angle, to show the yellows and pinks in their best light, planning to e-mail her the results. Is this crazy, this urge to document? It's all I have left of the beauty that was Maya, and the only physical evidence of a chance meeting that neither Julie nor I can—for the moment— truly assess.

What I know: When I look into Julie's face, I see a woman who could be my daughter, who reflects back to me the "what might have beens" of Maya's life.

Two minutes from now I will be on the phone with Meghan saying, "You'll never believe what just happened."

Forty-five minutes from now, when I reach her apartment in San Francisco, I will kiss her cheek and take Lucia from Meghan's arms and think what a very lucky woman I am to have my little family, my beautiful girls.

But right now, I climb in behind the steering wheel, settle into the driver's seat, and shake my head in wonder, whispering to the lingering wind, "Life is so strange."

November 2009—Lucia's birth

I enter the hospital room on tiptoe. Part of me longs to barge in, but the other part is hushed, contained. Meghan's bare shoulders and tangled hair remind me of when she was a little girl. She's wearing her black-rimmed glasses, which always make her look wiser than me. She gazes down at the wrapped bundle she holds at her breast. My granddaughter.

I pause and watch, taking in the image of a mother bending

over a brand new baby, worshipping. My baby has a baby, and life feels like a swelling wave lifting me as if I were a surfer so that I ride the wave higher and higher knowing the dangers of mother love but not caring because it's worth the ride.

I smile at my son-in-law who is watching the scene too, a few feet from the bed. We nod at each other, almost a bow, acknowledging the sacred. I hand him a bag of Noah's bagels, still warm, and a tray of foamy coffee drinks. My daughter murmurs, "Caffeine," and stretches out her hand, never taking her eyes from the baby's face. Her husband hands her a latte, and she sighs with pleasure even before the first sip.

When I approach the bed I look at Meghan, and then at the bundle, my vision double, my heart swelling like a balloon. And not some little party balloon but one of those giant gas-filled numbers that carries people aloft for miles, drinking champagne, and waving at the tiny fields and cars below.

Meghan hands me the bundle. I look into the little face, the swollen eyelids and rosebud lips, already in love.

"Hello, little one," I say. "Welcome to our world."

Her mouth twitches and I somehow think it's for me, a little smile, and I give myself totally, wholeheartedly to this little being. Even though I've known her for less than a nanosecond, I already adore everything about her. Her smell, the tiny ball of her fists, her little pointed chin.

"She's beautiful," I breathe.

Todd comes and looks over my shoulder. I feel his happiness, his breath on my neck.

I look back at him. "Congratulations," I say, meaning "Thank you."

Then I hand the baby to her father and finally do what I've been meaning to since I came in: throw my arms around my amazing warrior woman daughter, whose face is tired and radiant, remembering exactly what that face looked like on the day she was born.

"I love you," I say, ruffling her hair. "Good job—she's a beauty."

"What should we call her?" Meghan asks, and I know she's asking her husband, but including me too.

There's been a long debate over this, and a decision to wait until the baby has arrived to choose. Todd gazes at his daughter.

"Lucia," he says. "She looks like a Lucia."

"Yes," Meghan agrees. "Lucia!"

She calls her daughter for the first time, stretching out her arms, and her husband places the baby in them.

"Lucia," I say, leaning over the baby again, stroking her forehead, the skin velvety as a butterfly's wing.

Lucia opens her eyes for just a second, and Meghan and I both laugh and then look into each other's faces, wide-eyed with wonder.

June 2007—Meghan and Todd's wedding

Willowy as a sapling, twenty-six-year-old Meghan walks towards us in a cloud of satin and lace, her dark hair bound up in white ribbons. She joins hands with her groom. Todd stands at attention, ramrod straight in his black suit.

Meghan and Todd speak vows they have written: "Before our friends and family, I choose you as the One. The One I will love, encourage, and comfort, when life is easy and when it is hard, when our love is simple, and when it is an effort."

Meghan has planned every detail—each white hydrangea centerpiece, black sateen ribbon, and romantic French song. On this June evening in San Francisco, I marvel at my daughter's self-assurance.

I flash back to the spring afternoon fifteen years ago when I came home to find my sixth-grader huddled in the corner of the sofa, fidgety and pale. As a latchkey kid, she had answered the phone when the hospital called. An emergency room nurse said her older sister had been critically injured in a fall from a horse. Meghan shouldered the terrible job of breaking that news to me.

Four days later, when Maya died, Meghan became my only living child.

Loving Meghan gave me the strength to go on and a reason to get out of bed each morning. Now, as Meghan and Todd exchange wedding rings, I realize again that love is the most powerful force on earth. It holds us together even when grief tears our hearts apart.

Since Maya's death, no family celebration has been as it appears on the surface. There's always a missing person. I feel like a tightrope walker, balancing conflicting emotions: grief versus love, despair versus hope. Somehow love and hope always win in the end.

Five years to the day of their very first kiss, Meghan and Todd embrace as husband and wife. "I have a son now," I whisper to myself.

Cheering erupts as the bride and groom walk down the aisle. I follow, almost soaring, and a new wave of cheering begins. In front of two hundred people, I jump for joy. Love's gravity brings me back to earth. It's what holds me here.

April 2004—Publication of *Swimming with Maya*

What did I expect to feel? Relief? Check. Pride? Check. Terror? Underline and double check. I lie awake at night trembling. Anyone can read about my most private moments, my most insane decisions, our family secrets, loves gone wrong, losses that have shaped my life. I've just published a history of my own craziness.

I want to shout, "Stop the presses!"

The cat bolts off the bed. I get on my knees by the side of the bed and pray. Please put this book in the hands of people who need to read it. Give me courage, God, to go out there in the world and talk about Maya, about life and death and recovery. This will be a sleeping pill night.

But in the morning the sun rises as usual, and I have a radio interview to do. A station in Reno, Nevada. The interviewer has read the jacket notes and nothing else. I have to tell the story in two-minute intervals interrupted by commercial breaks for breast augmentation. It's so awful it makes me laugh. When I'm back on air I manage to keep it together, and I realize, hey, you've survived the worst already. How bad can this be?

Several weeks later, I read to six people in a Borders bookstore in Davis, California. The piped-in elevator music almost drowns my voice, despite the lapel microphone. I've driven an hour and a half to get here and a friend helps me set up the folding chairs. When it's over, people ask me to sign copies of the book, and I do, always with the same salutation, "Love heals!"

A teenage girl comes up to me and hands me a copy of *Swimming with Maya*.

"I just started reading your book, and I can't stop," she says.

I think I might burst into tears. "Thank you," I say. "I hope it helps you."

Face to face with the girl, I remember what is true and universal. We all lose those we love. I hold the copy of her book for an extra moment, glancing down at the picture of Maya on the cover. My baby. Wading in Cedar Lake in Minneapolis all those years ago. Moments after that picture was snapped, Maya hurled herself against my shoulders, throwing her arms around my neck.

I remember the joy.

I hand the signed book to the girl. She cradles it against her heart and walks away.

Reading Group Guide

1. What is your reaction to *Swimming with Maya*? Did you have any unexpected feelings or responses?

2. What does the title of the book mean?

3. How do you feel about Eleanor's decision to donate Maya's organs? What would you do if you were in the same situation?

4. If you donated the organs of a loved one, would you want to be in contact with the recipients? Why or why not?

5. Do you want your organs to be donated after you die? Have you discussed your wishes with those who are close to you? If not, why not?

6. What do you think Maya would say about this book?

7. What are the pros and cons of having a child who is high-spirited, seeks adventure, and takes risks?

8. In what ways are Maya and Meghan different? How are they similar? How does Maya's death affect Eleanor's thoughts and feelings toward Meghan?

9. Maya's death causes Eleanor to re-examine their relationship. They were mother/daughter, but Eleanor says they were also friends. Was theirs a healthy relationship? How does it change over time?

10. Maya's death also causes Eleanor to re-examine her own life. How did Eleanor's experiences as a child and as a young woman affect her approach to motherhood?

11. Do you think that writing this story was helpful/cathartic to Eleanor? How does writing aid healing? How do you deal with grief or trauma in your life?

About the Author

ELEANOR VINCENT was born in Cleveland, Ohio. She graduated from Baldwin-Wallace College in 1970, attended the University of Minnesota School of Journalism, and completed her MFA degree in creative writing at Mills College in 1995. Her work has appeared in the *San Francisco Chronicle*, the *San Jose Mercury News* and a variety of anthologies including *At the End of Life: True Stories About How We Die,* edited by Lee Gutkind; *Impact: An Anthology of Short Memoirs;* and *This I Believe: On Motherhood.* Her poetry and essays have been published by *Five Fingers Review, The Santa Barbara Review,* and the *Napa Review*. She lives in Oakland, California. Visit her at www.eleanorvincent.com.

CPSIA information can be obtained at www.ICGtesting.com
Printed in the USA
LVOW121915140513

333655LV00002B/49/P